KU-269-252

1968
and after

1968
and after

Inside the Revolution

TARIQ ALI

Blond & Briggs

Also by Tariq Ali

Pakistan: Military Rule or People's Power
(Jonathan Cape Ltd)
The Coming British Revolution
(Jonathan Cape Ltd)

Published in 1978 in Great Britain by Blond & Briggs Ltd
London, and Tiptree, Colchester, Essex
© Copyright 1978 by Tariq Ali
SBN 85634 082 0
Printed in Great Britain by
The Anchor Press Ltd and bound by
Wm Brendon & Son Ltd, both of
Tiptree, Essex

Short Loan Collection
WITHDRAWN

Contents

For CLIVE GOODWIN, friend and comrade,
who died suddenly in November 1977

Preface

Revolutionary socialism was reborn in 1968. Its inspiration came from the battlefields of Vietnam and the Sierra Maestra in Cuba, from the barricades of May–June 1968 in France and from the courageous Czechs who confronted Soviet tanks not with grenades, but with political arguments. This book analyses those developments a decade later. It evaluates their strengths and weaknesses in the wake of what followed in Chile, Britain and Portugal. It is not intended as a comprehensive survey of world politics and economics. Its aim is modest: to attempt a preliminary survey of revolutionary socialist politics over the last decade. The stability of the bourgeois political order has been threatened in the heartlands of capital in Western Europe, but the ability of bourgeois-democratic institutions to deflect every challenge so far has posed some awkward questions for the followers of Marx and Lenin.

This book explains some of the weaknesses of revolutionary strategy and tactics over the last decade. In that sense it is a self-critical evaluation of the revolutionary left. The dress-rehearsals of 1968 raised many questions of strategy and tactics for the far left. This book argues that we now have the accumulated experience which enables us to answer some of these questions and move forward. I hope it will spark off a discussion on how socialist democracy can be achieved in the West. This is no longer an abstract discussion confined to small sects. The crisis of the system is confronting workers' parties throughout Europe with a stark choice. Either they continue to manage capitalism and become responsible for the crisis or they change course and embark on a new direction. The next decades will pose an even sharper question: socialist democracy or barbarism?

I would like to thank Oliver Macdonald for reading the chapter on Czechoslovakia and Robin Blackburn for reading the entire manuscript and suggesting some useful additions. Thanks

vii

also to: Geoff Bell, Richard Carver, Steve Potter, Geoffrey Sheridan and Dodie Weppler, all members of the *Socialist Challenge* editorial staff, for permitting me to abdicate my responsibilities as Editor while the book was being written. Myra Trevelyan insisted on reading the manuscript simply to check that "no sexist language was used". She declared herself satisfied. I would also like to thank Tony and Judith Shaw for letting me stay in their house in Mid-Wales so that the book was written in isolation.

Tariq Ali
March 1978

In Lieu of an Introduction

Prague is a city for all seasons. Aesthetically it is the most pleasing in all Europe. In December 1966 it was enshrouded in snow. I was there on a journalistic assignment for *Town,* a magazine happily now defunct. My thoughts, I confess, were not on the task in hand, but on a war taking place in a not-so-small country in South-East Asia, thousands of miles away from Prague or London.

There were undercurrents at work in Prague, though I was not aware of them at the time. Most of the Czechs *I* met displayed no interest in politics. Those who mentioned Vietnam did so mainly as a complaint at the large amount of aid their government was providing to that country. The most politically aware people I met in Prague that winter were West German students on holiday. They were totally alienated from European politics. Germany was too staid, France too dull and Britain too uneventful for their tastes. Their minds were further away. They were enthusiastic about the Cuban revolution, and speculated avidly on the whereabouts of Che Guevara. They followed every development of the war in South-East Asia. They were members of the SDS (German Socialist Students) and they heralded a new wave of internationalism throughout Western Europe.

My tasks in Prague completed, I was preparing to return to London, when I received a telegram from the Bertrand Russell Peace Foundation in London, asking me to go to Cambodia and North Vietnam and join an investigating team of the Vietnam War Crimes Tribunal.

Russell was a veteran dissenter and the only survivor of the old radical tradition in English public life. He had been so deeply affected by the war in Vietnam that he had taken the initiative in setting up a War Crimes Tribunal to try the United States government for war crimes and genocide. He had been backed by Jean-Paul Sartre and Simone de Beauvoir from

ix

France, Vladimir Dedijer from Yugoslavia, Isaac Deutscher from Britain and many other public figures throughout the world. For this show of audacity, Russell had been much derided and reviled by the British press, which tended to be more loyal to the White House than the *New York Times*. The Labour Government of Harold Wilson had refused permission for the Tribunal to meet in London; de Gaulle had forbidden it to assemble in Paris. It was finally held in Sweden, where the government ably resisted pressures from the State Department.

Russell, a lifelong member of the Labour Party, had been so disgusted by Wilson's servility towards the United States in Vietnam, that he had publicly burned his Labour Party card at a meeting in the London School of Economics. When Richard Gott and I met Russell in 1966 this old but tireless philosopher was in fighting form. His scorn and contempt for Wilson were boundless. He despised men who were "small and petty", and Wilson, for him, was the epitome of such a person. Russell described how he had refused to shake Wilson's hand: Russell was leaving the Ghanaian High Commission after meeting Kwame Nkrumah and Wilson was just entering. "I just could not bring myself to shake that man's hand. He came forward and said 'Hello, Lord Russell'. I put my hand behind my back and walked out." When questioned he admitted that of all the Labour Prime Ministers whom he had known — and he had known them all — Ramsay MacDonald, the first, was the worst — much worse than Wilson.

Russell's passions were inflamed by the Vietnam war. He saw what would happen many years before the My Lai massacres and the Ellsberg revelations in the United States and he acted to try and stop it. At one stage he sent an angry letter to the Soviet leader Kosygin, asking why the Soviet Air Force was not defending Hanoi. The reply was respectful, though characteristically evasive.

As part of the preparation for convoking the Tribunal, several teams of investigators were sent to Cambodia and Vietnam to bring back evidence from their tour. The teams consisted of writers, journalists, historians, lawyers and scientists from different parts of the world, including the United States. I had been asked to join one of the teams in Cambodia.

Prince Norodom Sihanouk ruled Cambodia in every sense of the word. He was Head of State, Head of the government, the top musician, even the top film director. He was also desperate to keep Cambodia out of the war in South-East Asia, and for that reason he wanted the United States to withdraw its troops from Vietnam. He had stated that the Russell Tribunal would be welcome in his country and could travel around freely to ascertain whether or not Cambodia was being used as a sanctuary by the communist partisans of the South Vietnamese National Liberation Front. Soon after our arrival the Cambodians insisted that we inspected the border zones for ourselves.

We spent ten days in Phnom Penh. My team-leader was Lawrence Daly, the Scottish mineworkers' leader. Other members of the team were Carol Brightman from *Viet-Report*, a radical anti-war magazine in the United States, Dr Abraham Behar from the Unified Socialist Party (PSU) in France and Gustavo Tolentino from Canada, a doctor on the eve of qualification. Lawrence Daly had thoughtfully brought a bottle of the finest Scottish malt whisky as a gift for Ho Chi Minh. When he realised that we were to carry out a ten-day tour of duty in Cambodia he decided, wisely, that another gift would have to be found for the Vietnamese leader.

The United States had revealed a communications route to the NLF from the North which cut through Cambodia. It was called the Ho Chi Minh trail. The Cambodians refused to acknowledge its existence. Cambodian interpreters angrily denied the "Ho Chi Minh *piste*". The first occasion on which they did so Lawrence Daly collapsed with laughter. His one-track mind had interpreted the Cambodians' remark as : "Tomorrow you will go to see Ho Chi Minh pissed."

We did eventually visit the so-called trail, talked to numerous Cambodian military officers, carried out an inspection of an area where the Americans claimed that North Vietnamese planes had landed, and saw the rising smoke from the fires on the other side of the Cambodian-South Vietnamese border — the result of American bombing missions. We were quite sure that the trails we had seen could not have been used by a large convoy of North Vietnamese trucks, but at the same time it was clear that the United States had bombed the particular trail we were following. So while we had no hesitation in testifying to the indiscriminate character of American bombing raids, some of us believed that the NLF was using Cambodian

xi

territory as a sanctuary and that the Northern régime was sending to the South weapons, volunteers, medicines and other supplies via the same route. What was irritating was that this could not be publicly admitted. Why should there be such a veil of secrecy shrouding the aid which the North was providing the NLF in the South? This question was not to be satisfactorily resolved on this particular trip.

We spent ten exhausting and politically inconclusive days in Phnom Penh, before we left for Vietnam. Sihanouk was not in Cambodia at the time and so we did not meet him. His government ministers were hospitable, though uneasy, and divisions were evident within the Cambodian ruling circles. Attitudes towards the Tribunal varied from antagonistic indifference to restrained neutrality. It was clear that we were being received as guests because Sihanouk had so willed. Otherwise we would have not been allowed to enter the country by those who claimed to be his followers. By the time Sihanouk discovered that there was a right-wing plot to depose him it was already too late.

A few days before we left Cambodia, we spent a day at the old Khymer palaces of Angkor Wat. It was a surrealistic occasion. Not far away we could hear the sounds and feel the impact of a brutal war. And yet Angkor Wat exuded peace and tranquillity. We saw the sun set and the moon rise; we watched the most exquisite folk-dancing in the light of the moon: the image remains vivid in my mind. It could have been the seventeenth or the eighteenth century. However, the dream could not last despite all Sihanouk's efforts. A war on the scale of the US-Vietnam conflict has a logic of its own. It is impossible to remain "neutral": one has to take sides. Sihanouk discovered this too late.

There was only one way of getting to Hanoi from Phnom Penh: this was on a regular flight made by the plane belonging to the International Control Commission* — the only useful service this august body provided. It was a five-hour flight, not counting the three-hour stop-over in the Laotian city of Vientiane — a town crawling with CIA and other intelligence operatives, who scrutinised every traveller to Hanoi and took the necessary photograph for the computer files back at head-

*A powerless body set up in 1962 to prevent truce violations in Laos. Its members were Canada, India and Poland.

xii

quarters. Ever since an ICC plane had disappeared in 1965 over Laotian air space all visitors to Hanoi were somewhat tense in Laos. Rumour had it that the plane had been shot down by the Pathet Lao guerrillas whose hatred of aircraft was legendary. The three-hour wait at the airport was for the sun to set — it was not safe to fly to Hanoi during daylight. Hanoi airport was in darkness as we approached it, but just before we landed the lights were switched on and immediately we set down they were extinguished. Vietnam was at war. No chances were taken, and they were extra careful with visitors from the West.

The most galling aspect of our visit was a feeling that we were mere spectators. The entire nation was helping in the fight against the United States, but we were scrupulously kept out of the way during bombing raids. Nor were we allowed to participate in any defence operations. The Vietnamese insisted that our task was to observe, take notes and report back to "Lord Russell's Tribunal". On one occasion I remember trying to persuade a Vietnamese Major Van Bang in the southern province of Thanh-Hao to take us into the city. He maintained that Vietnamese radar had sighted a bombing mission. We were supposed to have been in Thanh-Hoa hospital at 2.30 p.m.; we did not arrive until 4.30. It was a smouldering wreck. It had been bombed at 3.00 p.m. I can still see the sad smile on Van Bang's face as he said: "I was right, wasn't I, comrade?" That was the last argument *I* had with Van Bang about our movements.

On another occasion we were visiting the mines north of Haiphong. The bombing had been so severe that the miners were living in caves on the coast. The sight of coalminers being bombarded day and night visibly moved Lawrence Daly. He made a powerful speech on internationalism to the Vietnamese miners. He questioned the arrogance of the United States in stationing their aircraft carriers off Vietnamese shores and sending in the planes to bomb workers and peasants. He wondered why those who claimed to be in fraternal solidarity with the Vietnamese were not doing more to help? "Where," roared Daly, "is the Soviet Navy?" There was a momentary silence as the interpreter translated what had been said, and then spontaneous and tumultuous applause. Daly wept as he was embraced by the Vietnamese miners and news of what he had said travelled far and wide. But there was fire in his belly in those days. If someone had suggested then that within a decade Daly would become a tame supporter of a reactionary Labour government, I would not have believed him.

This question of internationalism was raised again when we met the North Vietnamese Prime Minister, Pham Van Dong. I suggested that brigades from all the five continents could in a direct and concrete way help to win the war. Pham Van Dong walked up to where I was standing. He embraced me. This was to show sympathy for our predicament. He then explained how the war in Vietnam differed fundamentally from the Spanish Civil War. This was a war fought with the most technologically advanced weaponry and methods. The tactics of the Spanish Civil War could not be repeated. He told us quite bluntly that international brigades would be more of a liability than a help in military terms. He also implied that a call for international brigades in the year 1967 when the army of the Chinese People's Republic was not far away might be misinterpreted in some quarters. But he stressed time and time again that what was needed was a solidarity movement all over the world, and visits such as ours helped establish important links between the Vietnamese and their supporters in the West. "That is a task we cannot carry out from here, but you can." We took these words to heart. Earlier the same year Ho Chi Minh had been asked by a visiting Italian Communist Party delegation how best they could help the Vietnamese. He had replied: "The best way would be by making the revolution in Italy!" The Italians had been somewhat embarrassed.

Hanoi was a ghost city. Most of the children had been evacuated to safer spots. The shops opened every day for a few hours only. One could hear the noise of bombing throughout the day. Sometimes it was so close that the windows rattled in Reunification Hotel. And then for four days there was a ceasefire for Tet, the Lunar New Year. Suddenly everything changed. Hanoi was a bustling city once more. There were courting couples on the side of the Lake of the Restored Sword. The city was suddenly crawling with children, and the shops were open all day. There was even a hastily organised entertainment in the old French theatre, which was packed with soldiers and children. A Cuban orchestra received the most applause. It was Tet 1967. The full impact of the war had not yet been felt in the United States of America. In exactly one year a politico-military offensive by the liberation forces was to transform the war in a decisive fashion, which would reverberate throughout the world. But none of this was foreseen by us in Hanoi that year. Though even then the Vietnamese officers we met were modestly confident that the United States could not win the war.

We had endless discussions with Vietnamese military and political officials. We tried to find out from our interpreters how the war was affecting their personal lives. Even when they felt unable to reply they treated us with patience and courtesy. What was obvious was that the war had immeasurably strengthened the Ho Chi Minh régime. There was massive popular support for the war; there was overwhelming opposition to the Americans. The links between the party, army and the masses were closer than they had been since 1954, when Vietnam was divided into two by the Geneva Accord. There was little doubt that the country was committed to war — there was no democracy, but what was the option in *that* period? There is no other way to fight a war. The problems of bureaucratism only became a major obstacle *after* the successful liberation of Saigon and Southern Vietnam.

On our return from Vietnam we prepared our evidence for the War Crimes Tribunal in Stockholm, engaged in activities designed to convey the importance of the Vietnam Solidarity Campaign and went on endless speaking tours to describe what we had seen in Vietnam. It was the routine, everyday activity of full-time political activists. Vietnam was the most important struggle taking place in the world at that time. But it was not the only one. 1967 was a curious year in that sense. It saw a number of defeats: the Israeli victory in the Six Day War seemed to have destroyed all hopes of a Palestinian revival; Che's death in Bolivia at the hands of US-trained Rangers was another blow; the premature death of the distinguished Marxist historian, Isaac Deutscher, seemed to set the seal on the year 1967.

In their different ways Che Guevara and Isaac Deutscher exercised an enormous influence on the radical youth that took to the barricades in May 1968 in France and subsequently in other parts of Europe. The man of action and the man of ideas died within weeks of each other. Like most activists of that period, I too was heavily influenced by both of them. It was part of a process which drew one closer to revolutionary Marxism. It is therefore useful to try and explain what they both represented.

Che's prestige was linked to the success of the Cuban Revolution. His name, together with that of Fidel Castro, was known throughout the world. The Cuban revolutionaries had audaciously created a revolution under the very nose of the United States. The fact that they were linked neither to Cuban or Russian Stalinism had freed the revolution from dogma and bureaucratism. Castro's speeches and Che's writings in the early sixties and late fifties reflected this important fact. They were remarkably fresh and exhilarating.

Not surprisingly the Cuban revolution gave new hope to millions of oppressed people throughout Latin America. The insistence of its leaders that it was merely the first step towards the liberation of Latin America helped to create a new internationalist political current in Latin American politics. Neither Mao Tse Tung nor Ho Chi Minh had spoken in such a fashion about the international impact of their respective revolutions. They were conceived and carried out as revolutions in one country. The ideological dogmas of the Stalinist family forbade any mention of spreading the revolution. Fidel and Che were not bound by this catechism. They spoke openly and they spoke aloud. What they said, in the first years after the fall of Havana, pleased neither Washington nor Moscow. Washington attempted to crush them through subversion, attempted invasions and plots to assassinate Castro. They all failed. Moscow provided them with invaluable economic and military aid. The American blockade made this aid vital. The Russians exploited this unfortunate dependence to try and put the revolution in a straitjacket of its own brand of bureaucratic and stultifying "orthodoxies". It had greater successes than its North American enemy.

The attraction of Che Guevara was that he attempted to put his ideas into practice. He was disgusted by the lack of *effective* solidarity with Vietnam from its "fraternal friends". His message of "Create, Two, Three, Many Vietnams" to the Tricontinental Congress was motivated by the purest feelings of internationalism. Sentiments which had been virtually obliterated from the international workers' movement by the combined onslaught of Stalinism and social-democracy. Che felt that direct aid had to be provided for the Vietnamese. He attempted to open a second front in Bolivia with the approval and support of the central leadership of the Cuban revolution. He gave up all his official positions inside Cuba and left for other fronts. He fought with liberation fighters in Africa, but his heart was in Latin America. He was convinced that Bolivia offered the best conditions for repeating the Cuban experience. He was not so wrong in assessing Bolivia as a weak link of the Latin American chain. The Bolivian tin miners had a record of tenacious and protracted struggles as well as victories. The mines had finally been nationalised under a form of workers' control (with their own radio stations). They occasionally defended themselves against military incursions with machine guns and sticks of dynamite. What the oligarchs feared most of all was an army of miners descending on the capital city of La Paz. Che was, however, wrong in imagining that the Cuban model could be reproduced in Bolivia. He lacked a *political* strategy and he lacked a political organisation. These two weaknesses were to cost him his life.

Che had been joined in Bolivia by militants from other Latin American countries. Amongst them was a young French journalist Régis Debray. Debray and an Argentinian were asked by Che to leave the guerrillas and leave Bolivia. While they were attempting to do so they were arrested by the Bolivian military. Fortunately for them their arrest was witnessed by a journalist, otherwise they would probably have been shot. The arrest of Debray aroused a great deal of concern in the West. Reluctantly, the Bolivian government agreed to a trial under pressure from various quarters, including de Gaulle. In Britain the Bertrand Russell Peace Foundation set up a Commission of Inquiry. This consisted of Ralph Schoenmann (Russell's secretary), Robin Blackburn (a friend of Debray who could provide evidence to sustain the latter's claim that he was a journalist), Perry Anderson (Editor of the *New Left Review*), Lothar Menne (a German journalist), and myself.

When we arrived in the Bolivian capital of La Paz we were told that no journalists were allowed into Camiri, where Debray was being held. It was part of the guerrilla zone and, as we were all journalists, we needed credentials authorised by General Ovando, the head of the Bolivian army. These were eventually obtained. We hired a small plane and flew over the Andes to Camiri. From the very beginning the military understandably disliked us. We were not the sort of journalists they were accustomed to meeting, and they had not heard of the esoteric magazines and newspapers we represented. My task was to photograph all the top military officers in Camiri so that we could identify the men in charge of the anti-guerrilla operation. This turned out to be a more perilous undertaking than we had assumed. The first occasion on which I photographed a senior officer — from a distance and with a telephoto lens — he pulled out his revolver, walked over to me and coolly informed me that the next time I shot him with my camera he would shoot me with his gun. A few days later I was arrested and charged with being a Cuban guerrilla called Ponbo, who was, in fact, Che's bodyguard. After four hours I convinced them that I did not speak any Spanish and they finally released me. It was agreed by the Commission that I should leave as soon as possible. The words of Reque Teran, the commanding officer who led the anti-guerrilla campaign, were still ringing in our ears: "Our constitution is too democratic and I don't like democracy. I want a strong dictatorship which would give me authority to shoot Debray. Of course, he should be shot and if it was up to me he would have been shot long ago."

Meanwhile Debray's trial had been indefinitely postponed. Before I left Bolivia, I met Richard Gott from *The Guardian* in La Paz. We exchanged notes on the Bolivian military. A few hours later both of us were surprised to see another familiar face: Feltrinelli, the left-wing Italian publisher. I can still see him, sitting in the foyer of the Hotel Copacabana with an array of maps laid out on the table in front of him as he studied the terrain where Che's guerrillas were fighting for their lives. Feltrinelli had arrived with a large amount of money and quixotic notions of rescuing both Che and Régis Debray. "After all, they are both my authors," he had said in all seriousness. He was arrested and expelled from the country a few weeks later.

Blackburn and Anderson had both managed to see Debray. They had obtained the story of his arrest and imprisonment, which was subsequently published in *The Observer* and other papers. Ralph Schoenmann was the only member of our expeditionary force who actually attended the trial of Régis Debray.

He revealed his identity and attacked the trial procedures in his inimitable, forthright fashion. The Bolivian government arrested him and deported him to the United States. When Schoenmann attempted to return to London, where he was based, the Labour government declared him an "undesirable alien" and barred his entry into the United Kingdom.

It had become clear to us in Bolivia that Che's mission was doomed. The Bolivian officers were systematically capturing the guerrillas. They told us that they had Che surrounded. We hoped they were lying, but every new strand of evidence suggested that they were not. The CIA had sent in some top operatives to help supervise the kill. To add insult to injury they had sent a Cuban exile, now in their pay, to watch while Che was captured. A few weeks after we had returned to Europe we heard that the guerrillas had been defeated and Che captured. They were too scared to keep him alive for long. The generals arrived from La Paz with their CIA colleagues. They stared at Guevara in amazement. He stared back and spat at them. A non-commissioned officer named Mario Teran came and shot him dead in a deserted school room. Others arrived and each fired a shot into his dead body. They later claimed that he had been killed in battle, but no one believed this story. Some months later, a defecting Bolivian government minister told the truth and gave Che's diary to the Cuban government. In Britain the complete diaries were first published by the revolutionary newspaper *The Black Dwarf*.

Ironically enough Che's death transformed him into a cult figure in Bolivia. The workers who overthrew the military dictatorship and set up a Popular Assembly in 1971 paid open homage to Che Guevara. They pledged to avenge his death, but in fact they suffered a severe defeat as an even worse military dictator, Banzer, mounted the saddle. Che's tactics were certainly misguided, but his resolute internationalism and his fear that a Cuban revolution, isolated for too long, would suffer in the process deserve our admiration and respect. Che had written:

"The guerrilla is a liberation fighter *par excellence*: elected of the people, vanguard combatant in their struggle for liberation. Guerrilla warfare is not, as often thought, a small-scale war, a war conducted by a minority grouping against a powerful army. No, guerrilla warfare is war by the entire people against the reigning oppression. The guerrilla movement is their armed vanguard; the guerrilla army comprises all the people of a region or a country. That is the reason for its strength and for its eventual victory over whatever power tries to crush it; that is, the base and grounding of the guerrilla is the people.

"One cannot imagine small armed groups, no matter how mobile and familiar with the terrain, surviving the organised persecution of a well-equipped army without this powerful assistance."

In Bolivia Che thought that the conditions for a launching of armed struggle were already favourable. It could be argued that in an objective sense he was correct. But the struggle to create the necessary political instrument which could win the support of the masses did not take place. The *political* arming of the masses was ignored, with tragic consequences. The limitations and inadequacies of Che's legacy were further borne out in the inability of his followers to develop the necessary strategy for a revolution in conditions of mass struggle. Che's close friend, Salvador Allende, was installed in the Moneda Palace in Chile through an electoral victory. The strategy and tactics necessary to transform that win into a mass struggle for socialism and workers' power eluded both Allende and Che's followers in the MIR (Movement of the Revolutionary Left). Similarly in Argentina a failure to grapple with the complex problems of revolutionary tactics and strategy led to the elimination of the militants of the People's Revolutionary Army (ERP).

And yet despite these shortcomings and weaknesses, which Che himself would have been the first to acknowledge and correct if he had lived, his humanity and his belief in the international character of the revolutionary process stand out sharply in a world dominated by chauvinism and nationalism. These qualities were revealed in a letter which he left behind for his children in Cuba before he left:

"Dear Hildita, Aleidita, Camilo, Celia and Ernesto. If one day you read this letter it will be because I am no longer with you. You will almost not remember me and the littlest ones will not remember me at all. Your father has been a man who acts as he thinks and you can be sure that he has been faithful to his convictions. Grow up to be good revolutionaries. Study hard so that you can master the technology that will permit you to control nature. Remember that the Revolution is what matters and that each one of us alone is worth nothing. Above all, always be capable of feeling deeply any injustice committed against anyone anywhere in the world. That is the most beautiful quality of a revolutionary. Farewell children, I still hope to see you. A big hug and kiss from Papa."

If Che was essentially a man of action, his contemporary Isaac Deutscher was indisputably a man of ideas. He died in August 1967, a couple of months before Che and yet, despite the fact that his death was mourned largely amongst small circles of Marxists, his influence will probably last the longer. I have not provided a biographical sketch of Che because numerous books and articles have been written about him; newsreels on his life and death have been distributed by the Cuban government; and his origins are well known. The same cannot be said for Isaac Deutscher. He was attached to no state and to no political organisation. His only loyalty was to the ideas of Marxism. A brief and schematic sketch of his life is necessary if we are to comprehend the impact which his ideas have had on hundreds and thousands of people over the last two decades.

Isaac Deutscher died on 19 August 1967. It was a sudden and unexpected death and left deep wounds in the hearts of all those who had known him or read his writings. His work in the fifties and sixties did more to lay the basis for a lasting and viable anti-Stalinist Marxist tradition than all the empty rhetoric of many of his sectarian vilifiers on the left. He was, in my opinion, wrong on a number of important questions. (They were, incidentally, errors which would have been corrected by the passing of time.) But that in no way detracts from his stature as an outstanding Marxist historian, a writer of flawless English prose and a farsighted political analyst. The fact that Trotsky's leading role in the Russian revolution, hidden from many by the tyranny of Stalinism, is today almost universally, though grudgingly, acknowledged by the Communist Party intellectuals in the West is history's own tribute to Isaac Deutscher.

Deutscher was born in Cracow, Poland in 1907. He came from a strong rabbinical background. He recorded his early conflicts with Judaism, displaying both honesty and wit, in *A Non-Jewish Jew and Other Essays*. In 1926 he joined the

Polish Communist Party and found himself confronting a world where there was a great deal of theoretical confusion. In May 1926 the Polish CP had supported a military *coup d'état* led by Pilsudski against the Polish gentry. Following this appalling decision a debate began among party leaders aligned to rival factions within the Soviet Communist Party (the supporters of Bukharin and Zinoviev). But the discussion was unsatisfactory and Deutscher was later to describe it as a "quarrel of damned souls imprisoned within the enchanted circle of Stalinism".

A few years later the Stalinised Communist International changed course yet again. It forbade any collaboration with social-democratic parties which were termed "social-fascist". From his exile Trotsky denounced this turn. He called for a working-class united front against the growing threat of fascism. His appeals fell on sympathetic ears in Poland. A third of the Warsaw membership was inclined to agree with him, but the party leadership began to hound the dissidents. Those who wanted to fight fascism in alliance with social-democrats were themselves denounced as "Pilsudskist-Trotskyist-fascist agents" and were rapidly isolated. A hard core remained, which included Deutscher, and joined the Polish wing of the International Left Opposition against Stalinism. In 1932 Deutscher was expelled by the Polish Communist Party. His independent mind was not welcome. Only six years later the entire leadership of the Polish party was found to be too independent-minded. Having fled to Moscow to escape repression, they were arrested on Stalin's orders and executed. The Polish Party was dissolved by orders of the Comintern. Deutscher was shattered. He had strong disagreements with the Polish Communist leaders, but to hear them referred to as "fascist agents and traitors" was outrageous, to say the least. Deutscher recalled his memory of one of them:

"I remember the image of Warski at Theatre Square on 1 May 1928. He was marching at the head of a huge banned demonstration, through the hail of machine-gun fire and rifle shots with which we were greeted (by Pilsudski's militia). While tens of hundreds of wounded were falling in our ranks, he held up his white-grey head, a high and easy target visible from afar; and he indomitably addressed the crowd. This was the image of him I had in my mind when, some years later, he was announced from Moscow as a traitor, a spy, and a Pilsudskist agent."

The victory of Hitler in Germany provided a further vindication of Trotsky's critique of the suicidal practice of the Comintern. Deutscher accepted the critique, but disagreed with Trotsky that the time was right to set up a new Fourth International. He deliberately chose to devote himself to writing and withdrew to what he called the "watchtower". It is easy, in retrospect, to say that he should have remained an activist and a scholar, but given what he produced it would be foolish, in the extreme, to describe the course he took as dishonourable.

Several months before the Nazis invaded Poland, Deutscher left his native country and sought exile in Britain. He was seconded into the Polish army-in-exile, but he spent most of the war as a journalist. He had read references in Marx's *Kapital* to *The Economist* and it was in that journal that his first article was published. He wrote regularly on Eastern Europe and the USSR for both *The Economist* and *The Observer*. It was a stimulating discipline and it displayed all his talents as a contemporary political analyst. He knew no English when he arrived in England, but he soon developed an amazing mastery of the language, displaying a talent not dissimilar to that acquired by a fellow-Pole of the preceding generation — Joseph Conrad.

Deutscher began his main political project in the post-war period, at the start of the Cold War. His monumental Trotsky trilogy (published by the Oxford University Press) took on the Herculean task of replying to the mountains of slander heaped on the shoulders of the organiser of the Red Army: an accumulated product of the Stalinist propaganda machine, which functioned on a world scale. The completion of the three-volume biography of Trotsky was a remarkable feat. The books were written during a bleak period in international politics, and their audience was limited to semi-academic circles. The biography was a powerful assault on both the crude anti-Marxism of the Cold War historians and the vulgar apologetics of Communist Party intellectuals, who justified every Stalinist atrocity. The Trotsky trilogy soon became widely recognised, though this was not acknowledged at the time, as a political and literary classic. Deutscher was attacked from all sides: by the CIA through its Congress for Cultural Freedom; by the Stalinists through the Communist Party press; and the Trotskyist groups were angry because Deutscher refused to accept as the gospel everything Trotsky wrote.

It is not easy today to evoke the conditions under which Deutscher worked. The British intelligentsia was uniformly hostile to him. He received no grants from academic bodies, no university professorships from the educational establishment, no regular appearances on television as an authority on the Soviet Union. The élite of the British academic intelligentsia were also exiles, but reactionary émigrés from the East — Berlin, Popper and their associates — held complete sway. They were envious of Deutscher's achievements, and they were enraged because this particular émigré from the East was of a different generation — he spoke a different language: the language of Marxism. Deutscher's intellectual prowess threatened to break their monopoly of politics and history on the university campuses, so they treated him as an outcast. Isaiah Berlin blackballed Deutscher's appointment at Sussex University, and legend has it that this great believer in freedom and democracy was opposed to a Marxist teaching Soviet history. An honourable exception was the distinguished historian E. H. Carr, who openly acknowledged Deutscher's merits and helped him when he could. As a result, Deutscher's research work had to be constantly interrupted by writing articles for the press in order to earn a living. This hardship makes his ultimate achievement all the more courageous and worthy of our respect.

In a sense, the conditions in which Deutscher worked are similar to those in which Trotsky wrote *The History of the Russian Revolution* from his exile on the island of Prinkipo. Two decades later his biographer would write from a similar state of enforced isolation, induced by a similar political situation. Both Trotsky's *History* and Deutscher's trilogy must rank as the two finest examples of contemporary historical writing within the tradition of classical Marxism.

Deutscher's last years were spent on research for a biography of Lenin. It would have been a critical work and would have provided a powerful counterbalance to those who have transformed Lenin into an icon in their totally uncritical biographies as well as the cold warriors. His work on Lenin was interrupted by the war in Vietnam. He threw himself fervently into the anti-war movement. He responded to Bertrand

Russell's appeal and served as a judge on the International War Crimes Tribunal. I remember how sharply he responded to what he thought was a loose formulation in my testimony to the Tribunal. I had let drop the remark that there was a very strong racist content to the Vietnamese war and that the United States could not have got away with napalm and terror bombing in any white country of Europe or North America. Deutscher, hostile to any manifestation of nationalism, disagreed and a brief exchange took place in which neither of us conceded. It was clear that the struggle of the Vietnamese had moved him to commit himself to active politics for the first time since the thirties.

Before he could return to his biography of Lenin, Deutscher died and the international workers' movement lost its most gifted historian. It was doubly cruel and tragic because Deutscher's audience had grown by tens of thousands in just under a year. He died before the French general strike of May/June 1968 and before the Soviet invasion of Czechoslovakia. He would have been deeply affected by these developments. He used to believe that the bureaucratic régimes in the USSR and the East could be reformed "from above", from within the party apparatus.

What would he have felt as the young Czech communists — who were serialising his last completed work, *The Unfinished Revolution* (an important critique of the USSR) in the pages of *Literarne Listy* — were crushed by Soviet tanks? One of their crimes was listed as, in the words of the misnamed *Pravda,* publishing works by the "notorious anti-communist Isaac Deutscher".

Would not he have come down from his "watchtower" as tens of thousands of young students and workers flocked to join revolutionary organisations throughout the world? Deutscher's thoughts were anything but static. 1968 would have exercised a strong pressure on him to re-evaluate some of his political positions. Trotsky had been involved in the revolutionary upsurge which had shaken Europe in 1905-18, and then he entered the "hell-black night" of the thirties, and in his biographer's words he confronted a desperate scene:

"All anti-Stalinist forces had been wiped out . . . Trotskyism, Zinovievism, and Bukharinism, all drowned in blood, had, like some Atlantis, vanished from all political horizons . . . and he himself was now the sole survivor of Atlantis."

But Trotsky had a brain which continued to function as an important arsenal of revolutionary ideas. That is until Stalin's agent drove an ice-pick through it in 1940. It was the heritage of these ideas which provided a thin, at times almost invisible, continuity with the real traditions of revolutionary politics. Deutscher had emerged from that same "hell-black night" and taken a conscious decision to restrict his activities to theoretical production. But just as the night was ending and the rays of a new sun could be sighted on the distant horizon, he died. Many of those who have been won over to socialist politics in the last decade have essentially been wooed by the power of activism. This is positive and healthy, but it can only be lasting if these new militants can imbibe ideas not only related simply to what they are currently involved in. They could do worse than study the writings of Deutscher in the same critical way as he studied those of Marx, Lenin and Trotsky. The sad fact is that there is an objective gulf between the new generation of militants and the old, especially in Britain and West Germany. While the new revolutionary vanguard has a few, limited toeholds in the working classes, as this book argues, a gulf still remains. Until it can be bridged there will be no easy road to revolution.

The year 1967 witnessed a number of defeats and losses. Two years before that the Americans successfully invaded Santo Domingo. In that same year — 1965 — the United States had scored another major victory in Indonesia. The overthrow of Sukarno had been accompanied by the killing of over half a million communists and socialists. Two years later Bolivia had been "saved" and Guevara executed. American policy-makers could be forgiven for thinking that these "successes" could be repeated in other parts of the world.

But towards the end of 1967 the tide was beginning to turn. A new and politically aware generation, mainly students, was beginning to challenge the dominant assumptions of bourgeois society. In October 1967 there were demonstrations in Europe, America and Japan against the Vietnam war. In Britain it was the first major demonstration sponsored by the Vietnam Solidarity Campaign: 10,000 people marched behind banners proclaiming their solidarity with the Vietnamese. They were turned back at Grosvenor Square, but only after they had carried the flags of the National Liberation Front right up to the steps of the granite citadel. In Japan hundreds of thousands of workers and students demonstrated their contempt for their Prime Minister's departure on an official visit to Saigon. There were massive demonstrations in all the advanced capitalist countries of the world. It was a harbinger of what was to come.

The central argument contained in this book is that 1968 marked a turning point for the rulers and the ruled throughout Europe, East and West. It is true that no revolutionary upsurge succeeded. But on the other hand it is equally true that virtually none of the governments of Europe have succeeded in returning to pre-1968 "stability". What has happened in the ten years that have followed 1968 has required a readjustment of tactics in a whole number of cases. It has in no way demonstrated that the aims and aspirations of those who fought in 1968 in different parts of the globe were utopian and thus not capable of being fulfilled. Chile and Portugal, in their different ways, exposed the bankruptcy of traditional reformist politics. But they also revealed the far-left at its political weakest, unable to provide a fully worked-out alternative.

The aim of this book therefore is not to gloss over the mistakes and weaknesses of the revolutionary left, or to idealise them. It is to try and explain where we went wrong and to explore how we can move forward. Those readers whose only knowledge of Marxism and Marxists comes from a hostile mass media or from columnists whose main task is to denigrate our ideas, might be surprised by what we have to say. In order to help them further I have appended a bibliography which they might find useful.

Prologue

In 1968 the ruling classes of Western Europe governed with a certain degree of complacency. The preceding two decades had enabled them to establish social peace. It was a tranquillity aided by the cynical agreement reached at Yalta in 1945 and the economic boom of the post-war years. There had, however, been trouble in the East. In East Berlin a workers' rebellion demanding more democratic liberties had been crushed by Soviet tanks occasioning a sharp response from the pen of Bertholt Brecht. Then in 1956 the Hungarian masses had risen in arms determined to overthrow Stalinist tutelage. They too had been subjugated by Soviet tanks. In Poland a year later conflict had been avoided by the granting of reforms from above. As the bourgeoisie of the West witnessed these rebellions in the East they could not but congratulate themselves on the fact that their rule had so far proceeded fairly smoothly. There had been no pre-revolutionary upsurge in the capitalist West since the Second World War.

The Conservatives and Social-Democrats who governed Western Europe, mainly on their own, but sometimes in coalition with one another, were not completely dissimilar in outlook from the monarchs and despots who had presided over Europe following the Peace of Vienna in 1815. Yalta in a number of ways was the modern equivalent of Vienna. Those who signed their initials on a scrap of paper or embedded their seals on the parchment before them were not to know that the masses had and still have an awkward way of making themselves heard above the roars of the loudest cannon or gunfire and at a time when it is least expected of them. Time and time again the masses have disrupted the most carefully laid plans of their masters. They have insisted on determining the course of events. They have mostly been unsuccessful but that has not prevented them, after a lapse, from trying again.

In 1848 a mass revolutionary upsurge had resulted in a chain reaction, which almost assumed the dimensions of a continental earthquake. The democratic aspirations and demands of the Parisian masses had led to immediate tremors in Italy, Germany, Austria, Bohemia and Hungary. More distant echoes were felt in Switzerland, Denmark, Rumania, Poland and Ireland. Nothing as widespread or as interconnected as this had ever been seen in Europe before. While there was a set of specific indigenous particularities in all these cases, no one disputed the strength of the Parisian example. The wave of revolutions in 1848 subsided in time, but in a number of cases certain limited democratic reforms were implemented. It was the last occasion on which a liberal segment of the ruling classes took to the barricades against absolutism. From thenceforward they were to confine their activities to the parliamentary assemblies they had helped to create. And, more to the point, they were to react with a ferocious violence in defence of their property against the plebeian masses who challenged it in the name of egalitarian principles.

The year 1848 dented the absolutist régimes even if it did not completely eliminate them. It revealed the rulers in a state of despair. The Belgian monarch, sick with fear lest the impact of the Parisian "mob" make itself felt in Brussels, wrote to his niece, the British Queen Victoria, in February 1848: "I am very unwell in consequence of the *awful* events at Paris. . . . What will soon become of us God alone knows; great efforts will be made to revolutionise this country; as there are poor and wicked people in all countries it may succeed." Several months later Victoria replied to her uncle: "Since 24th February I feel an uncertainty in everything existing, which one never felt before. When one thinks of one's children, their education, their future — and prays for them — I always think and say to myself, 'Let them grow up fit for *whatever station* they may be placed in — *high or low*.' This one never thought of before, but I *do* always now. . . ."

Victoria was being unduly pessimistic. The heyday of Chartism had already passed. The upheavals in Paris gave the Chartists their last card. They played it by organising a mammoth demonstration on Kennington Common. A confrontation might have led to further resistance, but the instinct for self-preservation of the British ruling class proved as formidable as ever. Victoria's husband, Prince Albert, sent a private letter to the Prime Minister, Lord John Russell, on the actual day of the Chartist assembly: "I don't feel doubtful for a moment who will be found the stronger, but should be exceedingly mortified if anything like a commotion was to take place." Albert went further and advised Russell to cut down the level of unemployment in order to decrease the level of working-class discontent: "I find, to my great regret, that the number of workmen of all trades out of employment is *very* large, and that it has been increased by the reduction of all the works under governments, owing to the clamour for economy in the House of Commons. . . . Surely this is not the moment for the taxpayers to economise upon the working classes."

Britain avoided a major confrontation in 1848, but most of Europe saw street-battles and clashes. Its "rulers, who neither see, nor feel, nor know, but leech-like to their fainting country cling" were in the case of France overthrown and replaced. In other countries reforms were conceded to avoid further pressure from below: within the next three decades parliaments based on a partial franchise existed everywhere except in Spain and Tsarist Russia.

The Europe of 1968 was, of course, totally different in most respects. The contrast with 1848 is of interest only because the ruling classes in both cases were taken by surprise. Furthermore the upheavals occurred in times of "peace". There were no continental wars weakening the social fabric of Europe and creating conditions of instability which could bring about a radical shift in the consciousness of the masses. In that sense the events in 1968 were different from the wave of strikes and upheavals which shook capitalist Europe at the conclusion of the First World War; and markedly different from the situation which existed at the end of the Second World War. 1968 was not so much an echo from the past as an image of the future. That is what gave it its originality. Any serious analogies would have to compare France in 1968 with the Russia of 1905-06, though even here the differences outweigh the similarities. The main characteristic of the explosions that marked 1968 was their universality. They were by no means restricted to Europe. As a matter of fact the main inspiration for the radical left in Europe before the May Events in France came from Cuba, Vietnam and China. For two and a half decades the left in Europe had been discussing the events in other continents.

Suddenly they found the revolution on their own doorstep.

A number of "new left" theoreticians had attempted to theorise the long detour of the world revolution — i.e. the fact that after the Second World War the epicentre of struggle shifted to the "third world" — and had maintained that there was no hope of revolution in the West. The best known of these theoreticians, Herbert Marcuse and C. Wright Mills, denied that the working class in Western Europe and North America had any revolutionary potential whatsoever; it had been integrated into the structure of the bourgeois state. These rationalisations of isolationism and pessimism were given a further boost by an important leader of the Chinese People's Republic, Marshal Lin Piao. In a sensational, though mis-guided, text entitled *Long Live The Victory Of The People's War,* Lin Piao attempted to give the Chinese revolutionary experience a universal character. It was the *only* recorded instance by a major Chinese leader which tried to develop an internationalist perspective and map out a strategy for world revolution. The attraction of Lin Piao's theses lay in their simplicity. They were devoid of any incomprehensible jargon. The position they argued was stated simply in the following way: in China the revolution had engulfed the cities from the outside; the Liberation Armies had marched in from the countryside and liberated the cities. Without probably realis-ing it Lin Piao was also pointing at another indisputable fact: the passivity of the urban proletariat in China in 1949 and the failure of the Chinese Communist Party to mobilise it for decisive action. Could this strategy not, argued Lin Piao, be transposed to the world at large? Europe and America were the fortresses of imperialism. Their working class was quiescent and docile. A growing wave of social revolutions in the "Third World" could surround and isolate Western Europe and North America. It was the most advanced theory for the "Third World" to emerge from within the orthodox communist move-ment. It was readily embraced by the radical youth of the West.

Capitalism had been born in Europe. It created and sus-tained exploitation on a global scale, at the same time creat-ing the material and social prerequisites for liberating people from hunger, misery and the drudgery of repetitive labour. It also subjected the colonial peoples to almost permanent vio-

lence. It was, therefore, hardly surprising that its first successful defeats took place at its periphery rather than its centre.
Lenin had used the phrase "the weakest link of the chain will
break first". Marx had already said that "violent outbursts
take place sooner in the extremities of the bourgeois organism
than the heart, because here regulation is more possible". But
despite this, Marx and Lenin both knew that as long as its
heart was functioning capitalism would remain alive. Despite
the long delay was it possible that the working class in the West
had ceased to exist as a class? Marxists in the classical tradition rejected this strongly, amongst them Isaac Deutscher
and Ernest Mandel. The latter maintained that the post-war
economic boom was not the result of pure economic factors
but had been made possible by two vital political decisions that
had been taken respectively by Stalin and Truman. The Soviet
Union had agreed at Yalta that Western capitalism would
maintain its rule in France and Italy. The Communist Parties
of these two countries had therefore disarmed their partisans
and extinguished the flames of the rising masses. The communists had served in national governments at a crucial stage for the
rehabilitation of capitalism. The United States had decided
that the economies of war-torn Europe had to be reconstructed
because of the existence of a growing bloc of post-capitalist
nation states. It had therefore put the overall political interests
of world capital before its own narrow national interests, and
revived the economies of its European and Japanese rivals.
In these conditions capitalism thrived once again. But both
its technological developments — what Mandel describes as
the "third industrial revolution" — and the growing intervention of the State gave it new and important characteristics
which prevented slumps and crises of the 1929 variety, but
instead laid the basis for permanent inflation. The wave of
recessions which began in Europe in the late sixties marked
the end of the boom. They also confronted a working class
who had been led to believe that full employment and rising
living standards were a permanent feature of late capitalism.

At the same time a new intermediate layer, created because
of the new needs of the system, came into its own. In 1967
there were 6 million university students in the United States,
2½ million in Western Europe and 1½ million in Japan. It
proved impossible for late capitalism to integrate this grouping

into the functioning of the system. The character of the education system — justifying the status quo — combined with the growth of unemployment and the world political situation resulted in this particular stratum developing a consciousness and political sensitivity which was soon to erupt in every capitalist city. German and Japanese students had already unleashed a movement of opposition to their government's policies in South-East Asia. The first street-battles had since the late fifties and early sixties taken place in Tokyo. The emergence of these leftist student *samurais* with their helmets and staves revealed the extent of anti-United States feelings which existed in Japan: the war in Vietnam exacerbated these a hundredfold. The predominantly proletarian origins of the Japanese students provided an immediate link with the domestic workers' movement, and a number of joint student-worker actions against the war preceded similar developments in parts of Western Europe.

There were three definite sectors on the map of the world since the Second World War. There was the capitalist world proper: North America, Australia and New Zealand, Japan and Western Europe. Then there was the USSR and Eastern Europe: the latter had been collectivised (with the partial exception of Czechoslovakia and the total exceptions of Yugoslavia and Albania) by the entry of the Red Army in pursuit of the disintegrating legions of the Third Reich. The third sector was the largest and most heavily populated: the continents of Africa, Asia and Latin America. These were colonies of the imperialist powers. (Most of the direct colonies gained political independence at the end of the Second World War.) In China and Vietnam there were indigenous, popular revolts leading to social upheavals and victories on the European scale of October 1917. In the Korean peninsula the intervention of the Red Army was decisive in carving out an Eastern European type of state in the North, which proved incapable of winning the necessary level of mass support in the South to defeat the neo-colonial US-backed administration.

All three sectors were shaken in 1968: that is what makes it a unique year in the annals of world revolution. The May Events in France were preceded by the military offensive of the Vietnamese revolutionaries in Southern Vietnam and succeeded by the "Prague Spring" and the subsequent Soviet invasion. The impact of one was felt on the other and while France was clearly of the greater political significance it cannot be understood or explained in isolation. In 1968 internationalism reached a new peak. Those who sought to isolate one country from another were to be found in the ranks of the counter-revolution. This new internationalism revived the lost traditions of the Russian Revolution. It frightened both the ruling classes of the West and the bureaucracies of the East. *Pravda, Le Figaro* and *The Times* marched shoulder to shoulder. The language was different but the aim was the same: at all costs the unruly and undisciplined masses must be brought to heel: they threatened both the existence of capitalism *and* the system of bureacratic domination exercised by Stalin and his heirs in the USSR and Western Europe.

1. The Offensive in Vietnam

For the five decades before 1973, Vietnam was under continuous attack. No other country has been subjected in this century to so many wars by a succession of imperialist powers. The French, the Japanese, the British, the French again and finally the Americans have attempted to subjugate this Indo-Chinese peninsula, which has been defended by the most tenacious and courageous guerrilla fighters in the history of modern capitalism. The Communist Party in power had made a number of crucial political mistakes over these five decades — a result of the strategic political line dictated by Moscow. They paid dearly for every mistake. In the thirties the Party had destroyed the unity of Saigon's working class; in the forties it had, at the end of World War Two, welcomed British troops led by General Gracey into Saigon and permitted them to establish a bridgehead for the return of French troops. An ungrateful Gracey had turned on them and executed a savage bloodbath. In the fifties they had accepted the conditions of the Geneva Agreement of 1954, even when victory was within their grasp. They had accepted what they thought would be a temporary partition of the country in the hope that free elections within two years would resolve the issue. They might have done, but the United States had successfully sabotaged free elections because, in Eisenhower's words: "ninety per cent of the people would have voted for Ho Chi Minh". On all these occasions the Vietnamese had disobeyed their own political instincts and accepted the dictates of Moscow or, as in 1954, Moscow *and* Peking.

The growing Sino-Soviet split in the sixties enabled the Asian post-capitalist states to exercise a certain degree of flexibility. As the divisions in the Stalinist family led to an open break between Moscow and Peking, the Vietnamese leaders clearly saw the dangers inherent: imperialism would successfully exploit these differences and attempt to fill the

1

vacuum which they had created. It is futile to speculate too much on this question, but it is not impossible that a strong united front between Moscow and Peking resisting any further encroachments on Vietnamese sovereignty could have deterred the bombing raids launched with increasing ferocity by the United States on North Vietnam. However, there can be little doubt that the Sino-Soviet split enabled the Vietnamese to develop their own independent positions. They were able to successfully utilise the differences to resist the pressures from Moscow which constantly urged them to compromise. The whole strategy of "peaceful coexistence" was given a body-blow by the epic resistance of the Vietnamese. In that sense it has to be stated that the driving aim of the policy of the Vietnamese Communist Party was to reunify Vietnam and to abolish the imperialist-dominated economic system which existed in the South. These aims clashed with the global interests of the bureaucrats who sat in the Kremlin.

In the sixties the Vietnamese Communist Party did not repeat its mistakes of the preceding decades. It acted in accordance with the revolutionary needs of its own country. Everything was subordinated to the overall aim of driving the United States out of Vietnam.

The last imperialist power to invade Vietnam also proved to be the toughest. The United States was the most technologically advanced and powerful nation in the entire world. Its leaders imagined that a few thousand military advisers were all that was needed to shore up a corrupt and decrepit local dictatorship. Kennedy believed that given the massive economic aid which had already been provided, all that was necessary to defeat the communists was a small amount of military help. He was to be proved utterly wrong. The battle of Ap Bac in 1962 saw the communist guerrillas inflict a severe defeat on the local army and its American "advisers". It also marked a historic turning point for the Third Vietnamese War. The United States had to make an important choice: either they sent in more troops or they pulled out of the country altogether. There was no third way. But Kennedy and MacNamara were, like their French friends before them, not convinced that the Vietnamese communists enjoyed mass support, particularly in the countryside. They believed that a combination of internal repression and international economic

2

and military aid would solve the problem. They decided to send in more troops. After Kennedy's assassination, his successor, Lyndon Baines Johnson, continued this policy. From December 1963 to December 1967 the American leaders pledged that this was the last Christmas the "boys would be spending away from home". For four years they systematically lied to their own people about the Vietnam war. These lies were increasingly exposed by hard-hitting reports from journalists working for the *New York Times* and the CBS television network, and the Saigon administration regularly expelled the odd American or French journalist who was getting too inquisitive and embarking on an independent investigation. But the overwhelming impression which American citizens nonetheless obtained was that created by the Pentagon and the State Department.

In his New Year message to the President of the United States in January 1968, the Commander-in-Chief of military operations in South Vietnam, General William Westmoreland, sent a characteristically optimistic despatch. He assured the American President that light was at last visible at the end of the tunnel, that the United States was winning the war and the "enemy" was on the verge of defeat. Westmoreland stated that the communists had been forced to retreat to their border sanctuaries and he predicted that they would not be able to mount any major attacks from bases inside South Vietnam in 1968. He did not even consider possible the risk of an attack on the major cities of Southern Vietnam. He was convinced that the half-a-million American soldiers and technicians present on the battlefront would increase the war-gains already made in 1967.

Three weeks after Westmoreland's last despatch the Vietnamese revolutionaries struck the United States a stunning blow. On January 30 they sent the world their Lunar New Year (Tet) message setting the tone for the whole of 1968. They celebrated Tet by launching simultaneous military assaults on twenty-six provincial capitals. The ancient imperial capital of Hue passed under their control as did large parts of Saigon itself. Many local towns and airfields were also attacked, throwing the United States forces into utter confusion. Despite all their intelligence operations, despite their torture of prisoners to elicit information and despite their bases in every city, the United States were taken completely by surprise. It

3

was a remarkable tribute to the National Liberation Front and an indication of the support they enjoyed in the cities and the countryside. They had managed to keep their movements completely secret. To further stress their contempt for Westmoreland's rosy estimates, twenty heroic fighters captured the American Embassy in Saigon. US troops had to fight a long gun-battle before they could recapture the citadel. In Saigon itself it was the working class suburb of Cholon which proved the most resistant to attempts to restore American hegemony. It was bombed continuously for two weeks after January 30. Hue, too, was recaptured, but only after bloody battles.

James Reston, the well-known political columnist, wrote in the *New York Times* of February 4, 1968:

> "Something has happened here in the last few days, some conflict between logic and events. How could the Vietcong launch such an offensive against the American Embassy and the American bases all over South Vietnam? How could the North Vietnamese, who were supposed to be getting weaker, like the Vietcong, gather a force large enough to challenge the US Marines at the demilitarised zone?"

Reston rejected the arguments of the apologists who maintained that this was the "last gasp" or "the death rattle" and showed the weakness of "the enemy".

> ". . . neither of these explanations satisfies Washington. The dramatic events of the last few days have given it the feeling of dealing with something wholly alien and inexplicable and therefore with forces entirely unpredictable."

In reality there was no conflict between "logic and events". There was nothing that was "alien and inexplicable". The Pentagon and the State Department of the United States like other imperialist nations before them had become hypnotised by military arithmetic. Because they had half-a-million troops and the most advanced technology, they should by rights be the winners. Their problem, however, was that they were not playing a game of chess on a gigantic board, but were confronting the social forces of a revolution. They had intervened in a civil war to defend and sustain a neo-colonial administration which could not have lasted without American aid for more than a few months. The logic of war dictated that the Americans *should* win, but this logic had been superseded by

4

one superior and infinitely more powerful: the logic of revolution. It remains a logic which can never be properly understood: its richness and diversity always excludes the minds of its opponents.

In an interview with Madeline Riffaud of *l'Humanité* a few months after the Tet offensive, the Vietnamese leader, General Vo Nguyen Giap, who masterminded the successful assault on Dienbienphu in 1954, gave his answer to James Reston and other American commentators. Giap claimed that the Americans had, in fact, lost the war and explained why:

"Our people are fighting for our national cause but also for socialism and for the other peoples in the world struggling for their liberation. The myth of the invincibility of the USA, this colossus supporting itself impotently on the H-Bomb, is collapsing irretrievably. No matter how enormous its military and economic potential, it will never succeed in crushing the will of a people fighting for its independence. This is a reality which is now recognised throughout the entire world.

"Why did the United States think it would be victorious? It deployed an enormous war machine in our country. Westmoreland is a general who has found a way to boost the US expeditionary force from 20,000 men to more than 500,000 without offering Washington anything in return but a light at the end of the tunnel. The Americans based their confidence that they would win the war on their superior numbers, their overwhelming armament, their riches in dollars and in tons of bombs they are dropping.

"Finding themselves in a more and more difficult situation, they are now accusing their generals of trying to settle things arithmetically — for example, in the matter of the balance of force — while the Vietnamese have a trigonometric strategy. That is not correct. Our strategy is neither arithmetic nor trigonometric. It is quite simply the strategy of a just war, a people's war. They will never be able to understand that."

The Pentagon had declared that it had five military objectives in Vietnam. These were the "pacification" of the countryside; to blockade the South; to destroy the economic and military potential of the North; and to consolidate the Saigon government. The Tet offensive destroyed three of these objectives overnight. The "pacified areas" in the countryside simply disappeared. The blockade of the South was shown to be farcical as Hue and Saigon themselves came under siege.

5

As for the consolidation of the Saigon régime the liberation forces made it their prime target. The majority of their military actions were directed almost exclusively at South Vietnamese military and governmental installations. American airfields and helicopter pads were certainly attacked and, in most cases, destroyed, mainly to prevent the despatch of reinforcements.

In other words the entire Tet offensive was not simply a military operation. It had important revolutionary *political* motivations. The political aim of the offensive was to defeat and demoralise the Saigon régime and its armed forces. This was done for two reasons: in the first place to demonstrate to both the American soldiers and the American population back home that the government they were defending had little popular support and could be swept aside without too much difficulty; secondly to appeal to the Saigon soldiery itself and in a fashion which it would understand. The NLF appeal which accompanied Tet exhorted the South Vietnamese military to join the resistance and bring about the rapid downfall of the Thieu-Ky clique. Both political objectives were achieved over the coming months. The turn of 1968 provided the Vietnamese revolution with a much-needed impetus. It took the initiative, which it held on to even through the worst period of saturation bombing which was to take place throughout the country in the coming years. Two months after Tet the American anti-war movement compelled Lyndon Johnson to publicly announce his impending departure from national politics. A few days after that announcement General Westmoreland was withdrawn from the battlefield and replaced. The epic resistance of the Vietnamese had ended the careers of the American President and its top military commander alike!

In addition several important newspapers and weekly journals demanded a major shift in war policy. In that sense Tet brought out into the open, and further exacerbated, growing divisions inside the American ruling class. *Newsweek* commented on March 18, 1968 that the balance sheet of the war from the United States' point of view was "dismal" and argued that "the war cannot be won by military means without tearing apart the whole fabric of national life and international relations". The *Wall Street Journal* reiterated these views and a number of military tops, the majority of members of the Senate Foreign Relations Committee and the two presidential

6

contenders, Eugene McCarthy and Robert Kennedy, were all moving to support the same thesis. It was a unique acknowledgement that the revolutionary political strategy adopted by Vietnamese Communism was successful.

The impact of Tet 1968 on both Europe and America was profound. In the United States, as I have indicated above, it gave a tremendous boost to an anti-war movement which was able in that very year to mobilise almost a million people against the war. Within the base of the expeditionary army, fissures began to appear as well. A number of serving officers declined to give distasteful orders; an even greater number of soldiers refused to obey those orders. There were a few hundred desertions from the American army to the National Liberation Front. Anti-war magazines circulated in the army giving rise to further anti-war sentiments. Soon, discharged Vietnam war veterans began to take part in demonstrations under their own banners. Limbless veterans came in wheelchairs, others came on crutches to join those who had escaped injury and declare an opposition to the war which had maimed them and killed tens of thousands of others. The size and influence of the anti-war movement in the United States were without precedent in a country at war. The Tet offensive unleashed the latent opposition amongst sectors that were already uneasy, because it had showed decisively that the United States could only win the war by using nuclear weapons. This public opinion at home and abroad, including the USSR and China, would not and could not permit the use of tactical nuclear weapons which was actually considered at one stage and rejected for political reasons. The war could *not* be won. That was the message of the Vietnamese offensive to the people of the United States and large numbers responded accordingly.

In Western Europe the effect of Tet was electric. Here its importance lay not so much in demonstrating the fact that the United States could not win. This was accepted widely even by those who sympathised with American war aims like Harold Wilson and Willy Brandt: British and German social-democracy remained utterly servile and prostrate before the Pentagon and the State Department. The situation had been brilliantly summarised in a cartoon by Gerald Scarfe depicting Wilson's long forked tongue licking the posterior of the American President, with the simple caption: "Special Relationship". No, the importance of the Vietnamese offensive was that it showed to millions of workers and students throughout Western Europe that the Americans *could* lose. Given the years of Cold War hysteria, of uncritical acceptance of "American ideals", of the belief that not only was the United States always on the side of good, but that it was also invincible; given the reactionary character of the bourgeois intelligentsia throughout Europe, the Tet offensive came as a brilliant political and ideological rescue operation. In West Berlin, the showcase of the West, 30,000 demonstrators marched with red flags and portraits of Rosa Luxemburg and Karl Liebnecht to proclaim their solidarity with those who were humiliating the United States in South-East Asia. The United States were so obviously on the wrong side and the Vietnamese so clearly on the right that anti-Stalinist leftists came into their own. Tet helped them to break out of decades of isolation. Who could blame them for feeling exhilarated and euphoric?

In another sense the historic importance of Tet assumed a broader and more profound importance, particularly in France and Italy. At the conclusion of the Second World War the Communist Parties of both countries (which had played a central role in the anti-Nazi resistance) militarily and politically disarmed the working class. While both parties made public protestations of loyalty to the new bourgeois order, within their own ranks they explained matters in a slightly different fashion. Angry militants in both parties were told that any communist-led mass upsurge which posed the question of power would lead to immediate military intervention by the Americans. This was the trump card of the party leaders. In its own way it was a sly recognition of the fact that in both France and Italy a pre-revolutionary mood was developing. Any communist party worth its name would have attempted to transform this situation into one where the masses would launch a struggle for working-class power. In Italy in 1948 after an assassination attempt on the Communist leader, Palmiro Togliatti, the masses did not content themselves with token strike action. They occupied railway stations, factories and power stations. So the "American troops argument" was a fairly decisive one. It had an element of truth in it, but no more.

Naturally neither the French nor the Italian masses wanted

8

a new, protracted war and it was precisely the threat of such a war that was invoked by the party leadership in a determined and successful attempt to preserve the new status quo. This argument had seeped into the consciousness of whole generations of workers. It had been the sole explanation for the incomplete Liberation of France and Italy provided by older communists for their children, who were by now asking awkward questions.

Given all this the impact of a small, essentially peasant nation inflicting a political, psychological and a partially military defeat on the colossus which had after the Second World War held back the massed ranks of the armed French and Italian working classes, was a profound and a lasting one. The Lunar New Year in Vietnam had given life to a new generation of revolutionaries throughout Europe and America. Socially they were at the extremities of the bourgeois system, but they were beginning to affect its heart. In March 1968 almost a million people marched in the capitals of Europe to stress their solidarity with Vietnam. It was the most massive display of sympathy for a "foreign" revolution since the fall of Petrograd in 1917.

Tet had an international impact. A few days after Johnson's announcement that he would not stand for the Presidency of the United States, a hired assassin shot dead the black civil rights leader, Dr Martin Luther King. Dr King had begun to attack the war in extremely strong language. The black reaction to King's murder was phenomenal: there were rebellions in over 100 American cities. Black America took to the streets. The United States government called up 65,000 soldiers to deal with the largest mobilisation in peacetime since the American Civil War. Forty-three people were killed. The flames of burning buildings (mainly white businesses) could be seen ten blocks from the White House in Washington. Ironically enough many of the black militants who served as snipers during the rebellion had served as GIs in Vietnam. The chickens had come home to roost with a vengeance.

In Black Africa the guerrillas fighting in what was then Portuguese Guinea and Mozambique heard the news of the Tet offensive on their radio sets in the jungles. Spontaneous applause and jubilation greeted the announcement of the NLF victories. Tet had become truly international.

9

2. The May Events in France

"Revolutions are festivals of the oppressed and exploited . . . At such times the people are capable of performing miracles, if judged by the limited, philistine yardstick of gradualist progress. But it is essential that leaders of revolutionary parties, too, should advance their aims more comprehensively and boldly at such a time, so that their slogans shall always be in advance of the revolutionary initiatives of the masses . . . We shall be traitors, betrayers of the revolution, if we do not use this festive energy of the masses and their revolutionary ardour to wage a ruthless and self-sacrificing struggle for the direct and decisive path. . . ."

V. I. Lenin : *Two Tactics of Social-Democracy*, 1905

"What we call the beginning is often the end
And to make an end is to make a beginning."

T. S. Eliot : *Little Gidding*

France in 1968 was a model capitalist state. Its proudly vaunted prosperity was the envy of Western Europe. Britain was in the throes of a chronic economic crisis — the United States was crippled by a costly war in Asia. France, by contrast, gave the appearance of total stability. Its supreme leader, General Charles de Gaulle, was admired throughout the world. Tories in Britain, nationalist politicians in Quebec, uniformed despots in Asia and Latin America, all looked towards the General with differing degrees of reverence and respect. De Gaulle presided over a state whose economic "plan" was cited as the most striking demonstration of the successes of late capitalism.

The post-war economic boom which revived capitalism in Western Europe and Japan had created a largely industrialised France. In 1968 most of the French people lived in towns. Industrial workers employed by large-scale capitalist enterprises represented forty-one per cent of the total population; white-collar workers accounted for a further fifteen per cent. Together they represented the majority class in French society. Meanwhile six per cent of the population was engaged in small-

10

scale production, while the majority of the peasants owned their own land in the countryside. The traditional petty-bourgeoisie was the second largest social group in France. It was these groups that had provided the social base of the main bourgeois party of the Third Republic, the Radical Party. Capitalists in France had, since the Second World War, been unable to find a stable political party which directly represented their interests. This vacuum in French bourgeois politics helps partially to explain the instability of the political institutions of the Fourth Republic. The annual making and breaking of new governments was more typical of an Asian or Latin American banana republic than a bourgeois-democratic state situated at the heart of capitalism. India was, in fact, a more stable bourgeois state in the post-war period than the French Republic.

The Algerian war, ensuing political crisis and the paralysis of the Communist Party provided big capital in France with a new opportunity. It helped to bring about the birth of the Fifth Republic in 1958. All decisions were to be arbitrated through aloof and arrogant de Gaulle himself. The latter had always aspired to the role of a Bonaparte. French monopoly capitalism was prepared to pay this price in order to end its social isolation and gain a period of political *and economic* stability. De Gaulle's idiosyncrasies in the realm of foreign affairs were accepted without serious dissent, even though his nationalism and anti-Americanism ran counter to the interests of big capital, which favoured European and Atlantic integration. As long as his domestic policies suited French needs — and until 1968 they suited perfectly — French capitalists had no other option but to accept de Gaulle's special position. The Fifth Republic needed a strong person at the helm and de Gaulle was the only one who could take that responsibility. His position thus made up for the lack of a strong bourgeois party, which could unify the French ruling class on the model of the Italian Christian-Democrats or the British Conservative Party. He provided a temporary bridge. While he was seen to organise a political party of sorts, it was essentially a subordinate instrument of Gaullism. De Gaulle spoke directly to the masses through the tame mass media. His press conferences were accompanied by a pageantry and charade more suitable for a monarch. They were transformed into events of enormous political importance. His television broadcasts were projected

11

in a religious and adulatory fashion. The Gaullist state was thus not dependent on any political party, not even the General's own party. It was, however, in need of a bureaucracy strengthened on every level to meet the needs of the "strong state". This bureaucracy formed the lynch-pin of the Gaullist apparatus. But it also, of necessity, insulated Gaullism from the masses. In a crisis this could prove to be fatal.

Towards the end of 1963 a draconian wage-freeze had been imposed on the workers. In 1968 the unemployed counted half a million. The Fifth Republic had weathered its first five years, but it was now beginning to run out of breath. The development of French capitalism had necessitated a big expansion of the student population in order to meet the needs of the new technologically developed industries which required skilled labour. The number of students in France had rocketed from 200,000 in 1961 to 500,000 in 1968 making them an important intermediary between the contending social classes in the main urban centres, especially Paris. The result was massive over-crowding. France was unable to meet the needs of the new students — housing, grants, canteens, buildings or laboratories. Education was totally authoritarian, reflecting the needs of the thirties rather than the sixties: the system of instruction and examination was hopelessly out of date.

Towards the end of 1967 there were signs of increasing tension in the factories. The workers demanded better wages and an end to the wage-freeze. At the same time there were a number of student actions demanding better conditions. The students were arguing that less money be spent on nuclear weapons and more on education. On November 20, 1967 there was a large student strike in Nanterre, involving 10,000 students. On December 13 of the same year there was a nationwide day of action by university students, later regarded as an important success. On February 21, 1968 another massive demonstration of students took place showing solidarity with the Vietnamese partisans. The Latin Quarter of Paris was renamed: "Heroic Vietnam Quarter". At this demonstration a number of student leaders belonging to the National Vietnam Committee were arrested. On March 22 at Nanterre there was a large protest against these arrests. The university was occupied as was its broadcasting station and the "March 22

12

Movement" was formed at the conclusion of a massive student assembly. Its main leaders were Daniel Cohn-Bendit, a student with anarchist leanings, and Daniel Bensaid, a leader of the Young Revolutionary Communists (JCR), an organisation which attempted to synthesise the writings of Leon Trotsky and the actions of Che Guevara. The students designated March 29 as a day for "political discussion". The Rector at Nanterre decided to close down the university for two days. When it reopened, the students decided that May 2 and May 3 should be days devoted to the struggle against imperialism. The Rector decided once again to close down the university. The action went ahead, but the arena was shifted to the Sorbonne in the heart of the Latin Quarter in Paris. A demonstration of university and high school students was attacked by the police on May 3 and a number of leaders arrested. The Sorbonne was closed down and sporadic fighting continued on the streets.

Demonstrations continued over the next few days demanding both the immediate release of the imprisoned students and the reopening of Nanterre and the Sorbonne. Both demands were arbitrarily rejected. On May 9 it was agreed to call a mass mobilisation for the following day. The same evening a packed meeting organised by the JCR in the Mutualité was told that airport police had refused to allow two leaders of the German SDS (German Socialist Students), Bernd Rabehl and Christian Semmler, to enter France. The meeting erupted.

May 10 was a decisive day. 35,000 students defied the police and assembled at the Place Denfert-Rochereau. They marched to the Santé prison where their comrades were being held and demanded their release. They marched into the heart of the Latin Quarter. To their surprise they began to get support from many bystanders.

The police were beginning to surround the Latin Quarter. They were not the ordinary French police; they were the hated CRS (Compagnies Républicains de Sécurité), an armed security police force created specifically in 1947 by the Social Democratic Interior Minister, Jules Moch, for use against communist workers on strike. As such the CRS was hated by the most militant sections of the French working class. On May 10 they were preparing to do battle against a newer and as yet unpredictable enemy, though the CRS thought that time would defeat the students. They were, after all, in the words of the physically gifted, but mentally deficient cadres of the CRS, merely "mamas' boys", "privileged ones". The CRS were banking on a retreat by the students. As the negotiators came out of the Sorbonne and announced that the Rector was refusing to accept their demands, the majority of students decided that this was the time for action. A group of pro-Chinese students and the Revolutionary Student Federation (FER), a sectarian and neanderthal Trotskyist grouping, stated that it was wrong to participate in an "adventure", and marched away. The bulk of students stayed and constructed barricades. Over sixty started going up at 11 pm. The first organisation to set up a mobile headquarters in the Latin Quarter was the JCR. They got permission from some local inhabitants to use an apartment. They rigged it up with a public loudspeaker system, through which they explained what was happening.

The French Communist Party (PCF) had consistently attacked the student movement during the preceding months. On May 3, the leader of the PCF had written an article in *l'Humanité* entitled: "Unmask the Pseudo-Revolutionaries!" In it this soulless and dull bureaucrat penned some sentences he had no doubt learned by rote from the handbooks provided by the Stalinist apparatus in Moscow for use during the thirties and forties. He accused the students of being *provocateurs*. He insisted on belittling their strength. He appealed to French chauvinism by portraying the students as being interested basically in the "immigrant workers" and he referred to the German origins of Cohn-Bendit:

"In spite of their contradictions these grouplets — a few hundred students — have united into what they call the 'Movement du 22 Mars Nanterre', led by the German anarchist COHN-BENDIT. . . . These false revolutionaries must be energetically unmasked; for, objectively, they serve the interests of the Gaullist government and the big capitalist monopolies. . . .
"The views and activities of these 'revolutionists' are laughable; inasmuch as they are generally the children of big bourgeois, contemptuous of students from working-class origins, who will soon dampen their 'revolutionary flame' to go and run papa's business and exploit the workers in the best traditions of capitalism . . ."

This was the language of sectarianism and fear. Small wonder that the 35,000 children of "big bourgeois" tended to treat the leaders of the PCF with utter contempt. But even the PCF could not disguise reality from its members for ever. They did not have, as their friends in Moscow, a monopoly over the channels of information. And even from the bourgeois press the workers could get a better picture of what was actually happening in the Latin Quarter.

To return to the night of May 10, 1968. At 2 am the loud-speaker announced that the PCF had just declared its solidarity with the students. The students sang the "Internationale" to celebrate. They knew that this retreat on the part of the PCF leadership had been brought about by pressure from below, from the ranks of the party membership. It was also a sign that the workers would soon be moving into action. Sure enough the largest trade union federation, the CGT (Conféd-ération Général Travail — aligned to the PFC), announced soon after that the workers would strike in solidarity with the students on May 13. A *one-day* general strike! News of these developments gave further impetus to the embattled students. Victory was in the air.

At 2.30 am the CRS were ordered to smash the barricades. They began their attack with tear-gas and smoke-bombs. An amazing spectacle followed. As the gas descended, some doctors and medical students appealed to the local population for help. Warm water was promptly rained down from the apartment windows of the Quarter, followed by sheets, rags and plastic sacks. These were handed out to students who had no protection against the gas. Earlier the residents of the Quarter had provided the students with coffee, water and food. Their aid was of key importance in maintaining both the political and physical morale of the students. As the CRS attacked they confronted barricades at which there stood hundreds of activists, a third of whom were women. When retreats were necessary from one barricade it was set alight to delay pursuit. The students had been on the streets since 6.30 pm.

By 5.30 am, almost twelve hours later, the following morning there was still fighting. The CRS had now started to use chlorine in a desperate attempt to disperse the students. It failed. The students had organised messengers on motorbikes flying red flags, to main contact between the barricades. At 5.30 am

15

the barricade on the Rue Gay-Lussac, the scene of many a heroic battle, fell to the CRS. But elsewhere the fighting continued. As dawn broke students and CRS could be sighted on the roofs of the apartments where the pitched battles were raging. Nearly 400 students had now received wounds, some of them serious.

The fact that no life was lost on the night of May 10 is a tribute to the extremely efficient medical organisation of the students rather than the cool-headedness of the CRS, a fact acknowledged by their opponents. By 8 am on the morning of May 11 the students were still fighting. At this point the government decided to release the students' leaders and accede to their central demand. It was capitulation, pure and simple. The night of the barricades had ended in victory. Two days later there was a general strike and a mass demonstration attended by a million workers who marched from all over Paris to assemble in Place Denfert-Rochereau. It was a moving tribute to those whom the PCF leaders had reviled and slandered only ten days before. The red flag flew that day over the Sorbonne and the Place de la République. But the struggle had only begun. The students of France had joined their fellows in Asia and Latin America in the revolutionary struggle. They were not imaginary monsters of conformity, but had become, in the words of Tom Nairn: "real monsters, walking paragraphs from the *Manuscripts of 1844* and the *Grundrisse*".

The élite structures of Gaullism now revealed the isolation and vulnerability of the Fifth Republic. The government had hoped that its belated concessions to the students would bring the movement to a halt. In reality the demands of the students had now been completely superseded. The important fact was that the government had acceded to them under threat of violent street confrontations. The Night of the Barricades acted as a detonator. It lit a spark which travelled right into the heart of the French working class. The PCF and CGT had called a one-day stoppage in solidarity with the students. On the actual day of demonstration a group of menacing PCF marshals had erected a physical barrier to prevent the students from fraternising with the workers. But ideas do not respect barriers as numerous dictatorships have discovered.

Workers, especially the younger ones, visited the Sorbonne in droves. Building workers inspected the barricades and, in

16

some cases, awarded their seal of approval. What the workers found in the Sorbonne was in sharp contrast to their own trades union structures. A militant from the CGT was used to receiving orders from a superior official. If a pertinent question was raised the person concerned was asked: "Are you in touch with some ultra-left group?" It was a deadening and bureaucratic atmosphere; whereas in the Sorbonne political ideas were being debated and discussed. With a few exceptions complete democracy prevailed in the "Sorbonne Soviet". The workers who attended these sessions and heard the ardent pleas of the students for unity with the working class could not help but be impressed by what they saw. Their leaders had told them that the student riots were started by a "handful of agitators", but thousands of students had triumphed by actually fighting the hated CRS there on the streets. Their leaders had told them that these were the pampered children of the bourgeoisie, but in the Sorbonne itself these "pampered children" were obsessed with one thing: how they could achieve unity with the working class. This mood was transported from the Latin Quarter into the factories by thousands and thousands of young workers. The result was stupendous.

The day after the one-day strike there was a beginning of spontaneous factory occupations. The first two factories to be occupied were an aircraft plant in Nantes and a Renault factory near Rouen. It was clear from the start that the occupying workers had no clearly defined economic objectives. Within the following week there was a tidal wave of factory occupations. The French working class was in revolt. Memories of previous revolutionary outbreaks reduced the French ruling class to a state of near paralysis. The ghosts of 1789, 1848 and 1871 were coming to life again. How far would they go? Already the workers had paralysed the communications system by halting railways and public transport. The shipyards, power stations and the printing presses had all come to a standstill. The post and telegraph services followed. Within twenty-four hours the scale of the strike had become clear. *It was a spontaneous general strike from below.* It involved 10 million workers. This made it the largest working class action in the history of capitalism. What was even more astounding was that it soon became clear that the workers wanted a fundamental change in society. Ten years of Gaullism and the stultifying atmosphere of the Fifth Republic had finally brought them to this situation.

The Gaullist state trembled. It was in a state of suspension. Isolated and paralysed by the strike it was at the same time not yet under frontal attack. What should it do? How should it strike back? Pompidou, the Gaullist Prime Minister, was called back from a foreign visit. He confided to the chief of police that France was in a "pre-revolutionary" state. He advised that there should for the moment be no action by the State — no provocations — otherwise the situation could get worse. At the same time Pompidou began daily discussions with the representatives of the French Communist Party. De Gaulle himself some weeks later left for Baden-Baden to consult with the French Generals stationed there and discuss emergency plans. The French Bonaparte realised that at a time when the police were threatening a strike if they were sent into the factories, the conscript units in the French army could not be trusted. The professionals at Baden-Baden agreed with his analysis, but laid down a few conditions of their own. The first was that the notorious semi-fascist General Salan (who had attempted a right-wing putsch against de Gaulle himself) and others arrested at the same time be released in the near future. De Gaulle agreed. His side of the bargain was kept.

But the soldiers were not needed from Baden-Baden on this occasion. The generals of the French working class had decided not to fight any battles whatsoever. Even *The Observer* was led to comment in an on-the-spot report by two of their senior journalists: "The Communist Party thus stood revealed as the ultimate bastion of the consumer society which the student Bolsheviks were pledged to destroy. It is as if Washington and Moscow had got together to put down North Vietnam . . . the communist unions and the Gaullist Government they appear to be challenging are really on the same side of the barricades. They are defending French society as we know it." For the reality of the situation was that the leaders of the French Communist Party had decided that May 1968 must not be allowed to extend itself. They deliberately and ruthlessly sought by every means possible to direct the general strike down the familiar channel of higher wages. The French workers were chanting one slogan above the others in their

18

occupied factories: "This time we will go all the way." The leader of the CGT, Seguy, explained it: " 'All the Way' for us trades unionists means the satisfaction of the demands for which we have always fought but which the government and bosses have always refused to take into consideration. . . . 'All the way' means a general increase in wages — no wage less than 600F a month. ....." Every demand raised by French communists ignored the meaning of the struggle that was taking place in France.

There were isolated incidents of factories where workers had started producing goods which met the real needs of the community. There were others where local peasant groups blocked the roads and linked arms with urban workers to provide supplies for towns. The literature on the upheaval which shook France is enormous and needs to be studied in detail to get a composite picture of the opportunities which lay before the left for three weeks in May. Only the students and the small "groupuscules" offered an overall alternative. But the bureaucrats of the CGT prevented them from entering the factories. The PCF and CGT leaders finally negotiated a deal with Gaullism. Their narrow economist aims were conceded at Grenelle by a grateful French ruling class. But now the situation became more tense. Throughout France, in factory after factory, the workers rejected the Grenelle agreements. The government was now threatened. It was at this stage that de Gaulle made his celebrated secret trip to Baden-Baden. Soon after, supported by the army and the PCF, he made an appeal on television. He promised reforms and gave the date for new general elections. The PCF immediately accepted the offer and slowly, but surely, the movement was dismantled by the unions. On the day of de Gaulle's broadcast his supporters came out on to the streets. They were a strange lot: veterans of the OAS from the Algerian débâcle; local French fascists; luminaries of the Gaullist party; government bureaucrats; plainclothes policemen; military officers out of uniform. One of the slogans they chanted was "Send Cohn-Bendit to Dachau". A month later de Gaulle won a record electoral majority at the polls. The French ruling class heaved a sigh of relief. The Fifth Republic had been saved. It was a strange paradox, but it did not defy explanation.

"In practice a reformist party considers unshakeable the foundations of that which it intends to reform. It thus inevitably submits to the ideas and morals of the rulling class. . . .
"People do not make revolution eagerly any more than they do war. There is this difference, however, that in war com-do war. There is this difference, however, that in war compulsion except that of circumstances. A revolution takes place only when there is no other way out. And the insurrection, which rises above a revolution like a peak in the mountain chain of events, can no more be evoked at will than the revolution as a whole. The masses advance and retreat several times before they make up their minds to the final assault."

Leon Trotsky: *History of the Russian Revolution*

"A Frenchman travelling abroad feels himself treated a bit like a convalescent from a pernicious fever. And how did the rash of barricades break out? What was the temperature at five o'clock in the evening of May 29? Is the Gaullist medicine really getting to the roots of the disease? Are there dangers of a relapse? Even if these questions are not put directly, one can read them on the headlines displayed in all the news-stands and bookstalls.
"But there is one question that is hardly ever asked, perhaps because they are afraid to hear the answer. But at heart everyone would like to know, hopefully or fearfully, whether the sickness is infectious."

Robert Escarpit, *Le Monde*, July 23, 1968

Paris was not Petrograd. May 1968 was not October 1917. But France had been perilously close to a revolution. It had disproved all the models erected by bourgeois sociology and recycled versions of the same peddled by certain socialist theorists. It constituted a social experience which left its mark on both the rulers and the ruled. It *was* infectious. While the temperature of Italy did not attain French heights millions of Italian workers nonetheless responded eagerly to the "French sickness" in 1969. France in May 1968 was a political laboratory. The experiments taking place there were first sabotaged and later stopped. But they nevertheless indicated what was possible, provided all the ingredients were properly assembled.

The most obvious and natural analogy was with the Russian Revolution. It was made often enough in the months that followed May. Many of the points established were correct, though banal. There was no Bolshevik Party in France, there were no Lenins and Trotskys. The wave of factory occupations had no coherent, unifying set of economic or political demands. The French Communist Party consciously sabotaged the struggle. All these facts are indisputable. But there are other facts, equally indisputable, which need to be analysed and explained so that the lessons of May are not obscured by a heady rhetoric or by the repetition of correct, but limited and partial features of the struggle. How similar was France to Tsarist Russia? Why did the French Communist Party, which clearly betrayed the aspirations of the masses, not suffer any major split? What was the evolution of the far left itself? How did Gaullism win the elections after it had almost lost a State? Will a revolution in the West be a simple repetition of the storming of the Winter Palace?

In the ten years that have followed the explosions of May 1968 a wide-ranging debate has been taking place on the left on the question of socialist strategy in the West. We have seen the emergence of "Eurocommunism" and the growing divergences between Moscow and the European Communist Parties; we have witnessed the development of "Eurosocialism" as reflected in the tactics of Portuguese, Spanish and French social-democracy and we are still in the midst of a debate between revolutionary Marxists and centrists on the question of revolution. Of late there has not been much reference made by the reformists and centrists to May 1968 except in derogatory terms: it was utopia. For some it almost didn't take place. A conscious attempt is being made to treat the May Events as an atypical aberration. A leading theoretician of the British Communist Party, Eric Hobsbawm, who was excited by May but critical of the role of the French Communist Party (1) is today a leading Anglo-Saxon apologist of the "Italian Road" and an eloquent spokesman for the strategy and tactics of the PCI (Italian Communist Party), which in some ways is to the right of the British Labour Party. It is therefore essential to restate some elementary axioms of Marxism.

What is the basic task of the socialist revolution? In my opinion, and this has always been the viewpoint of classical Marxism, it is to *overthrow and defeat the state apparatus of the ruling class that organises its violence on a world scale.* Every capitalist state, including the most democratic, rests

(1) See article in *Black Dwarf*, No. I, May 1968.

21

ultimately on coercion. It is this *fact,* which gives an international dimension to the struggle for power. It was this universalist function of the revolution that was highlighted by Lenin in one of his later works, *State and Revolution.* The tasks adduced by Lenin in this little book are equally applicable to Britain and Zaire, France and Paraguay, Sweden and Singapore, Belgium and Pakistan. Without doubt the tactics in each of these countries will vary greatly, but the strategic aim remains the same as do the *measures* necessary to bring that aim to fruition. It is worth stressing that Lenin was not, in this particular instance, developing a new theory "based on Russian conditions"! He was merely repeating what had already been established by Marx. The necessity of a working-class revolution and the establishment of a dictatorship of the proletariat were themes Marx had developed in relation to France and Germany, two Western countries. The notion that these two basic and fundamental tasks were only applicable to Russia is both spurious and unscientific.

May 1968 in France provided us with a new opportunity for assessing the form a revolution in the West could take and contrasting it with the Russian model of 1917. The first and obvious comparison is on the level of the State. Tsarist Russia was dominated by a repressive and feudal State apparatus, which had revealed its vulnerability during the upheavals of 1905, but had survived and consolidated its rule through a more repressive dictatorship. At the same time the industrialisation of the country was proceeding apace. Foreign investments were creating large and concentrated industrial plants in Petrograd and Moscow, thus creating a new proletariat which from the beginning was faced with extremely cruel working conditions. The particular feature of Russian capitalism, brilliantly analysed and described by Trotsky in *1905,* was a socially and politically weak industrial bourgeoisie. The late industrialisation of Tsarist Russia necessitated state intervention and financing from the very start. This meant that the new bourgeoisie was economically dependent on Tsarism, which acknowledged its own strength by denying the former any significant political powers. The post-1905 reforms in the Russian countryside were limited; they did not ease the conditions of feudal or capitalist exploitation under which the former serfs lived. The hatred against the landlords *united* the poor

22

peasant, the agricultural worker and the rich peasant. Eighty-five per cent of the Tsar's population lived in the countryside; fifty-seven per cent of the population as a whole was non-Russian. It was ruthlessly oppressed by the Great Russian chauvinism of the autocracy. At the top of the pyramid was the institution of the Tsar itself symbolising, through the absolute monarch, all the vices of the autocracy. The supremacy of the Tsarist dynasty was ideologically buttressed and sanctified by the Orthodox Church and its hierarchy of priests. Absolutism, religion and national oppression went hand in hand, giving the Russian State its own specific features. The combination of economic retrogression in the countryside and large-scale industrial enterprises in the cities had its political counterparts as well. *The most backward state in continental Europe possessed the most advanced revolutionary political organisation in the world.* The leadership of this organisation had been formed in the matrix of the mass strikes and struggles which characterised Tsarist Russia in the first two decades of the twentieth century *and* the development of Marxist theory on the continent. The latter was eagerly assimilated and developed by the exiled Russian revolutionaries. The decaying and almost somnolent character of Tsarist absolutism was reflected not only in the growing inefficiency and corruption which characterised its state apparatus, but in the remarkable lack of care taken in relation to its political prisoners. The fact that the majority of Bolshevik leaders throughout Russia survived the repression was an indication of the complacency and isolation of the autocracy: It was a mistake not made by the other ruling classes in the world after the revolution until the Cuban dictator Batista spared Castro's life in 1953.

The internal contradictions of Russian society were accumulating at a rapid pace. By the First World War Russian absolutism and its armies were no match for the troops of Imperial Germany. The succession of defeats suffered by the Tsar's armies helped to radicalise the peasants. It was in the army at the front that Bolshevik agitators established a real contact with the peasantry. The party itself was virtually non-existent in the countryside — a weakness often presented by its apologists as a virtue.

The February Revolution in Petrograd was brought about by mass discontent in the factories and at the front. There

23

was in addition a bread shortage in the city of Petrograd. The masses rebelled. Their vanguard were the workers of the giant Putilov plant: all 30,000 had been locked out. Their leaders toured the factories to spread their discontent. The Tsar was not in the capital. He sent his message from afar: the demonstrators must be repressed at all costs: officers ordered their soldiers to open fire on the crowds. A series of mutinies now shook the Tsarist army, already demoralised by the state of the war. From barracks to barracks the revolt gathered speed. The soldiers retained their arms and disarmed their officers. Within twenty-four hours the Tsar's ministers had evacuated the imperial capital. As jubilant crowds of workers, soldiers and sailors celebrated on the streets, two counterposed powers were attempting to fill the vacuum. On the one hand a group of bourgeois notables and, on the other, soldiers and workers organised in the Petrograd Soviet. Three days later the Tsar abdicated. The autocracy had been overthrown. In its wake the weak and dispirited bourgeoisie attempted to create a bourgeois state proper. But it was from the beginning denied the chance to do so by the ghosts of 1905. What has been called the dress-rehearsal of 1905 was of vital importance to 1917, and not in some romantic, utopian or abstract sense. In 1905 the spontaneous uprisings had led to the creations of *soviets*: representative bodies based on direct elections. These soviets had fulfilled a real need: they had organised the struggle against the autocracy and been accepted by the mass of workers as real representative organs, infinitely more democratic than the most generous Tsarist reform. The February Revolution of 1917 was to remain haunted by the soviet until the demise of the Provisional Government and the outbreak of the October Revolution. The formation of soviets in 1917 was almost automatic.

The combination of soviets and Lenin proved too powerful for the weak bourgeoisie. From February to October the revolution had its ups and downs. The Bolshevik Party consisted of only 30,000 members in March 1917. By October it had doubled. What sealed the fate of the Kerensky government was its insistence on continuing the imperialist war. This provided the Bolsheviks with their final slogan: peace. Together with the other demands of land and bread coupled with effective Bolshevik agitation, Lenin and his comrades

24

established a majority in the key soviets of Petrograd and Moscow. Once *this* majority had been established, they began to prepare the seizure of power. It was managed by the creation of a Military Revolutionary Committee responsible to the Petrograd Soviet. Its most prominent member was Leon Trotsky who organised the insurrection. When the Bolsheviks finally struck on November 7 they had already won over to their cause most of the soldiers and workers. The storming of the Winter Palace was a moment of high *political* drama. Its military significance was virtually nil. The Red Guards created by the Soviet united with the soldiers to ensure the seizure of power. There was some fighting in Moscow, but in most centres the Bolsheviks assumed power peacefully. The violence was to come six months later when the imperialist powers decided to intervene in force and provide the counter-revolution with a foreign head.

If we contrast May 1968 with October 1917 we notice a number of important dissimilarities, most of which can be explained by one crucial determining factor. This was succinctly expressed by the Italian communist leader Amadeo Bordiga at a meeting of the Executive Committee of the Communist International in 1926:

> "We have in the International only one party that has achieved revolutionary victory — the Bolshevik Party. They say that we should therefore take the road which led the Russian party to success. This is perfectly true, but it remains insufficient. The fact is that the Russian party fought under special conditions, in a country where the bourgeois-liberal revolution had not yet been defeated by the capitalist bourgeoisie. Between the fall of the feudal aristocracy and the seizure of power by the working class lay too short a period for there to be any comparison with the development which the proletariat will have to accomplish in other countries. For there was no time to build a bourgeois state machine on the ruins of the Tsarist feudal apparatus. Russian development does not provide us with an experience of how the proletariat can overthrow a liberal-parliamentary capitalist state that has existed for many years and possesses the ability to defend itself. We, however, must know how to attack a modern bourgeois-democratic State that on the one hand has its own means of ideologically mobilising and corrupting the proletariat, and on the other hand can defend itself on the terrain of armed struggle with greater effi-

cacy than could the Tsarist autocracy. This problem never arose in the history of the Russian Communist Party." (2)

The scale of mass mobilisations in Gaullist France was superior to those of Romanov Russia. The ten million workers involved in the strike in 1968 represented the most vital section of the population. The memory of the French working class was however not of setting up soviets, but of occupying factories. That is what they had done in the upsurge of 1936 and that is what they moved towards instinctively when they wanted to challenge the government. That these occupations formed the basis for a qualitatively higher form of democracy is indisputable, but here the French workers confronted another set of obstacles. First they lacked a revolutionary political organisation with implantation in all the key factories and capable of both unifying the struggle by giving it a political focus and thus posing a clear alternative to the reformists of the PCF. The second interrelated obstacle was the hold of reformism itself. The small revolutionary organisations existed, essentially, outside the working class. The PCF ensured that they remained that way by physically obstructing their attempts to enter the factories.

The arguments of reformism were expressed in a clear fashion by the secretary-general of the PCF, Waldeck-Rochet:

"In reality, the choice to be made in May was the following:
— Either to act in such a way that the strike would permit the essential demands of the workers to be satisfied, and to pursue at the same time, on the political plane, a policy aimed at making necessary democratic changes by constitutional means. This was our party's position.
— Or else quite simply to provoke a trial of strength, in other words move towards an insurrection: this would include a recourse to armed struggle aimed at overthrowing the régime by force. This was the adventurist position of certain ultra-left groups.
"But since the military and repressive forces were on the side of the established authorities, and since the immense mass of the people was totally hostile to such an adventure, it is clear that to take such a course meant quite simply to lead the workers to the slaughterhouse, and to wish for the crushing of the working class and its vanguard, the Communist Party.

(2) Quoted in Perry Anderson: 'The Antimonies of Antonio Gramsci', *New Left Review*, 100.

"Well, we didn't fall into the trap. For that was the real plan of the Gaullist régime.

"Indeed, their calculations were simple: faced with a crisis which they had themselves provoked by their anti-social and anti-democratic policies, they reckoned on taking advantage of that crisis in order to strike a decisive and lasting blow at the working-class, at our party, and at any democratic movement."

Leaving aside the fact that Waldeck-Rochet's democratic rhetoric did not extend to defending the democratic rights of the revolutionary organisations that were banned, or protesting the deportation of Daniel Cohn-Bendit and hundreds of foreign workers, his remarks are a remarkable indictment of his own party. The PCF leader erects a straw argument and then proceeds to explain why his party was opposed to it. The choice he offers the French working class is economic demands or immediate insurrection. The whole operation we are told was "a trap" and the PCF avoided falling into it. Bravo! The reply to Waldeck-Rochet's argument printed in *l'Humanité* of July 10, 1968 (it is interesting that he even discussed the question of power given that it was only the dream of small groups of "ultraleftists") was provided by Ernest Mandel, a leading Marxist theoretician and a central leader of the Fourth International, to which one of the "ultraleft" groups so derided by Waldeck-Rochet was affiliated. Mandel wrote:

"When the bourgeois régime is stable and strong, it would be absurd to hurl one's forces into a revolutionary action aimed at the immediate overthrow of Capital; by doing this one would plunge to certain defeat. But how will one move from this strong and stable régime towards a régime which is weakened, shaken, disintegrating? By some miraculous leap? Does not a radical modification of the balance of forces necessitate decisive, staggering blows? Do not such blows open up a *process* of progressive weakening of the bourgeoisie? Is it not the elementary duty of a party which claims to be that of the working class — and even of the socialist revolution — to push this process to its furthest extent? Can this be done if one excludes automatically all struggles except those for immediate demands . . . for as long as the situation is not ripe for an immediate armed insurrection, with victory fully guaranteed?

"Does not a strike of ten million workers, with the factories occupied, represent a considerable weakening of the power of

27

Capital? Should one not concentrate all one's efforts on an attempt to enlarge the breach, to gain a hold over the enemy, to make sure that Capital will no longer be able rapidly to re-establish a balance of forces which favours it? . . . The entire history of capitalism bears witness to the latter's capacity to give way on material demands when its power is threatened. It knows only too well if it can preserve its power it will be able to take back in part what it has given (by increased prices, taxes, unemployment, etc.) and in part to digest it through an increase in productivity. Besides, any bourgeoisie which has been scared by an exceptional strike, but which has been left in possession of its State power, will tend to go over immediately to a counter-offensive and to repression, as soon as the mass movement starts to ebb. The history of the working class movement goes to demonstrate it: a party enclosed in Waldeck-Rochet's dilemma will never make the revolution, and will inevitably be defeated."

In addition it should be pointed out that while no doubt sections of the students believed that an insurrection was imminent or should be launched, this was not the position of the most influential of the far-left groups, the JCR. In its declarations issued on May 21 and distributed in hundreds of thousands, the JCR maintained that the next step was the creation of elected "rank-and-file Strike Committees in the factories and Action Committees in the universities and neighbourhoods that will encompass all the workers in Struggle". They called for nationalisation of all the major occupied factories; for the establishment of democratic workers' control; for the publication of all company secrets; etc. On the political front they called for de Gaulle's withdrawal and the "establishment of a *workers' government*". They insisted that this government should base itself on the grass-roots committees elected in the universities, factories and neighbourhoods. It could be argued that these demands were unrealistic given the fact that neither the JCR nor any other far-left group had the necessary proletarian infiltration to argue and fight for them, but that does not make them incorrect. Nor, incidentally, do they even mention the word "insurrection". What the JCR was calling for was the creation of organs of dual power. Clearly these could not be willed into existence. For them to come into being would have necessitated the establishment of a clear

28

political focus for the general strike. The removal of de Gaulle, the dismantling of the undemocratic structures of the Fifth Republic, large-scale nationalisations, disbandment of the CRS and the creation of a new popular Assembly elected on a democratic basis could have provided the thrust needed to organise organs of power independent of the bourgeois state. In any event the only organisation in a position to ensure that these objectives could be achieved was the French Communist Party. It refused to do so because it *accepted* the constitution and sanctified the existing bourgeois institutions.

The general strike was defused not by repression (even the banning of the far-left organisations was essentially a formality as they regrouped under new names a few weeks later). It was brought to a successful conclusion by French reformism accepting the constraints of the bourgeois-democratic state. Elections that ended May 1968. Gaullism was prepared for a frontal clash, but took great care not to initiate one. The ten million workers wanted a change, but saw no reason for a frontal assault at that stage. The French Communist Party won a massive wage increase for the workers and at the same time enabled (through the Grenelle Agreements) the unionisation of a further million workers. The workers were disappointed, but did not regard the events as a defeat. A minority did, however, regard the PCF's actions as a conscious betrayal. Most of these were probably outside the Party in the first instance. They were now to become increasingly responsive to the initiatives of the far left groups and they provided the latter with an important toehold inside the working class.

The French working class held out for nearly three weeks. It then accepted the legitimacy of bourgeois-democratic institutions. It was offered no other alternative. The French far left unanimously screamed "betrayal". In a sense it was correct to do so, but what it failed to perceive was that there was an objective basis for the "betrayal". In other words the reason that the mass of workers did not regard the actions of the French Communist Party as a "betrayal" was because the hold of bourgeois ideology had been weakened, but not broken. Nor could it be broken simply by propaganda. For a decisive break to take place the mass of workers had to understand the practical importance of constructing new organs of power. If that stage had been reached and the PCF had then tried to dismantle these organs the impact could well have created a vital disjuncture between the party's social base and its leadership and political line. Precisely because bourgeois-democracy offers a limited choice it helps to sustain the illusion that the masses are in reality the final arbiters in bourgeois society. Instead of using a unique opportunity to shatter this illusion the French Communist Party actively sought to sustain it. Waldeck-Rochet stated in the few minutes allowed him on television on the eve of the election:

> "The truth is that throughout the grave events which we have just lived through, the French Communist Party conducted itself as a responsible party. . . ."

This "responsibility", displayed by the French Communist Party, was of vital importance to the Gaullist State. A similar responsibility had been displayed by the communist leader Thorez at the conclusion of the Second World War. De Gaulle had paid tribute to his skills and explained in his memoirs that "France benefited" from Thorez' actions and the political line of the PCF. Two decades later France was to "benefit" again from the politics of the French communists. The point is that there were two Frances in May 1968 and they were in open conflict. The PCF's actions benefited capitalist France. Of that there can be little doubt.

May 1968 revealed in the space of two weeks all the problems of strategy which confronted revolutionary socialists. Bordiga's remarks addressed to the Comintern leaders in 1926 thus take on a significance which has only recently begun to be fully grasped by European Marxists. The Fifth Republic proved to be a more dangerous and a more resilient enemy than Tsarist Russia. Its "outer ditch" was the entire system of modern representative bourgeois democracy. Its inner fortifications were the French Army on the Rhine. No revolutionary party existed in France. Even if it had its task would not have been as simple as it appears. May 1968 revealed that a revolution in the West would happen only with the support of the majority of workers or not at all. Petrograd had fallen to a revolutionary party basing itself on a *minority* of the population. It had then sought to woo the majority, aided in the process by the First World War and a series of bold, revolutionary agrarian reforms.

In the West the opposite will be the case. The majority of

the population will have to be involved from the beginning and the minority will possibly be won over at a later stage. This elementary lesson, which was provided by May 1968, was not universally absorbed as we shall see later when we discuss the dynamics of the Portuguese upheaval. The corollary to this is the fact that the masses will only move towards a socialist revolution when they have either *experienced* socialist democracy in action for themselves (clearly through organs of autonomous workers' power challenging the bourgeois state from within) or through the overthrow of the bureaucratic régimes in any of the countries of Eastern Europe or the USSR. In that sense the fate of revolution in the West is intimately correlated to the degrading and alienating experience of Stalinism in the East. Whereas the bourgeois democratic states are based ultimately on coercion, their routine existence is dependent on the *consent* of the masses. A failure to understand this results in petty bourgeois revolutionism, which is characterised by a failure to grasp the key importance of the working class as the only agency of social change under late capitalism and by a political impatience with the existing situation. A belief that "heroic actions" by a minority will open the gates of the bourgeois fortress — the "detonator" impact of the student struggle — was to be theorised by a number of groups in this fashion. Their conclusion was to either lead them out of politics altogether or subject them to violent repression. In either event they remained totally isolated from the mass of workers. This "suicidal" political streak was certainly present in May 1968, but not dominant. It reached its climax not in France, but in the German Federal Republic with the series of armed action undertaken by the Baader-Meinhof group — actions which were and remain totally counter-productive.

In the East the Stalinist bureaucratic caste rules without any form of consent. The occasions on which the masses have succeeded in winning some concessions and opening the way to more fundamental changes has only led to the coercive entry of Russian tanks. The case of Czechoslovakia is therefore also of vital importance in the development and understanding of a global strategy for the socialist revolution. In that sense a working class victory in any Western country and the establishment of socialist democracy would have a profound and immediate impact on the bureaucratic states in the East.

3. The Invasion of Czechoslovakia

"We must distinguish between the nationalism of an oppressor nation and the nationalism of an oppressed nation, the nationalism of a great nation and the nationalism of a small one.

"As regards the second sort of nationalism we, as members of a big nation, have almost always in historical practice been found guilty of an endless chain of oppression, and what is more we still commit acts of oppression and behave offensively without realising it ourselves . . .

"That is why the internationalism of an oppressor, or if you like 'great', nation (sometimes great only in the extent of its oppression like a 'great tyrant') must consist not only in the maintenance of a formal equality of nations, but also in such a degree of inequality as will allow the big, oppressor, nation to compensate for the inequality created in practice. Anyone who fails to understand this has failed properly to understand the proletarian standpoint on the question of nationalities; he has to all intents and purposes retained a petit-bourgeois standpoint and is therefore bound at any moment to go over to a bourgeois standpoint."

V. I. Lenin : *The Question of Nationalities or
"Autonomisation"*, Volume 36, Collected Works,
December 1922

"When I use a word," Humpty Dumpty said, in rather a scornful tone, "it means just what I choose it to mean — neither more nor less."
"The question is," said Alice, "whether you *can* make words mean so many different things."
"The question is," said Humpty Dumpty, "which is to be master — that's all."

Lewis Carroll : *Through the Looking Glass*

On August 20, 1968 the armoured cars, tanks and soldiers

of East Germany, Bulgaria, Poland, Hungary and the Soviet Union, under the military command of Soviet generals, invaded the Czechoslovak Socialist Republic. This brutal violation of Czechoslovak national sovereignty was not resisted by Czech border guards. Soviet tanks reached Prague without opposition. The headquarters of the Central Committee of the Czech Communist Party where a meeting of the Presidium of the Central Committee was in progress was one of their first targets. The central leaders of the party, Alexander Dubcek, Josef Smrkovsky, Frantisek Kriegel and Oldrich Cernik, were arrested. Dubcek was brutalised by three security officers brandishing guns. They handcuffed him after they had knocked him to the ground. The emissaries of Leonid Brezhnev were in the process of unseating the First Secretary of the Czechoslovak Communist Party, the most popular leader in the country's postwar history. The Tet offensive had revealed the weaknesses of United States' imperialism; the May Events had shown the vulnerability and the resilience of the bourgeois democratic state in the West. Prague was now to reveal the deep crisis which was shaking the Stalinist system. The *first* seeds of "Eurocommunism" were sown on that fateful night of August 20.

The process of reforms initiated by the Dubcek leadership under the rubric of "Socialism with a human face" began on January 5, 1968, when a meeting of the Central Committee voted to remove Novotny from the position of First Secretary. Simultaneously the Central Committee accepted the draft of an Action Programme designed to democratise political life in the country. However, the hesitations and a certain lack of determination on the part of the reformers and divisions in the Central Committee between those for and against changes, meant that there was a time-lag of four months before the discussions of the Central Committee and the Action Programme were transmitted to the masses. The disputes of the Central Committee were ultimately resolved by two important decisions. The first was the abolition of censorship of press and television and the second, even more important, was the decision in June to call an Extraordinary Congress of the Party in September 1968 to ratify the changes and attempt a new phase of political, social and economic development in the country. The result of these measures was to involve important and growing

33

sections of the masses in the debates which had hitherto been the preserve of leading bodies of the Communist Party. It was also clear that the September Congress would remove the hard Stalinists from the party leadership.

Of all the countries of Eastern Europe, Czechoslovakia was the most industrially developed and politically advanced. Czech communism had mass roots which stretched back to 1921. The Stalinisation of the Party was completed by 1929, an event which lost it over sixty per cent of its membership and reduced it to the level of a sect, materially and politically dependent on Moscow. It was the anti-Nazi resistance which was greatly to aid the recuperation of the party and restore its link with the masses. It is worth noting that some of the central leaders and inspirers of the "Prague Spring" of 1968 had been heroes of the Resistance. One of them, Smrkovsky, had been imprisoned by the Stalinist régime after the seizure of power in 1948 and classified as "an agent of the Gestapo". A set of spontaneous popular uprisings in 1944-45 was launched against the will and advice of the Russians. Like the Warsaw uprising they were defeated. Prague was not to have the advantage of being liberated by its own partisans. The Red Army was to carry out that basic task, though the exact details are still disputed.

The formula of Czech communists and Moscow was that what was needed in the country was a "national and democratic revolution". It was a meaningless formula for what it could only mean was the creation of a viable bourgeois-democratic state. The existence of such a state would have suited neither the interests of the Stalinest bureacracy in Moscow nor (and for completely different reasons) the interests of the Czech working class. Stalin could not have exercised any effective control over a bourgeois state. The Czech workers had seen the bourgeoisie discredited and compromised. The most advanced sections amongst them wanted a workers' state. The international needs of Great Russian chauvinism coincided temporarily with the basic autonomous thrust of the working class in Czechoslovakia. It was this combination that produced 1948. The dominant partner was, from the very beginning, Stalinist Russia. The Czech workers were armed, but not encouraged to develop their own autonomous organs of power. The Red Army provided the ultimate military backing to sustain the overthrow of a weak and debilitated Czech capitalism.

What was created in the aftermath of 1948 was a monstrosity. To inflict the Stalinist model of political and economic structures on any country (including, incidentally, the USSR) was a crime of major proportions. To do so in a country which was heavily industrialised and had a certain tradition of bourgeois democracy was to turn history upside down. In their own bizarre way the Stalinist apparatchiks who were to rule Czechoslovakia were aware of this contradiction. Their first acts of violent repression were carried out against Marxists who challenged their monopoly of political power and demanded workers' democracy. The Trotskyist poet and writer, Kalandra, posed these questions. He had edited the party's theoretical journal in the thirties. He was arrested in 1948 and executed. Numerous other Marxists who opposed Stalinism were arrested and shot. Finally those members of the Communist Party itself — solid and ardent Stalinists — who had been abroad, as a number of Jewish communists, or had fought in the Spanish Civil War were rounded up and eliminated. The process of liquidation which had marked Stalinism in the USSR was now transplanted in Czechoslovakia. These Stalinised communists were shot not because they were proving to be "troublesome", but because they could have presented at some future, unspecified, time a potential threat. A sordid and grotesque parody of the Moscow Trials was carried out in Czechoslovakia. After the events in Hungary and Poland in 1956-57, a member of the Czech Central Committee, Kopecky, remarked at a meeting of that august body that the only reason Czechoslovakia had been immune to the process of uprisings was because the leadership had "liquidated all its potential political opponents physically" whereas in Hungary and Poland some of them had merely been put into prison. These were the reflections of the police mind of a bureaucrat: Kopecky. Both he and his boss Novotny were far too complacent and like most bureaucrats displayed complete and utter contempt for the political capacity of the masses, whilst nourishing these false hopes.

On the economic level the straitjacket of Stalinism was to hinder economic progress. Bureaucratic planning without any form of workers' control or participation was ruthlessly implemented. By the beginning of the sixties the economy was stagnating, with the accompanying effects on the standards of living of the masses. Essential consumer goods were obtainable only in the black market or in the special shops for party bureaucrats. The system of bureaucratic management generates a humiliating form of corruption. Spivs, touts and black marketeers flourish in the USSR and Eastern Europe, a damning indictment of the planning models operated in these countries. The technocratic wing of the Czechoslovak bureaucracy realised that a series of reforms was necessary. They understood that the total suppression of initiative at regional and plant level was an important factor inhibiting economic growth. Most of the technocrats wanted to allow greater initiatives and incentives, but only to the managers in charge of plants and enterprises, not to the workers. The dilemma was aptly summarised by Ernest Mandel:

"Under the concrete conditions of the economic situation in the CSSR of 1966-68, an increase in decentralisation, and an in-increased use of market mechanism in the field of consumer goods, was probably unavoidable to bring the economy again into focus with the main goals of harmonious and accelerated economic growth. But this was not the main social question involved in the reforms. 'Decentralisation' can mean two things. It can mean strengthening of *factory managers* both with regard to planning authorities and to workers; it can also mean the creation of workers' power at factory level. The first trend would be viewed with utmost distrust by the workers, especially if it implied the right of managers to fire workers, change wage rates, increase 'labour discipline', etc. The second trend is a first step in the direction of socialist democracy. During the major part of 1968, it was not clear to the Czechoslovak workers which of these two reform trends would prevail, and Dubcek was by no means identified with the second one."

As a matter of fact during the early days of the "Prague Spring" the conservative and ultra-Stalinist wing of the bureaucracy had taken advantage of the workers' uncertainty on the question of "liberalisation" of the economy, and swung them against the accompanying democratisation process. But once this process had started, the discussions which took place completely isolated the orthodox Stalinists. From now on the "Prague Spring" acquired a dynamism of its own. It was beyond the control of those who had initiated the process. It opened up the

36

richest and most creative period to be seen in any non-capital-ist country since the Second World War. It transcended the limited de-Stalinisation programme inaugurated in the Soviet Union by Khruschev in 1956. It is impossible to understand the reasons for the Soviet invasion unless one fully compre-hends the complexity of what was taking place in Czecho-slovakia from March to August 1968, in itself a response to growing dissatisfaction amongst the masses building up since the preceding year.

An important characteristic of the bureaucracy which rules in post-capitalist societies is its total monopoly of all channels of information. The press, television and radio as well as cultural magazines and the majority of films are under the iron control of the ideological commissars of this corrupt and unrepresentative governing caste. It is an extremely jea-lously guarded preserve. The reasons for this particular mono-poly are obvious. It helps to institutionalise a situation in which the masses are excluded from all forms of political participa-tion; it legitimises the one-party state; it provides the main link with developments in the outside world; and it provides a justi-fication for every policy twist of the government. The decision taken by the January meeting of the Czech Central Commit-tee was destined to have far-reaching effects. In that sense we can say that the developments in Prague were of a more lasting and fundamental character than the East Berlin uprising of 1953, the Hungarian revolt of 1956, the "Hundred Flowers" period of the Chinese Revolution, or the various waves of workers' revolts which have periodically shaken Poland since 1957. The reason for this is not that these other events were un-important. In one sense they posed the question of overthrow-ing bureaucratic rule more strongly than in Prague in 1968. But they were all of an episodic character. They, of necessity, with the exception of Poland in 1956-57, could last for only a short period before they were confronted with tanks.

The Czech developments lasted for over a year. They spread throughout the country and the debates which they unleashed were responsible for the increasing political awareness of the entire country. It should be stressed that there was no political current inside the Czech Communist Party which favoured restoration of capitalism. Outside the party the restorationist groups were small and unrepresentative at the time of the invasion. The latter provided them with their biggest boost since January 1968.

The decision to convoke an Extraordinary Congress of the Party in September 1968 was designed to provide legitimacy for the Dubcek turn and to approve the Action Programme already approved by the majority of the Central Committee. A debate was initiated throughout the country. It was not merely restricted to party members determining the basis on which to send delegates to the Congress — that in itself showed the absurdity of a one-party state. The mass media took full advantage of the ending of censorship and a wide range of views was expressed. A new magazine, one of many, entitled *Informačny Materiály* (Information Materials) was published which brought to the notice of the Czech people the views of anti-Stalinist Marxist currents. The June 24 issue, for instance, reprinted extensive extracts from a manifesto of the Fourth International specifically addressed to the workers and students of Czechoslovakia. The magazine's editorial board explained to its readers that while differences remained with the Fourth International and other currents, "However, we must take cognisance of their views (which, moreover, are often related and similar) and try, with the help of our own rich experience in integrating all concepts and programmes, to create a powerful ideological and practical school that can make possible the achievement of socialism and socialist man. Therefore, we are publishing here about two-thirds of an official declaration of the Fourth International which was published in the May issue of the Paris magazine *Quatrième Internationale*." The journal then printed an account of the May Events in France which was highly critical of the French Communist Party and Stalinism. The sections *not* printed were exclusively related to criticisms of the Kremlin. Another magazine, with a much larger circulation, *Literarni Listy,* had published some texts by Trotsky and Bukharin. It was serialising extracts from Deutscher's last major work, *The Unfinished Revolution,* at the time of the invasion. The Dubcek leadership was at pains to stress to journals of this character that they should proceed cautiously and not provoke the Soviet leaders. But the whole point was that the Soviet leaders had already taken exception to the decisions of the January plenum. Every measure that sought to democratise Czech society was regarded by them as a "provocation". Like Carroll's Humpty Dumpty they transformed the meanings of words to justify their repression.

What had antagonised the Russian bureaucrats was not the confused, liberalisation procedures envisaged by Otto Sik in the factories. These were only repeating what already existed, though to a lesser extent, in the Soviet Union, Hungary and East Germany. In fact Sik's "reforms" had already been accepted by Novotny as a way of meeting the economic difficulties of the country. Nothing comparable to the agreements negotiated between the USSR and the Fiat monopoly had been negotiated by the Dubcek régime in the field of economic collaboration with the West.

The main enemy of Soviet bureaucracy was socialist democracy. The Czech leaders continuously attempted to allay the fears of the Russian leaders. They insisted that the Czech reforms were specifically designed for Czechoslovakia and were not meant to be a model for the "socialist countries". But on this question the Soviet bureaucrats proved to be better materialists than their Czech opponents. Brezhnev understood that if the "Prague Spring" was institutionalised by a Party Congress it would spread like wild fire into the rest of Eastern Europe and parts of the Soviet Union itself. Already the winds of Prague were being felt in East Germany and the Ukraine. Ulbricht and the Ukrainian party boss, Shelest, were demanding action to curb the Czechoslovak "excesses".

The discussion on socialist democracy was no longer confined to small magazines. It had spread to the mainstream of the mass media and it had gripped both the universities and factories. The country was thinking along new lines. One example was the article published in June in the daily newspaper *Nova Svoboda* in which Professor Zbyněk Fišer made an impassioned plea for workers' democracy at every level of the state. He discussed the question of workers' self-management and subjected the Yugoslav model to a critique from the left:

"The Yugoslav factories are supposed to be run in accordance with the wishes of the self-governing workers. However, plant managers fire workers by the thousands in order to step up labour productivity. They keep quiet about the increased unemployment in the country. And they say nothing about the exporting of workers, which from the standpoint of the Yugoslav *state*, has become one of the main means for re-establishing the balance of its foreign currency account.

"In our circumstances, the programme of workers' self-management must have a totally different content. We must clearly understand that workers' self-management cannot be a merely formal institution. We must not forget that for Marx the principle of workers' self-management could only be effective once the entire political system of the society was in the hands of the workers, or rather of their political representative, which could be none other than a truly revolutionary party."

Language of this sort had not been heard in the international communist movement since Poland in 1956. If the students of Paris had been "walking paragraphs from the *Manuscripts of 1844* and the *Grundrisse*" were not the Czech workers and students striking chapters from *State and Revolution* and *The Revolution Betrayed*? Fišer, for instance, did not restrict himself to erecting a set of abstract criteria; he developed his argument further and raised a set of immediate demands:

"At the present stage of development an important problem is beginning to be posed. The question is whether, above and beyond the demand for workers' self-management, a demand should be formulated also — if only as a first step — for effective guarantees of the right to strike. In fact, if the new economic system proposed by Professor Sik is put into practice, the workers would be left with no social guarantees. (This problem was correctly handled by Robert Kalivoda in the Prague party conference. *Cf. Rudé Právo,* May 5, 1968.)

"Guarantees of the workers' social rights must be firmly demanded. Indeed without guarantees that the workers' economic interests will be satisfied, there can be no guarantees either that their political interests will be realised. Democracy as well as political and civil liberties *which are not based on real satisfaction of the needs and vital interests of the broadest strata of workers can be neither stable nor lasting*. This democracy and these freedoms would be only for socially privileged groups; they would not be the real freedoms expected from the democratisation process. They would only be a liberal caricature."

Another article by Václav Slavík returned to the subject of democracy in a text written for *Literarni Listy* a month later. Entitled "Where does the Power Lie?", Slavík's text once again posed a whole series of questions related to the past functioning of the party. In particular the author maintained that there had to be a separation between the Party and the State. He located the central defect of Stalinism in the equation of the two. It was but natural that as the discussion progressed currents would develop within the Party. On May 11, *Rudé Právo,* the daily newspaper of the Czech Communist Party, published a call for the formation of a left Marxist group. Following this appeal an association of left Marxists constituted themselves as the Prague Club, an organisation later to be attacked fiercely by ideological mercenaries in the pay of the Kremlin. The Prague Club, which consisted largely of members of the Communist Party, prepared a programme which they intended to submit to delegates attending the Extraordinary Congress scheduled for September. The intervention of Soviet tanks prevented the publication of this important document. It would have been undoubtedly rejected by the majority, but it would have nonetheless provoked a lively debate. It represented the most politically advanced group inside the Czech working class at that time. The official leaders of the reform movement criticised the Prague Club for "ultraleftism", but no attempt was made to censor its views, or to suppress it as an organisation.

It was not surprising that the Action Programme had initially sparked off a debate amongst the intelligentsia. If that debate had been concerned exclusively with rarefied or abstract economic concepts it would have remained isolated from the mainstream of the Czech working class. Its parameters were, however, much broader and embraced virtually every sphere of Czech social and political life. The workers began to discuss democratisation as it affected them. This led to the revival of trade unions. The role played by the latter in the months preceding the invasion provided us with a glimpse of the potentialities of bodies such as trades unions in post-capitalist societies. The first set of workers' councils were elected on July 1, 1968. Over the next few months they were to embrace 114 factories including giant plants such as the Skoda works. The laws proposed by the government were totally insufficient and reflected the preoccupations and concerns of the technocrats within the leadership, whose leading spokesman was Otto Sik, but who had the backing of Dubcek himself. These laws

41

amounted at best to co-determination: the elected workers' councils were seen as advisers and collaborators on management bodies rather than organs of management themselves. The congress of trades unions held *after* the invasion expressed its strong opposition to these laws and demanded that the workers' councils themselves should be the highest organs of management. The technocrats and Moscow tended to agree on one aspect of the economy: they both saw the choice (though not in these words) as being between bureaucratic centralisation or the "market economy". They deliberately ignored the third and Marxist choice, namely the transferring of all power to a nationally elected congress of workers' councils, which would make the final decisions regarding planning and investments. It was not a question of ignoring expert advice of professional economists. It was determining who would make the final decision. The matter was not settled by democratic votes; it was decided by Brezhnevite pro-consuls backed by an army of occupation.

The Soviet leaders applied maximum pressure on the Czechs to change course. At a meeting of Warsaw Pact leaders in Dresden in March 1968, the Czech delegation led by Dubcek was strongly criticised. The delegation unanimously decided not to transmit this displeasure to the Czech party or the press. They felt that to do so would only exacerbate anti-Russian sentiments and further provoke the Brezhnevite apparatus. It was to prove a crucial and costly error. The Czech leaders hoped that the Russians would not have the audacity to invade their country. Dubcek was until the last moment not totally convinced that a Soviet intervention was on the agenda. Jiri Pelikan, a member of the Central Committee of the Party, later revealed in a remarkable interview given to the British magazine *New Left Review* that Czech military intelligence had been aware of Soviet plans:

> "However, there were people like General Prchlik, who was head of the Department for Defence and Security, who wished to submit to the leadership a paper outlining the alternatives in case of a Soviet invasion. The army and the security forces had discovered that the objective of the Soviet army manoeuvres in Czechoslovakia in June and July had been to put itself in a position where it could control our communications systems. They had made maps of how this system worked,

they had laid cables underground and they had established the location of all telephone and postal facilities, including those only used by state organisations. This was known to the security forces, though since some of the security officers were Soviet agents there were conflicting reports."

Through their agents the Russians discovered that General Prchlik had submitted a contingency plan. They sent an Official Note to the Czech government complaining about Prchlik on some petty pretext. Dubcek now made his second mistake. He sacked Prchlik. Having politically disarmed the masses by not informing them of the intolerable pressures to which their leaders were being subjected, he now militarily disarmed the Czech State by refusing to consider defending Czech sovereignty against Soviet invasion. These two decisions were to provide the final go-ahead for Moscow.

The reasons given by Moscow for the invasion were unconscious imitations of Lewis Carroll. The propaganda department of the Soviet bureaucracy claimed that Czechoslovakia was threatened by internal "counter-revolution" and also by a possible West German intervention. They pointed to the large numbers of Western tourists in Prague and alleged that many of these were American "Green Berets in disguise". In reality the Czech Communist Party was more popular than it had ever been since 1948. The May Day demonstration in Prague in 1968 was in marked contrast to other Eastern European capitals. There were no tanks and soldiers on the streets: only the people. Thousands and thousands of students and technicians, their arms linked with tens of thousands of factory workers marched past the party leaders. Many contingents threw flowers at the dais as they went by as a gesture of approval for "socialism with a human face". At one stage Dubcek, moved by this display of approval, wept with emotion. It certainly was an unprecedented demonstration in the annals of Stalinism.

Moscow's justifications for the invasion were so patently absurd that they were treated with contempt both by socialists in the West and in Czechoslovakia. Not a single major Communist Party in the West, in marked contrast to Hungary, supported the invasion. The far left mounted massive demonstrations outside Soviet embassies in every capital city of Western Europe. We marched with red flags and portraits of Lenin,

Trotsky and Luxemburg to demonstrate our anger and disgust. Given our commitment to solidarity with the Vietnamese it was a trifle difficult for the Soviet press to denounce us as "agents of the CIA". And yet the Kremlin ideologues had no option. The top bureaucrats were not worried about the external reaction; it was the possible domestic repercussions which concerned them. For the rank-and-file soldiers and the junior officers the pretexts for invading another country had to be presented in a global ideological wrapping. The West German angle was useful because it brought back memories of the Second World War. In fact, amongst the top echelons of the Soviet army, Great Russian chauvinism is rampant. Pelikan revealed in his interview in *New Left Review* that "Soviet officers with whom we talked after the intervention claimed that Stalin's greatest mistake, after his failure to prevent the German attack in 1941, was his failure to incorporate the East European countries as constituent republics of the Soviet Union in 1945".

The actual reasons for the intervention, as I have already indicated, were the rapid moves towards socialist democracy. It has been privately argued by Czech revolutionaries that Moscow was too impatient. If they had waited another year, or even less, the internal mood would have been such that Dubcek would have been resisting attempts to completely dismantle bureaucratic power. At that time "Soviet help" might have been welcomed by at least an important section of the leadership. What this argument ignores is the international dimension of the "Prague Spring". News of what was really happening in Czechoslovakia was suppressed in the press of the USSR and Eastern Europe, but it was brought back to these countries by returning tourists and by the radio stations of the West. The Brezhnev leadership wanted, above all, to delay the Czech Party Congress scheduled for September. The Congress was bound to approve the course taken by the leadership, and remove all the pro-Russian elements from the party leadership. It would thus have provided the Dubcek administration with the legitimacy it needed. It would also have made an invasion more difficult to justify internally. In August the Soviet leaders made a last attempt to influence the Czechs. A meeting of the Politbureaus of the two Communist Parties met at Cierna. Brezhnev asked the Czech leaders to postpone the date of the party congress. They refused, although they agreed to other concessions. Their refusal sealed their fate. The meeting was adjourned. Contact was resumed again only after the entry of Soviet tanks into Prague.

Moscow had hoped that the Czech leadership would collapse after the invasion and they would be able to cobble together a government composed of collaborators. One of the pretexts used had been to imply that "progressive" elements within the Czech leadership had requested the invasion. However the Presidium of the party passed a resolution condemning the invasion and asked the Soviet troops to withdraw. There were elements within the Czech army who were even at that late stage prepared to organise an armed resistance, but they reluctantly accepted orders to remain passive. The armed resistance should have been prepared earlier when General Prchlik had sounded the tocsin. It could now only flow out of a mass political resistance to the invasion. Some members of the Central Committee pressed Dubcek to leave the headquarters via a secret exit and organise resistance from the CKD factory in Prague 9. Here Dubcek made his last mistake. He decided to stay because legally he was the First Secretary of the Party. By now he should have known that the Russians were no respecters of legality.

The choice Dubcek confronted on 21 August was one which has faced many political leaders at critical moments. Dubcek was clearly not a Lenin, but he also lacked the self-confidence of Tito or Mao. He had been politically formed not in the heat of a mass struggle, but in the conflicts which developed in the party apparatus. Having hoped against hope that there would be no Soviet military intervention, but at the most an economic blockade, he was now almost paralysed as Soviet tanks surrounded the headquarters of his Central Committee. His legal instincts compelled him to try negotiations once again, which he preferred to a public appeal to the masses for nationwide resistance. He probably thought even now that all they needed to do was postpone the Congress, make additional concessions and persuade the Russians to withdraw. He hoped that he could still play for time. But the game was over, at least temporarily.

A revolutionary leader would not have been content with simply condemning the invasion. He or she would have given some guidance to the masses to create the most favourable relationship of forces for pushing the Russians back to their own frontiers. Dubcek had believed that Brezhnev could not outdistance Stalin. After all, not even Stalin had dared invade Yugoslavia when it had embarked on its own "road to socialism". But what Dubcek and his comrades forgot was that Tito had got away with heresy because he had made it clear that any Soviet invasion would be resisted by the people. He had shown his confidence in the Yugoslav masses by arming them politically *and* militarily. The Yugoslav League of Communists had pledged to revert to partisan warfare if their country's sovereignty was usurped by Russian Stalinism. Tito's confidence was not a result of ideological anti-Stalinism. It had been bred in the mountains during years of resistance against the Nazi occupiers. Moreover Tito had not accepted the decision made at Yalta whereby Yugoslavia was assigned a different status and Stalin had agreed to restore the monarchy. The Yugoslav communists had made their revolution despite Stalin, even though they remained ideologically loyal to many of the central tenets of Stalinism. Thus their confidence was based on the prestige they enjoyed in their own country, and the rapport they had developed with the masses. Dubcek's prestige was also very high, but he lacked the will and determination necessary to organise the resistance. It was the best possible proof, in one sense, of the imbecility contained in the argument that he was "anti-Soviet". In any event Dubcek's thoughts were not on resistance on the night of August 21. Possibly he was pondering the fate of Imre Nagy, who had headed the Budapest government in 1956 and based himself on the Hungarian masses. Nagy too had been a veteran communist, but that had not prevented the Russians from describing him as a "counter-revolutionary" and executing him.

Dubcek was soon confronted by the perverted and debased standard-bearers of Brezhnevite "internationalism": three men with revolvers tore the telephone out of his hand, hit him with a revolver butt and, as he lay on the floor, they handcuffed him. He was taken to the airport where, together with the Prime Minister of the country and other leaders, he was thrown into a cargo plane and transported to a military airport in the Ukraine. If their lives were saved it was because of what happened in Czechoslovakia in their absence.

The Prague City Committee of the Party now took a bold and unique initiative. They decided to organise the planned Congress, which the Russian tanks had been sent to prevent, immediately and in Prague. This task was made much easier by the fact that the delegates had already been elected at city, district and regional level conferences during the preceding two months. The draft statutes of the new Constitution of the Party had been fully discussed in the national press. An appeal was broadcast convening the Congress. Its location was in the heart of proletarian Prague: the district of Vysočany. Delegates travelled as best they could. They had been instructed to report at different factories in the district from where workers took them to the location of the Congress itself. They were also aided by Czech soldiers and police. Within twenty-four hours of the broadcast appeal, 1,290 elected delegates (more than the two-thirds necessary to allow decisions to be binding) had reached Vysočany. The Congress was "underground" yet the knowledge that it was taking place was widespread. It was held in an empty factory hall, a symbolic demonstration of the fact that the Communist Parties of Eastern Europe, despite all their deformations, still rested ultimately on the working class. The Vysočany Congress was a direct challenge to the occupying forces. Almost half-a-million soldiers had been sent to prevent it, but they were unable to do so. If the tanks had been sent into Vysočany they would have been met by the vanguard of the Prague working class. Battles would have taken place, workers would have been killed and the effect on the Russian soldiers could have been dramatic. They had been told, after all, that they were defending the Czech working class against "counter-revolution". How would they have reacted on realising that *they* were the counter-revolution? In any event they decided not to disrupt the Congress with armed force.

The Vysočany Congress was described by Brezhnev as the "Vysočany Riot". For the invaders it did constitute a riot, but one which they could not quell. The Congress voted unanimously to condemn the invasion. It elected a new Central Committee; it adopted a new programme and constitution; and gave overwhelming support to the democratisation procedures which were already under way. It did not institutionalise workers' democracy, but it did adopt a thorough de-Stalinisa-

47

tion programme. As far as the occupation was concerned the Congress discussed whether to call a token one-day strike or a general strike. After a lengthy discussion it took the wrong decision. It called a token strike, which turned out to be a massive success, but could not, because of its character, change the situation. A general strike should not be used, many party leaders argued, because it was "the ultimate weapon". But at that stage they had no other effective weapons. It must have seemed somewhat bizarre for a Communist Party to call a general strike in a country where they already held power. But then the conditions confronting Czechoslovakia were also bizarre. It had suffered a "fraternal" invasion. The Vysočany Congress saved the lives of the imprisoned Czech leaders. It prevented the immediate establishment of a collaborationist régime. But it did not prevent, though it tried, the Czech President Svoboda from leaving for Moscow to negotiate with the Russians. A general strike would have possibly been more persuasive.

The young workers and students had spontaneously, though with the clear approval and support of party members, embarked on a process of fraternisation with the Russian soldiers. Many students who could speak Russian approached the soldiers as comrades who had been misinformed about the situation. "Where, comrades, is the counter-revolution? Where are the West German infiltrators?" they asked. They then explained what had been happening in Czechoslovakia. They suggested that the soldiers should fight for socialist democracy at home. The results were not disheartening. Many Russian soldiers wanted to know more. There were desertions from the occupying army and a few suicides. Moscow had to despatch over 200 secret police specialists to deal with the internal situation in the army. The troops who had initially entered Prague were withdrawn and replaced with fresher troops who were "advised" not to engage in conversation with the "young hooligans".

The mass opposition to the invasion and the virtual unanimity with which Czech communists had reacted made Moscow's task more complex. It released the imprisoned leaders and negotiated a temporary settlement. The terms of this became known as the Moscow Protocol. It was also the political death-warrant of both Dubcek and the "Prague Spring". At Moscow,

Dubcek and Svoboda signed an agreement compelling them to renounce their past; it reinstituted press and media censorship; declared the Vysočany Congress to be invalid; accepted the dismissal of Otto Sik and Jiri Hajek; and accepted the resignation of the Czech Interior Minister, General Josef Pavel, who refused to collaborate with the secret police apparatus of the Soviet Union. Dubcek was on the road to political extinction. The Moscow Protocol provided Moscow with its *first* political breathing space since the "Prague Spring". Until now it, had possessed limitless weaponry and fire power. What it sought was political ammunition. Dubcek's capitulation, for unfortunately there is no other way to view it, now provided the latter.

Despite the agreements, several months were to elapse before Moscow could begin to inflict its "normality" on Czechoslovakia. On Dubcek's return a meeting of the old Central Committee was convened with the addition of some delegates to the Vysočany Congress — a characteristic Dubcek compromise — in order to ratify the Moscow Protocol. There was only one voice which suggested an alternative solution even at that late stage. A young delegate from Moravia, Sabata, made a passionate attack on the invasion and the Protocol. He demanded that the leadership reject the agreements and organise a resistance. But the Central Committee, despite its hesitations, gave Dubcek a vote of confidence. Sabata and his entire family were not forgotten by the Russians and they were later to serve long prison sentences for their audacity.

It took several months more before the Kremlin dismantled the last vestiges of the "Prague Spring". In that sense the Czech events are of the utmost importance in preparing a revolutionary strategy for the overthrow of the Stalinist bureaucracy throughout Eastern Europe. For seven months the country's mood was precarious and uneasy. It was still militarily occupied. However at the same time the Czech press, despite the limited censorship, was the liveliest in Eastern Europe. The trades unions had not reverted to being empty bureaucratic shells and discussions on workers' self-management continued. It appeared almost as if the political and cultural life of the country was a permanent reality and that it was the Russian troops which would have to be withdrawn. When Moscow published its notorious document, "On the

Events in Czechoslovakia" (a document, incidentally, designed largely for visitors from another planet!) a reply was published in *Reporter*, the weekly magazine of the Czech journalists' union. In an article full of heavy irony, Jiri Hanak described the book as belonging to the realm of "science fiction". *Reporter* was suppressed, but only after it had reached the kiosks. The next day a new *Reporter* with the same date was published. Hanak's text had been replaced by an article on "currency convertibility". All this was taking place under the Occupation. The masses and large sections of the party membership refused to accept the Occupation. It was being defied in small and big ways. In January 1969 a young student had emulated the Buddhist priests protesting against the Americans in Saigon: Jan Palach burned himself as a moral gesture against the Soviet invasion. His body was taken to hospital, where he died hours later. His funeral was the first *mass* demonstration against the Russians. Throughout the country active hostility still persisted. On the night of March 28-29 the anger of the masses erupted on to the streets. A wave of spontaneous demonstrations shook the country. The Soviet trade mission and Russian tourist offices were destroyed. The barracks where the occupying soldiers lived were stoned and anti-Russian slogans were chanted throughout the country.

The Russians responded to this political crisis by despatching an emissary to Prague with an ultimatum that Dubcek must be removed from his position as First Secretary. The Soviet Defence Minister, Marshal Grechko, also arrived in Prague and was greeted at the airport by pro-Soviet Czech Generals, some of whom had replaced pro-Dubcek officers. Grechko's behaviour was that of a Viceroy. Czech oppositionists inside the Communist Party managed to send out of the country a number of accounts of what transpired during the weeks leading up to the Central Committee plenum of April 17, 1969. Grechko refused to negotiate with Dubcek. He met the Czech President Svoboda and presented him with the Soviet assessment of the situation: the "anti-Soviet provocations" had been encouraged by Dubcek, Smrkovsky, Cernik and other "extremists". Grechko denounced the failure of the party apparatus to intervene against the demonstrators and asked why the party organ, *Rudé Právo*, had not denounced the demonstrations. He also informed the Czech leaders that he had the authority to occupy Czech cities a second time and would do so unless the situation was resolved. He offered the Czechs three choices: (i) they should resolve the internal situation themselves in accordance with Soviet views; (ii) if they could not do so on their own they could ask for "aid" from the Warsaw Pact forces; (iii) if they did neither, then the Soviet army would intervene. Grechko further told the Czech leaders that in his personal opinion a mistake was made by the Soviet leaders in not settling the question at the time of the invasion. The Presidium of the Party met the same night (March 31, 1969) and decided that they would accept the first choice, but they opposed any immediate changes in personnel.

An outraged Grechko then made direct approaches to the Czech generals. He met General Martin Dzur, the Defence Minister, and made the following proposals: (i) the Soviet and Czech armies would organise a joint take-over of the country and in cities where Soviet garrisons existed the Soviet military commanders would become the "political commissars"; (ii) and an immediate task was to reimpose an absolute censorship and carry out a reorganisation of the party apparatus. General Dzur was unhappy with these proposals, but gave no direct answer except to declare that he could only accept orders from his supreme commander, President Svoboda. Grechko then gave support for action by pro-Soviet generals. A number of these — Mucha, Rytir, Bedrich, Dvorak and Rusov — now threatened a *coup d'état* to "restore normality". Some military divisions were moved to within fifteen miles of Prague. An emergency meeting of the Presidium was convened to draw up a declaration to respond to the Official Note of protest sent through normal diplomatic channels by the Soviet government. This response accepted the bulk of Soviet criticisms, spoke of "extreme right-opportunist forces" existing in Czechoslovakia, accepted the need for repression and publicly criticised Josef Smrkovsky (Dubcek, Slavik, Kabrna and a few others voted against this section), who was regarded, not without justification, as the Czech leader most opposed to collaboration. As one of the leaders of the anti-Nazi resistance during the Second World War, Smrkovsky enjoyed a certain popularity within the working class. The combination of the Presidium statement and the prestige of Svoboda in the Czech Army, defused the situation and the threatened *coup* was averted.

51

The following day (April 12) there was an official meeting between the Czechs and the occupiers. The Czech delegation consisted of Svoboda (President), Cernik (Prime Minister) and Dubcek (Party Secretary), while the occupiers were represented by Grechko, Semyonov, Chervonyenko (Russian Ambassador in Prague) and General Mayorov, commander of the Occupying Forces. The Russians accepted that the Czechs could settle the crisis, but they immediately afterwards met with pro-Soviet figures in the party to plan a thoroughgoing purge.

The Dubcekite wing of the leadership was now in full retreat. They met as a caucus on the evening of April 4 to prepare their response to the planned statement by the right wing welcoming the August invasion. Their response stated that the stationing of Warsaw Pact troops in Czechoslovakia was necessary for "strategic reasons". At the same time, this caucus planned to shifts its leaders into different posts in an attempt to appease the Russians. One of them summed up their tasks in the following way: "Let's play ice hockey with the Russians. We have to gain time." (The wave of demonstrations that had sparked off the political crisis of March 1969 had followed the victory of the Czech team against the Russians in ice-hockey!)

By the time the plenum of April 17 took place the Dubcekites were totally atomised. The plenum itself was completely rigged. The real decisions had been made in Moscow. The new leader was Gustav Husak. The disorientated Dubcekites had voted for him provided that he would prevent their supporters from being expelled from the Party. Husak gave this assurance, but naturally ignored it some months later. Despite this, twenty-two members of the Presidium voted against Husak and they were the last vestiges of the "Prague Spring". Dubcek, Cernik and others were removed from their posts. Husak flew to Moscow to present his credentials to Brezhnev. The latter is reported to have said that they would judge Husak on the basis of what he could *do*, not his intentions. Over the coming months over half a million members of the Czech Communist Party were expelled. The Stalinist winter had once again enshrouded the country in darkness. The more neanderthal of the bureaucrats came out of their caves once again. They are still ruling Czechoslovakia, but there is a growing opposition led by expelled members of the Communist Party, who have organised a Charter demanding democratic rights. The group of dissidents known as Charter 77 enjoy a great deal of popularity, not least in the factories.

The events in Czechoslovakia were a confirmation of the contradictory character of Eastern European post-capitalist societies. What was demonstrated in East Berlin, in Budapest and now in Prague, was the fragility of the State and its power. On all three occasions, but particularly pronounced in the cases of the last two, the State could not withstand mass eruptions from below. On all three occasions the Great Russian State had to intervene militarily to maintain the status quo. The reasons for the weakness of the Eastern European State and its vulnerability are a reflection of two inter-related peculiarities. The Eastern European bureaucratic State lacks the legitimacy of a popular revolution (Russia, China, Yugoslavia, Vietnam) and is not based on any form of institutionalised consent. Secondly, and this is a feature of *all* post-capitalist states, there is an equation between the party and the State on every level. The Brezhnev Constitution has further strengthened this equation, symbolised now by Brezhnev simultaneously holding the positions of Party Leader and Head of State. Thus, in a new sense, the "state is civil society" in the bureaucratic world of post-capitalist societies. This State form can at best be unstable. In the case of Eastern Europe the ultimate powers of coercion to maintain the bureaucratic form of State power rest outside the geographical boundaries of these states. (Though at the moment the only three countries where there are no permanent Soviet garrisons are Yugoslavia, Rumania and Albania.) In itself this is a recognition of the weakness of indigenous State power. This does not mean that the only task for revolutionary Marxists in Eastern Europe is to analyse the situation and wait for explosions in the USSR itself. What they need to do is to work out a strategic line which can politically weaken the Soviet bureaucracy at home. A revolutionary leadership in Czechoslovakia between February and August 1968 could have prevented the Soviet intervention. The mass mobilisations which confronted the invading troops and the fraternisation which followed provided us with another glimpse of the tactics which need to be fully worked out. The links between the Eastern European and the Soviet State force one to confront the necessity for an *internationalist* strategy. The refusal of Dubcek and his supporters to grasp this proved ultimately to be the

Achilles heel of Czech reformism. For their opponents, on this front, were more aware of the potential international impact of the "Prague Spring" and the threat is posed to the bases of bureaucratic power.

The developments in Czechoslovakia demonstrated in a striking fashion the continuing links between party and class in post-capitalist societies. In Hungary and in Czechoslovakia some of the most politically advanced cadres in the anti-bureaucratic movement emerged from within the ruling communist parties. This makes permanent coercion an extremely risky enterprise. In mass upheavals which do not pose a fundamental challenge to the bureaucratic State the tendency is to make big concessions as the Polish upheavals of the last decade have adequately demonstrated.

The bureaucracy, precisely because it is not a social class, but a caste representing a privileged minority, understands perfectly well that its State power and its political and material privileges would disappear with the eruption of socialist democracy. The main refrain of the Russians in Czechoslovakia after the invasion was: "Censorship, more censorship, total censorship". This absolute monopoly of information is vital for preserving and maintaining bureaucratic power over the majority of the country's citizens. Without this monopoly of information the entire justification for the monolithic one-party State begins to collapse.

The merit of the Czech events lay in the fact that they demonstrated these theses in a remarkably clear fashion. In that sense their impact has been more lasting and profound than any previous revolt against bureaucratic power and Russian tutelage in Eastern Europe.

4. The Lessons of Chile

"Proletarian revolutions . . . constantly engage in self-criticism, and in repeated interruptions of their own course. They return to what has apparently been accomplished in order to begin the task again; with merciless thoroughness they mock the inadequate, weak and wretched aspects of their first attempts; they seem to throw their opponent to the ground only to see him draw new strength from the earth and rise again before them, more colossal than ever; they shrink back again and again before the indeterminate immensity of their own goals, until the situation is created in which any retreat is impossible and the circumstances themselves cry out: *Hic Rhodus, hic salta!* Here is the rose, dance here!"

Karl Marx: *The Eighteenth Brumaire of Louis Bonaparte*

"Lenin very studiously followed all the elections and voting in the country, carefully assembling those figures which would actually throw a light on the actual correlation of forces. The semi-anarchistic indifference to electoral statistics got nothing but contempt from him. At the same time Lenin never identified the indexes of parliamentarism with the actual correlation of the masses. He always introduced a corrective in favour of direct action."

Leon Trotsky: *The History of the Russian Revolution*

On September 11, 1973 the Chilean army, instigated and backed by the Central Intelligence Agency and the United States government, carried out the *coup d'état* which it had been planning for two and a half years. The elected Popular Unity government was overthrown and the Chilean President, Salvador Allende, was shot dead by Captain Robert Garrido in his room in the Moneda Palace, a large section of which was destroyed by artillery and aerial bombardment. The *coup* signalled the end of the "Chilean Road to Socialism". It added new names to the growing scroll of Latin American martyrs who have died in the battle for a new world. The international impact of the *coup* was phenomenal. In the "third world" itself the ghost of Allende haunted the heads of virtually every civilian government. In Western Europe the fall of Allende resulted in a far-ranging debate on socialist strategy and tactics. It can be said that if the seeds of Eurocommunism were planted in Prague in August 1968 it was the sprinkling of Chilean blood which transformed them into saplings, well on their way to becoming trees. A discussion of Chile is thus of vital importance since that experience has helped to determine working-class strategy in several Western European countries.

Ever since the Cuban revolution, the more sophisticated sections of the American and Latin American ruling classes understood the importance of projecting an alternative model of development to that of Cuba, thereby creating a viable and alternative pole of attraction in the Latin American continent. It was a role not dissimilar to the one which India was assigned in relation to China in Asia. The influence and prestige of the Cuban revolution and its leaders (Castro and Guevara) were such that the United States were extremely concerned at the possibility of Cuban-style revolutions sweeping the continent. Their concern had only been enhanced by the creation of the Organisation of Latin American Solidarity (OLAS) and the openly declared internationalist aims of the Cuban Revolution. Important sections of the Chilean ruling class backed the Christian Democratic Party in the 1964 elections and ensured the victory of Eduardo Frei as President, a victory which was hailed by the American press as a "revolution in freedom". It was stated on numerous occasions that Frei was going to transform the economic and social structure of Chile. The Chilean rulers were playing the reformist card in an attempt to hold back working-class and peasant discontent and prevent it from overflowing into a popular revolt. A number of reforms were undertaken by the Christian Democratic government — the Agrarian Reform Law of 1967 made a start by expropriating land and distributing it among peasants; a rural unionisation law permitted the establishment of peasant unions; Chilean participation in the US-controlled copper industry was increased until the government finally owned a controlling share in both the Kennecott and Annaconda Copper Companies; an attempt

56

was made to devote more expenditure on social welfare measures.

Frei's reformism was supported by the United States. A number of changes had taken place in the location of imperialist capital investments in Latin America, which now concentrated more in manufacture than on primary materials, and by 1966 this had become the dominant area of investment. The United States could now *economically* afford to reach an accommodation with the new oligarchs who existed in the shape of bourgeois or military "reformism". In other words the objective basis for the alliance between the old oligarchies (based on land and mining interests) had been reduced. Needless to add, the old oligarchies were *politically* not outmoded as far as the United States was concerned. The changing investment patterns merely afforded the United States a much greater room for manoeuvre, though its final decisions were motivated by *political* considerations, themselves determined by the global interests of capital.

Thus Frei's policies in no way clashed with the interests of United States imperialism. What was vital for preserving a working relationship with the latter was not the number of reforms, but the ability to repress any mass movement which appeared menacing whenever the need arose. In this crucial arena Frei did not disappoint the United States. Working-class demonstrations were regularly attacked and teargassed by the police. Eight workers were shot dead at the El Salvador mine in 1966. Ten squatters who had claimed unoccupied land were massacred in Puerto Montt in 1969. The Frei reforms had stimulated working-class consciousness rather than contain it in the sense that many workers and even more peasants were not satisfied. It was in this context that the discussion on armed struggle first arose. Carlos Altamirano, a prominent leader of the Chilean Socialist Party, told the Cuban newspaper *Granma* (October 30, 1968) that there was a "progressive feeling of betrayal; . . . people, workers and youth seek true revolutionary methods of struggle, of action. In the country, as well as in the university, highly explosive forces are being formed."

Within the Christian Democratic Party itself a number of groups began to emerge which were extremely critical of Frei for pandering too much to the right. In May 1969 a leftist group split off and formed the *Movimiento de Accion Popular*

57

Unitaria (Movement of United Popular Action — MAPU). By 1970 it was clear that the Christian Democrats would not win the forthcoming elections, so they discarded Frei. Their new Presidential candidate, Tomic, used a rhetoric virtually indistinguishable from that of Allende. The experience of Christian Democracy in power had, however, disillusioned broad sections of the masses. Even the bourgeoisie was split and could not agree on a common candidate, an important factor which permitted Allende's electoral victory. The electoral result itself demonstrated the polarisation taking place in Chilean society: Allende obtained 1,075,000 or 36.3 per cent of the vote; the right-wing National Party nominee, Allesandri, obtained 1,036,000 or 34.9 per cent and Tomic was squeezed out with 824,000 or 27.8 per cent. Allende's victory was greeted with street parties, fiestas and demonstrations by the workers and the oppressed. A series of attempts were considered, including a possible *coup,* to prevent Allende becoming President, but rejected for a number of reasons. A lack of coordination between the Pentagon, the CIA and the Chilean Army led to the unauthorised assassination of the Chilean Commander-in-Chief, General Rene Schneider, as part of an overall plan to "destabilise" Chile.

The election of the Popular Unity (*Undidad Popular* — UP) — a coalition dominated by the Communist Party and the Socialist Party — was seen as an important step forward by the Chilean working class. Despite the reformist confusions contained in the Popular Unity programme it nonetheless transcended the reformism of Frei and pledged to create a new Chile. The programme promised to nationalise all foreign capital and foreign trade, to greatly extend the agrarian reform of Frei and to lay the basis for the creation of a new apparatus under the control of the working class. In other words the Popular Unity saw its electoral victory as the beginning of the process of a transition to socialism.

The political project of Allende moved peacefully and gradually, through a process of reforms (some of them structural) to socialism. In an extended interview with the French Marxist journalist and writer, Régis Debray, Allende stated that in the thirties their aims had been different from today: ". . we consciously entered into a coalition in order to form the left wing of the system — the capitalist system, that is. By contrast, to-

58

day, as our programme shows, we are struggling to change the system. . . . Our objective is total, scientific Marxist socialism." One aim of the social-democratic and communist parties during the thirties had been to preserve bourgeois democracy in alliance with major bourgeois parties against the encroachments of fascism. The changed relationship of class forces on a global scale since the mid-sixties necessitated a new project. It remained a reformist project, but its stated aims were different as were some of the actions undertaken. The Popular Unity was essentially a reformist united front composed of the two major working-class parties of Chile. Allende's electoral victory provided us with the closest equivalent to a workers' government in post-war history; a government of the left parties, which was the stated aim of a number of Western European Communist Parties before the Chilean *coup*.

Another important feature of Popular Unity was that it was not the Chilean Communist Party which represented its extreme left. It was the Chilean Socialist Party, to which Allende belonged, which was more radical on virtually every single political issue. This fact is important to understand why the UP was not in a position to contain the mass movement by selective repression or to outlaw the MIR (*Movimiento Izquierda Revolucionaria* — Movement of the Revolutionary Left), measures which would certainly have appeased the Chilean ruling class. It was the existence and presence of the Socialist Party which made the Unidad Popular an unsalvageable political operation for the more sophisticated and liberal sections of the ruling class (those represented politically by Christian Democracy). In the absence of a strong left-wing pole inside the Socialist Party it is quite clear that the Communists would have dragged the UP irredeemably to the Right in an attempt to drag the Christian Democrats into the coalition and transform the UP into a classical Popular Front of the type in which the Stalinist movement specialised in the thirties.

What then was the Chilean Socialist Party and what were its origins? It was founded in 1933 by a group including Salvador Allende. It was from the beginning a party which stated in its programme a commitment to Marxism: "The party adheres to Marxism as the method of interpreting reality and recognises the class struggle as the motive force of history." It was created because its founders felt that the Chilean Communist Party was, because of its dependence on Stalinist Russia, incapable of responding to the needs of the Chilean proletariat. The Socialist Party attempted to build a working-class party based on Marxism, but not under the domination of Stalin's Third International (the Comintern): a party, that is, which was able to devise tactics in relation to the needs of the Chilean class struggle and not in accordance with the twists and turns of Moscow. As a result, the Socialist Party was different from the traditional social-democratic parties of Britain, Germany, France and Italy. It did bear marked resemblances to the left wing of Spanish social-democracy. Allende stressed this difference in 1970 and maintained that the Socialists in Chile had nothing to do "with certain self-styled socialist parties in Europe". The Socialist Party (and here in marked contrast to the Spanish social-democrats) was never aligned to the Second International (it was the Radical Party which was the latter's Chilean section!). Its policies, for a period, were closer to Marxism than those of the Chilean Communist Party. Its internal life was considerably more open and democratic and many SP militants in the thirties, including Salvador Allende himself, studied not only Lenin, but also Trotsky, who was at that time regarded by the official communists as "an agent of the Gestapo".

Despite the fact that the Socialist Party was committed to Marxism by its programmes, it nonetheless had no coherent strategy for the seizure of power, and its political conceptions remained confined within the framework of existing institutions. In 1938 it had supported the Popular Front, which was under the hegemony of the Radical Party and its leader Cerda. The Socialist Party could, with justification, be characterised as a centrist formation constantly vacillating under the pressure of different class forces in Chilean society. This peculiar characteristic of Chilean socialism made the task of the Chilean Communist Party somewhat difficult as it was confronted with a mass party on its left, which made it difficult to bring either the masses or mass mobilisations to power.

The Communist Party had, since the thirties, been a party of abject class-collaboration. After its ignominious role in the Cerda Popular Front of 1938, a Front which did not carry out one *significant* reform in favour of the urban or rural poor, the Chilean CP continued to concentrate on electioneering. In

1946 it participated in the Radical Party government under the domination of the right-wing Radical boss, Gonzales Videla. This participation was justified by the Communist Party by extensive quotations from Videla's pre-election rhetoric, promising the working masses everything they wanted in addition to the moon. Videla was an artful political tactician, who wanted communist support in order to contain the mass upsurge. He gave the Communist Party three positions in his government, but once they had played out their role, they were unceremoniously discarded. The Communist Party was banned, a ferocious repression was unleashed against the trades unions, 1000 communist militants were arrested and 500 of them were sent to a desert concentration camp in the North. The ban on the Communist Party was not lifted until 1958. Immediately after its legal recognition the Party embarked on its old political course. Externally loyal to Moscow and internally reformist, the Chilean CP was not noticeably influenced by an important event which was taking place in its own continent, just off the shores of the United States: the Cuban Revolution. No lessons were learned; no questions were asked. To justify its reformist conceptions the argument of Chilean exceptionalism was repeatedly emphasised.

In polar contrast, the Socialist Party was engaged in a discussion on what had taken place. At its Twenty-First Congress in 1966 the SP drew the following conclusion on its tactics up to that date:

"The popular movement which we structured in accordance with our line on the basis of the parties of the working class, with a class programme, with the aim of establishing a truly people's government, has been orientated towards an electoral contest within the framework of bourgeois democracy. As a result, the working class has lost the possibility of coming to power for a period. It was not just one more loss of presidential candidacy, but the catastrophic culmination of a heap of weaknesses and mistakes which have led us from a correct perspective to the blind alley of bourgeois democracy. We were dragged through a false doorway with respect to bourgeois constitutionalism and the policy of the 'peaceful road'."

It is obvious that this anti-parliamentarist wave in the Socialist Party did not disappear with the victory of Popular Unity in

1970. On the contrary it became more vigilant, and one of its spokesmen, Carlos Atamirano (also the party's General Secretary) resisted the attempts of the Communist Party to drag the Popular Unity into the arms of Christian Democracy.

Salvador Allende was elected as President on the basis of a minority vote. The Chilean parliament endorsed this victory on the condition that Allende gave a number of crucial guarantees which were embedded in the Constitution. Allende accepted, and the Popular Unity pledged that it would maintain the system of "liberal democracy" and its state apparatus. The concession was strongly attacked by the MIR and the Socialist Party youth, but supported by the majority of the Popular Unity as a "tactical necessity". The assassination of General Schneider by right-wing squads demonstrated clearly that the threat to democracy was coming from the right and not the left. It thus put Allende, contrary to what the assassins had planned, in a relatively strong position in the first several months in office.

The first year of the UP saw the Allende government carrying out a number of important reforms as their electoral programme had pledged. There can be little doubt that most of these measures were immensely popular with the oppressed strata of Chilean society (the majority of the working population) and had a big impact. Beginning with free distribution of half a litre of milk a day for every child, a number of new laws were passed to increase and develop the existing social services. A ceiling was placed on all government salaries, forty-five political prisoners were released, the special mobile group of riot police (trained in the arts of repression by the US AID police training programme immortalised in the Costa Gavras film *State of Siege*) was disbanded. There was a sixty per cent increase in wages and most prices were fixed. In the first six months inflation was reduced to 7.5 per cent compared to the first half of 1970 when it had risen to 22 per cent. A set of major nationalisations was also begun. Within the first nine months a large proportion of the textile, iron, automobile and copper industries had been taken into public ownership.

In July 1971 an important threshold was crossed. The nationalisations were extended to the copper mines, including those owned by United States capital. Cerro, Annaconda and Kennecott were all taken over and no compensation was paid.

The Popular Unity argued that the profits which had been extracted out of the mines by their owners over the years amounted to more than ample compensation. Pressure from the army and the right-wing press continued to be exerted in favour of compensation. Allende resisted this pressure: "Here are four numbers the people should remember. These companies invested the sum of $30 million. In fifty years, they have taken out $4.5 *billion*. . . . We will not compensate Annaconda, or Kennecott, or El Salvador, but the debts of those companies are $736 million and it is logically foreseeable that we will have to assume those debts. Thus, *we will be paying an indirect indemnity* of $736 million to the copper companies who over a period of fifty years took out $4.5 billion." The argument had the desired effect. Neither the military nor *El Mercurio* were convinced, but the people were. What was lacking in most cases was democratic workers' control after the nationalisations. If measures designed to establish workers' control had been implemented, they could have been of the utmost importance in transforming a legal decree into a concrete measure, changing the overall relationship of class forces by drawing the copper miners — traditionally right-wing — closer towards the Popular Unity. It would also have provided a tremendous impetus to workers in privately owned factories. However, even the existing nationalisations without compensation had a favourable impact on working-class consciousness. In May and November 1971 two multinational companies were occupied by workers protesting against redundancies. The workers demanded that they be nationalised to save jobs. Both the factories — Ford Motor Co. and the local subsidiary of the Northern Indiana Brass Company — were nationalised by the government.

More significant was the seizure in May 1971 by the workers of fourteen textile mills. This action also led to the mills being nationalised in addition to five other textile plants. The combination provided a base for the new state-owned textile industry. These measures in particular worried the Chilean bourgeoisie. They were now convinced that the Popular Unity was not going to restrict takeover to such obvious anachronisms as the copper mines, but was determined to challenge the hegemony of the ruling class in the sacred sector of manufacturing. The United States was also enraged by these new nationalisations. They were always prepared to tolerate a certain measure of nationalisation provided that compensation was forthcoming (Peru is the latest example), but they expected that, at the very least, the reforming government would use these measures to contain the mass movement. In Chile it was an energetic mass movement which was in part initiating the nationalisations by action from below. Furthermore this was being done in the manufacturing sector and with multinationals: such interference was not readily brooked in the favoured continent of Latin America. The Popular Unity, however, was unable to oblige the United States on these matters. Even though their Communist leaders would have been prepared to hold back, their own base as well as large sections of the Socialist Party would not have accepted any further concessions. Least of all would they have tolerated any repressive action to crush the workers occupying factories even if the government had decided that it was a "tactical necessity".

Thus the Allende administration was unable to satisfy the needs of the United States or its Chilean clients. Its dilemma lay in the fact that by its very nature it was also incapable of satisfying the hopes and aspirations which it had aroused in the working class and peasant masses. Its vacillations were exploited by the military and the bourgeoisie as they planned, together with the United States government and multinational interests (of which ITT is only the most blatant example), to bring about an undemocratic overthrow of the Popular Unity government.

Allende's programme had stressed that the first stage of the Chilean process would be anti-imperialist and anti-oligarchic, but the whole development of capitalism revealed that there was no Chinese wall dividing the economic interests of imperialism from those of the local bourgeoisie. Over the past two decades the penetration of foreign and indigenous capital had increased by leaps and bounds. The possibility of important sections of the Chilean bourgeoisie balancing between the United States and Popular Unity in order to strengthen themselves was virtually nil. If anything the theory of progress by stages ("brick by brick") was more out of place today than it had been in the early years of this century.

What were the real problems which confronted the Popular Unity government? Fidel Castro expressed them succinctly in his speech about Chile in Havana on September 28, 1973. The speech was, of course, three years too late but the Cuban leader posed the problem in this way:

"In the first place there was an intact bourgeois state apparatus. There were armed forces that called themselves apolitical, institutional that is, apparently neutral in the revolutionary process. There was that bourgeois parliament where a majority of members jumped to the tune of the ruling classes. There was a judicial system that was completely subservient to the reactionaries. . . ."

All this was correct, but what Castro did not explain was that the leaders of Popular Unity, Salvador Allende and Luis Corvalan in particular, consistently stressed the "professional" and "neutral" character of the *Chilean* army. They agreed that armies in the rest of Latin America were agents of the guerrillas, but not in Chile. Robinson Rojas Sandford, a Chilean journalist, who specialises in the military and who was a supporter of Popular Unity, gives us an interesting insight into Allende's thinking in his recent book *The Murder of Allende* (New York, 1975):

"The following incident typifies Allende's attitude toward the armed forces. At the beginning of April 1971, Senator Alberto Jerez of the Senate Defense Commission and 'coordinator' between the generals and the Unidad Popular government called me to his office and told me: 'As you know, at the end of this month, Salvador is going to give a master class to the Santiago military garrison. The class will be held at the Army Academy of War, before some 800 officers. Salvador asked me to get the best information that exists on the Chilean armed forces . . . You've got seven days to do it.'
"In about twenty pages, I presented a summary of events between 1964 and 1970, including an interpretation of the situation pointing up the extreme danger to the stability of the Unidad Popular government posed by the continuance of the same high commands in the armed forces as had existed before Allende took power.
"At the end of April, during the course of a leftist journalists' meeting, Alberto Jerez gave me this message: 'Salvador was very grateful for your report, but he told me it wasn't useful to him, because you are talking about imaginary armed forces

taken out of books by Lenin, and he is dealing with flesh-and-blood human beings. He said to tell you that the Chilean armed forces are a special breed, not foreseen by Lenin in his books. . . .' "

The key problem confronting the Popular Unity was a hostile bourgeois state apparatus. This problem was at best understood by the major components of the Popular Unity in a gradualist, parliamentarist and constitutionalist fashion. There was a total failure to understand the nature and function of the Chilean Army. There was a total failure to understand that unless the Popular Unity electoral victory was used to construct new organs of power — more direct, more democratic and based on the factories, farms and neighbourhoods in contrast to the bourgeois democratic assembly — there could not be any chance of winning. Some sections of the Socialist Party clearly understood the need for this, but even this understanding was at best partial and the socialist left did not wage a crucial struggle in the issues at stake inside the Popular Unity coalition until it was too late. The Socialist Party Congress held in February 1971 backed Allende to the hilt, but also stressed the following points:

". . . We recognise as a form of self-criticism that some of the actions of the workers have gone beyond the political directions of Popular Unity and are in fact putting into the forefront the question of power . . .
"The presence of workers in the government cannot signify dependence of the mass movement on the governmental apparatus . . . The Socialist Party will fight to revitalise the committees of Popular Unity and to convert them into instruments of political power for the working masses in the new popular state. . . .
". . . the Socialist Party gives special priority to those programmatic measures that undermine capitalist power and connect the bourgeois-democratic tasks with socialist tasks in the same uninterrupted process. . . ."

These were well-meaning phrases, but what was lacking was a concrete analysis of the concrete situation: an understanding as to what constituted the vital next steps forward for the masses; a set of tactics which could, as part of an overall strategy, undermine and ultimately challenge the power of the

66

bourgeoisie. In short it was Leninism that was absent in Chile in the years 1970-73. The reformist parties were determined that *their* road was the correct road. The far left, represented by the MIR, was characterised by a political reductionism: its central demand was the armed struggle. The MIR was correct to stress the need to arm the masses. What they lacked was an overall political strategy that would politically strengthen the masses and prepare them for handling real weapons. The two processes were intertwined.

The first reaction of the United States to Allende's victory was to adopt a "wait and see" attitude. This period lasted between six and nine months and during this time Henry Kissinger's "destabilisation" plans were being made ready for application. The refusal of the CIA Director at the time, Richard Helms, to testify before a Senate Committee on Chile in October 1977, has deprived us of the details, but CIA and Pentagon interference have been publicly admitted by official representatives of the Carter administration. Towards the second half of 1971 the United States began to turn the screws. They showed signs of regret in not having accepted the advice of the ITT to prevent Allende taking office through activating a CIA plan. Once nationalisation began in earnest, the Americans declared economic war on Chile. All economic aid and credits were suspended and a *de facto* boycott of Chile by American capital was put into operation. Internally the agrarian bourgeoisie embarked on a course of sabotaging agricultural production and the urban bourgeoisie, in total control of the distribution networks, began to hoard and create a black-market in the cities on a vast scale.

An interesting sidelight to the whole affair is the fact that throughout the period of the Popular Unity government the United States did not for one single moment cut off *military* aid to Chile. They knew perfectly well how that aid would be utilised in the coming months. Having put the economic screws on Allende, they continued to strengthen the military apparatus of the Chilean state so that it could at the necessary moment apply the military screws and throttle the Popular Unity. In October 1971, a well-known expert in repression (politely termed as a "troubleshooter" in the American press), Nathaniel Davis, was appointed the Ambassador of the United States in Santiago. His previous posting had been Guatemala, where his timely "advice" to the army had resulted in the crushing of the mass movement in that country. In December 1971 two White House aides, Messrs Finch and Klein, returned from a "fact-finding mission" to Chile and proclaimed that "Allende won't last long". This was clearly a statement of fact and designed to reassure the giant US corporations which were being nationalised in growing numbers in Chile: Rockefeller, General Motors, ITT, Dow (the makers of napalm!), Du Pont were all beginning to demand action. They were informed that the "cavalry" was already there, but the trumpet would be sounded when the time was ripe.

James Petras and Robert La Porte, two American specialists on Latin America, summed up American policy aims:

"The overall purpose of US policy is to create economic disorder and provide a democratic social crisis that could lead to . . . the overthrow of the Allende government by a civil-military coalition made up of the Army, the Christian Democrats and the extreme right-wing National Party."

In February 1972 Nixon gave the official seal of justification to what was already United States policy when he declared:

"Henceforth, should an American firm be expropriated without reasonable steps to provide prompt, adequate and effective compensation, there is a presumption that the expropriating country would receive no new bilateral economic benefits . . . Similarly we would withhold our support for loans to that country in multilateral development institutions . . . and, because expropriation is a concern to many countries, we are placing greater emphasis on the use of multilateral mechanisms for dealing with this problem."

Presumably this was also intended as polite advice to the West German government (which also had heavy economic investments in Chile) to join in the economic blockade which had been mounted. But the message was frighteningly clear: the American monster was ready to move into action. The close relations between the multinationals and the American press were also revealed in the United States media as a concerted propaganda campaign against the Allende régime.

Given the preparations which the United States and their Chilean friends were making, the Popular Unity leaders showed little understanding of what was at stake. There were two clear-cut options in the face of this offensive. The first choice was the simplest: to capitulate to the demand of the United States. The only party which, in essence, favoured a political retreat was the Chilean Communist Party. This was impossible as it would have meant the internal disintegrity of the Popular Unity. The only other alternative was for the Allende government to go on the offensive, mobilise the workers, expropriate large sections of the private sector and establish a state monopoly of distribution and foreign trade. If this had been done during the first half of 1972 it would have severely disrupted the plans of the Chilean bourgeoisie, put it on the defensive and mobilised all the creative energies of the Chilean working class — a process which would have inexorably led to the formation of autonomous organs of popular power. But to do so would have required a break with reformist constitutionalism to which the Popular Unity leaders were addicted and which characterised the road to the socialist future which they had planned. It was this rigid reformism which proved to be the rock on which the Popular Unity foundered and was ultimately crushed. Moral exhortations and political propaganda were not enough. What was necessary was a set of transitional measures which could allow Allende to seize the initiative from the ruling class.

In the autumn of 1972 the Chilean ruling class unleashed its offensive: it went on strike against the Popular Unity government. The normal rule of class conflict in a bourgeois society had been reversed and the bourgeoisie was striking against a government which it did not regard as its own. What the Chilean ruling class forgot was that there is a small difference between the management and the workers. Without workers there can be no production. Without the management there can only be more production! When the Chilean capitalists locked out their workers in October 1972, they thought they would paralyse the economy and bring down Allende. They had underestimated the working-class capacity for independent mobilisation. The workers defended the government against the lock-out. They occupied factories and managed to keep production going. The question was posed as to how the goods being produced by the workers would be distributed. The government answered this query some weeks later. In the mean-time a number of occupied factories were nationalised and twenty-five days later, when the bosses ended their protest, a number of them had no factories to which they could return, though a number of factories were returned under pressure from the Communist Party. The Socialist Party paper, *Aurora de Chile,* which spoke for hundreds of thousands of Popular Unity supporters, wrote an anguished editorial in November 1972, one month after the bosses' lock-out:

". . . because we are sure that there is going to be another bosses' strike. The strike was called off but not ended, the rich said on Sunday night (November 5). We heard them clearly over the radio. Either the drones are going to leave the honeycomb or they will come back to rule the country with blood and fire. It is us or the rich . . . There is going to be another bosses' strike, and the government is handing the plants back to the fascists so that they can make another try. . . .

"The big problem is that we are in those plants and we are not going to give them back. What is the government going to do? Shoot us? . . .

"They didn't drive the rich out of the enclaves where they were holding the trucks [a reference to the CIA-backed truck-owners' strike which paralysed road haulage the previous year]. Are they going to drive us government supporters out of the plants? What a dilemma, Companero Presidente!"

From November 1972 onwards other attempts at sabotage were carried out and an overall economic deterioration took place, affecting the working class. In these conditions the government made a necessary, empirical turn to the left. Fernando Flores, the Minister of Housing, called on the workers and peasants to transform the JAP (Juntas de Abastecimiento y Control de Precios — Supply and Price Control Boards) from being mass watchdog organisations into more active bodies. Flores now said to the JAP: *"You* distribute." The results were dramatic. The JAP undertook the storage and distribution of goods to defeat the black-marketeers and the hoarders. It was a form of sectoral embryonic dual power. The JAP were most effective in the working-class areas and the shanty towns. They ensured that the basic necessities were available to workers and their families. On a political level they increased working-class combativeness because they showed what was possible on a national level when threatened with economic sabotage.

At the same time the government wanted to assure the bourgeoisie that these were merely defensive measures taken because of the "unreasonableness" of the ruling class. They accordingly invited the leading military and naval chiefs into the Cabinet in an attempt to "unify the nation" and ensure "stability". The generals accepted Cabinet posts, but immediately began to put intolerable pressure on the government. Before the government could respond to the military demands the decisive March 4 elections intervened. The leading bodies of the Chilean bourgeoisie — associations of capitalists and landlords — spent a great deal of money in backing the right-wing parties. The main slogan of the latter was: "Get two-thirds of the vote to oust Allende". The crucial importance of the March 4, 1973 elections was cogently underlined by the leftist daily paper, *Puro Chile*. Commenting on what were to be the last democratic elections in Chile the newspaper wrote:

"It doesn't matter to the Society for Industrial Development, the National Agricultural Society, and the National Confederation of Production and Commerce whether or not their politicians, among them Frei and Jarpa, ever get to the Senate to 'legislate'. They want them in to overthrow the Allende administration in a way that is cloaked in 'constitutionality'. Thus, for this country's right wing, obtaining two-thirds of the vote is essentially a mere accident of chance. It can happen or it cannot happen. If they get them, then Allende will be deposed after May 21. If they don't get them, they will nonetheless carry out their plot to depose him, turning to the fascist officers in our armed forces who have let themselves be seduced by their siren songs. The danger of a *coup* will begin on the night of March 4. The North American imperialists have already given the order to their lackeys in Chile to overthrow the constitutional government by any means. Thus the people must be on the alert. They must not let themselves be tricked by the idea that 'the elections will solve the problem of power'. The elections won't solve anything. The problem of power can be solved only by preparing to confront the fascists on their own ground, using their own weapons. Certainly, we must fight to make sure the enemy doesn't win a two-thirds majority in March. That will be easy. You can see it in the streets, in the communities, in the factories, and in the peasant settlements. What is hard is the other thing and this must be achieved. . . ."

Yes, the "other thing" was hard, but not because the masses were not ready or eager to defend their gains. It was difficult because Allende and the Communist Party believed that success in the March elections, coupled with what seemed a few irrelevant concessions, would solve everything. Little did Allende realise that his victory in March would seal his fate unless he was prepared to fight on the extraparliamentary front as well. The March elections gave Popular Unity 44 per cent of the vote. The masses were jubilant. In a flash of euphoria Allende declared: ". . . the meaning of the election results is clarified by the historic context in which the voting took place. The government's policy has been interpreted by the massive support received by the political parties that defend it, *the largest that any government has received in the last twenty years after twenty-seven months in office.* The Fourth of March has reconfirmed the Chilean way to socialism." In a triumphant mood Allende dismissed the arguments of the left. He was not going to "beware the ides of March". Instead of using the election results to mount an audacious offensive, Allende and the Communist Party turned on their own left flank, who were described by the "Comrade President" as the "lunatic fringe". From the bosses' lock-out of October 1972 to the March elections the working class had been on the offensive. After the elections they were demobilised in the name of constitutionalism. The JAP was in effect dismantled. It had, together with the elected workers' committees (*Cordones industriales* — industrial cordons), planned a mass congress "to analyse the election results and take a leap forward in forming the people's power", but their assembly was forbidden by the government they supported. Allende feared that it would be seen as a provocation. As a matter of fact the situation after the March elections was the last real opportunity for Popular Unity to go on the offensive. The correlation of class forces as well as electoral statistics was in their favour.

The military was disgusted with the election results. They realised, to paraphrase Brecht, that it was the people who would have to be dissolved in addition to Allende. They withdrew from the government. The official excuse was that the March elections had renewed the Popular Unity mandate and their presence was no longer necessary. The real reasons were somewhat different. The Christian Democratic daily, *La Presna,* observed:

"In a prolonged meeting in the middle of last week, the Council of Generals decided to call on President Allende to meet four demands. Failure to do so would mean that the men in uniform would leave the offices they held. The demands included the right to maintain effective surveillance of the armed groups; the end of the executive's use of legal loopholes to institute social reforms; and taking a technical and non-political approach to the questions relating to the food supply."

The withdrawal of the uniforms from the Cabinet was the beginning of a process which was to culminate on September 11, 1973 in a *coup d'état.* The choices posed by the political situation were reflected in divisions within the Popular Unity. The tussle between the right and left was reflected inside the MAPU. In November 1972 the left wing of MAPU, with positions close to those of the MIR, had won the majority at their annual congress. They had passed a resolution in favour of the "permanent revolution" and advocated uninterrupted socialisation and collectivisation in the towns and country. The right-wing leader Jaime Gazmur had been replaced by Oscar Garreton. The MAPU had polled 100,000 votes in the March election. Three days later the right-wing minority carried out a *coup* against the majority by occupying the three offices and the MAPU radio station in Santiago. The MAPU minority had the active backing of the Communist Party. It was a reflection of the growing crisis within the Popular Unity as the Socialist Party left supported Garreton.

Allende refused to accept all the demands of the military, but his action denoted that his government would make a number of concessions. Hugo Blanco, a Peruvian revolutionary in exile in Chile, reported to the American socialist weekly, *Intercontinental Press,* how the power of the JAP was being curtailed. The JAP had never been effectively generalised. They functioned most effectively inside the shanty towns where democratically elected and representative delegates gave them real weight. The strength of the MIR in these areas was a further factor of some importance. Blanco wrote:

"Once the JAP were permitted wide powers. But, following

73

this, their role was restricted, with many of their functions being handed over to the police at the same time that military officers were being brought into top posts in the distribution system. At their height, besides receiving the goods and taking them to the merchants, the JAP maintained supervision over the prices and weighing of products sold over the counter . . . Once things reached this level, the consumers saw that they were 'unpaid employees of the storekeepers', realising that merchants were unnecessary."

The emasculation of JAP by the introduction of police and military personnel was part of the whole strategic and political thrust embodied in the "Chilean road". This concession to the uniformed despots was a clear indication that the Popular Unity would not break with the state apparatus of the bourgeoisie. It was this as well as conjunctural errors which led to the clash with the copper miners as well as public sector workers in June 1973.

Confronted with growing inflation, the public sector workers staged a strike for higher wages. The government stupidly branded them as "agents of the right", a sobriquet also regularly applied to those who "illegally" occupied factories and land. The public sector workers replied by saying that they were supporters of the UP and were prepared to take over *El Mercurio,* the daily newspaper which ideologically organised the counter-revolution and which was owned by the Edwardes family. A strike of copper miners was organised by Christian Democracy and even by the fascist group "Fatherland and Freedom", and it is interesting to note why the strike leaders were so obedient to right-wing initiatives. The Popular Unity leaders could not understand that their refusal to go forward was leading to a deterioration of the economy. It was patently absurd to ask the miners to tighten their belts in a society where the bourgeoisie still held the reins of power, an intact state apparatus and owned a large section of the economy and seventy per cent of distribution. Of course the right-wing parties used this contradiction to increase their support. A set of bold measures was needed, designed to further challenge capital by institutionalising workers' control and factory councils, thus opening up the way to generalised organs of workers' power. The Popular Unity government turned its back on this path, which was clearly visible. Small bridges leading to this

74

path also existed, which the Popular Unity succeeded in dismantling. It may not have realised it, but it was also dismantling itself.

On June 29, 1973 the Second Armoured Regiment led an assault on the Moneda Palace. This attempted *coup* did not have the approval of the Military High Command. It was prepared essentially by officers in league with the fascists, whose organisation Fatherland and Freedom had carried out over 500 terrorist attacks on trades union and left-party headquarters in 1973 alone. Eighty-three fascists had been arrested, but every one of them had been released by Chile's "impartial" judiciary. So Souper, encouraged by the fascists, struck alone with his unit. He was clearly hoping that his actions would force the hand of the army. It was no secret in the army messes that a *coup* was being prepared, and Souper was fully aware of the moods of senior officers. The attempt was a miserable fiasco.

The most important feature of the abortive *coup*, however, was the reaction of the masses. It was greeted with factory occupations and a strengthening of the Cordones Industriales (Action Committees of Workers). Defence committees were further strengthened and new ones were established. The Chilean Trades Union Congress, however, did not call a general strike to prepare the workers for struggle. They asked workers to stay *inside* their factories. There were a few initiatives which were independent of the Popular Unity apparatus, but these had no national impact. Nonetheless the anger of workers at the attempted *coup* was reflected in a massive street demonstration the same evening. Nearly a million workers marched through the streets and demanded that Allende dissolve parliament and punish the plotters. Allende replied that the majority of the army had remained "loyal". The "loyal" army was ruthlessly applying the notorious "arms law" accepted by Allende, which enabled troops to disarm anyone who had unauthorised weapons. The situation had all the ingredients of a Greek tragedy: the main characters were now aware of the danger facing them, but they embraced it with an air of fatalism.

One of the independent initiatives from the base of the workers' parties, which did indicate that the more advanced workers were becoming conscious of the necessity of preparing the masses for civil war, was the action of delegates of the Vicuna Mackenna Cordon. A joint statement was drawn up

75

and signed in the Elecmetal factory on June 29. It is reproduced here in full to stress that there were other options even at that late stage. Only the will to resist was missing. It was not a question of tactical errors. The entire political strategy of the Popular Unity government was a major obstacle. The government could not even now see the limitations of bourgeois democracy. Only a vigorous socialist offensive could protect the democratic rights of the masses. The workers were beginning to realise this as the following statement indicates:

"We, representatives of the undersigned left wing parties, express our total support to the measures taken by the Command of the Vicuna Mackenna Industrial Cordon in its Instructions Numbers 1, 2 and 3 [a reference to factory takeovers and preparations to defend the cordon with all means available at a time when the attempted coup had not yet been put down].

"The workers will not allow the government, installed by us, to be overthrown by the bourgeoisie. We will not permit the gains we have achieved over long years of struggle to be swept aside by a fascist mob. The workers will crush sedition; we will make no truce with the bourgeoisie, but will crush it once and for all.

1. All plants will become part of the Social Sector of the economy; not one plant that is important for the workers will remain in the hands of the bourgeoisie.

2. Workers' leadership. Production and distribution will remain in the hands of the workers, and the people will exercise complete control over community territory.

3. Popular Militia. The organised people must protect their gains. Create a Defence Committee and arm it in every industry and neighbourhood.

4. The leadership of the defence, and the advance of the people will be assured only if they rest in the hands of the organised working class.

Eloy Bustamante, *Socialist Party*
Jose Urrutia, *Communist Party*
Augusto Alcayaga A., *Radical Party*
Sergion Sotomayor, *Christian Left*
Enrique Fernandes, *Fourth International*"

The Popular Unity did not pass the test of June 29, by failing to organise the extraparliamentary mobilisation of the masses, the only way they could have begun to reverse the bourgeois offensive. After June 29 the workers were prepared to make all sorts of sacrifices. This was a late opportunity for the Popular Unity government to convene a Congress of workers, peasants and students' delegates to oppose the ruling-class offensive. This was the opportunity for Allende to appear on television (as Fidel had done in Havana) to explain to the masses what was happening, to speak directly to the soldiers and sailors over the heads of their superiors. That is what a revolutionary leader and a revolutionary party would have done. A pause now would be dangerous; a passive marking of time would be fatal. Allende failed to seize the moment. Within days the bourgeoisie, amazed at the lack of a public counter-offensive in the wake of the débâcle of the attempted *coup,* resumed their offensive. The rapidity with which they did so alarmed Allende's Cuban friends. During his state visit to Chile several months before, Castro had, in a number of subtle speeches, warned the Popular Unity of the dangers behind the fascist and right-wing mobilisations. Now he despatched two members of the Central Committee of the Cuban Communist Party to Santiago with a personal letter to Allende. In this he wrote:

". . . and I can imagine that tensions must be high and that you want to gain time to improve the balance of power in case fighting breaks out and, if possible, find a way to continue the revolutionary process without civil strife, avoiding any historic responsibility for what may happen. Those are praiseworthy objectives. But if the other side, whose real objectives we are not able to judge from here, continues to carry out a perfidious and irresponsible policy, demanding a price which it is impossible for Popular Unity and the Revolution to pay, which is quite likely, don't ever forget the extaordinary strength of the Chilean working class and the firm support it has always given you in difficult moments. In response to your call when the revolution is in danger, it can block those who are organising a *coup,* maintain the support of the fence-sitters, impose its conditions and decide the fate of Chile once and for all if the need arises. The enemy must realise that the Chilean working class is on the alert and ready to go into action. Its power and fighting spirit can tilt the scales in the capital in your favour, even though other circumstances may be unfavourable. . . ."

Fidel Castro's advice was late, very late. But what it implied was clear. The Cubans advised Allende to mobilise the masses and prepare an offensive against reaction. They stressed the independent capacity of the working class to act on its own behalf and advised him to use this latent strength. But the Popular Unity was by now mesmerised by its own political impotence. In early July the bourgeoisie's favourite newspaper, *El Mercurio,* carried an article entitled "Anti-Communist Satisfactions". Its author wrote: "Travelling through anti-communist countries like Brazil offers profound satisfactions for those of us who have had to put up with the communists for almost three years. In the first place, you find the communists in their proper place, in hiding."

As late as July 31, the Communist leader, Luis Corvalan, was still trying to coax the military leadership. In a speech he reiterated several weeks later, the central theoretician of Chilean Communism said:

"They (the reactionaries) are claiming that we have an orientation of replacing the professional army. No sir, we continue and will continue to support keeping our armed forces strictly professional."

The attitude of the leaders of the Popular Unity convinced the military plotters that they would confront no serious organised or generalised resistance to their *coup d'état.* In collaboration with the United States and the Brazilian military dictatorship, the Chilean generals began to plan the last details of their takeover.

On September 4, 1973, over 700,000 supporters of Popular Unity marched past the Moneda Palace to commemorate the third anniversary of the Chilean experiment. Allende and other leaders were on the balcony acknowledging the acclaim of the crowd. In exactly a week the government would be overthrown and its leader dead. The mood of the demonstrators was militant. They chanted repeatedly: "Allende, the people are defending you. Hit the reactionaries hard." But there was no response. For a group of leaders dedicated to gradualism and compromise it was a cruel situation. All the reformist exits were sealed off. It was too late to effect any compromise with the Chilean ruling class and its parties. The only way forward was to mobilise the masses, organise and extend popular committees at the base and prepare to resist. Certainly this route did

78

not guarantee a victory. What it did, however, was to ensure that the masses would not be butchered in cold blood — they would not be defeated without a struggle. Even when the smell of a *coup* reached the executive committee of the Popular Unity, they made no real plans for mobilising the masses.

On September 11, the Chilean military struck. It was supported by the fascists, the Christian Democrats and the entire ruling class. At the Moneda Palace, the tragic figure of Salvador Allende resisted them with a machine gun in his hand. It was a moral gesture. Before he died he dictated a last message to his people: "That is how we write the first page of our history. My people and Latin America will write the rest."

The last few weeks of Allende's life remind one, despite the many differences, of the dilemmas and choices which confronted Alexander Dubcek, the deposed Czech leader. Both men submitted to the "inevitability" of their fate and were overpowered, although they both desperately hoped that their problems would disappear of their own accord. Both knew what was being planned for them but neither was aware of the exact timing. Both Allende and Dubcek found themselves powerless to act and were overwhelmed, the one by Soviet tanks and the other by Chilean military fascism.

They confronted different enemies in different political situations, but their ultimate choice was the same: should they throw their caution to the winds and issue a direct appeal to the masses and prepare a fight back? It was not an unprecedented course of action even for non-revolutionaries. After all, had not the Austrian social-democrats resisted clerico-fascism in Vienna with guns in their hands? True, they had been defeated, but the international relationship of forces was heavily weighted against them. Allende and Dubcek were both understandably desperate to avoid civil war and bloodshed. It is a terrible decision for any leader, revolutionary or not. The importance of Lenin, Trotsky and Castro is that they, in their different ways, placed their future in the hands of the masses. They were all responsive to the slightest changes in mass moods. Allende was destroyed by his constitutionalism; Dubcek by the fact that he had been raised politically within the apparatus of the party and the system which was being challenged. If we go to the masses, both men must have thought, what guarantee is there that they will remain with us?

Might not others arise who will offer more radical solutions? In other words for even the most radical and left-wing reformists it is extremely difficult to trust the independent political capacity of the working masses.

Naturally revolutionaries cannot be certain what will be the outcome of a particular struggle or battle. We are not soothsayers who promise success. What we do insist on is that our methods are more educative so that even in cases of defeats the masses, in reality, assimilate the causes of the setback and are better prepared for the next encounter. The Chilean masses suffered a terrible blow and went down without a fight. Was more blood spilled than if a struggle had been prepared? Who can tell? But the loss of life in Chile after the first month of the *coup* was truly horrendous: more people were lost than in a year of fighting at the height of the Vietnam war!

In Czechoslovakia we can say with more certainty that a mass mobilisation and preparedness to resist the invasion would have, in all probability, avoided an invasion. Tito had successfully resisted Stalin by threatening armed resistance. The geographical terrain favoured Tito. The Bohemian plains were not as well-suited to guerrilla warfare as the mountains of Serbia, but the *political* terrain was infinitely more favourable than in 1948 and Brezhnev was not Stalin. Allende lost his life. Dubcek was more fortunate (in itself a sign of the changed times). He was deprived of his job and was employed as a worker in a factory in an obscure Czech town.

In both Chile and Czechoslovakia a resistance is emerging under extremely difficult conditions. Whether all the lessons of the débâcles suffered by the working-class movement in both countries will have been learned when the resistance finally erupts in mass dimensions we still have to wait and see.

The overthrow of Allende posed a whole set of questions for socialists throughout the world. Chile had been, after all, the country which was cited most frequently as an example by Communist Parties throughout Western Europe of the most advantageous road to socialism. The question which arose was whether or not the Communist Parties in the West would re-evaluate their strategy in the light of the Chilean events. The answer was not long in coming. The Italian Communist Party developed a set of theses which, in effect, completely excluded the possibility of socialism. Instead it advanced the notion of the "historic compromise": a coalition government consisting of the Christian Democrats and the Communist Party. Communist leaders seemed to imply that the main problem with the Allende régime was that it moved too rapidly to the left.

What was inevitable was a settling of accounts with the "armed bodies of men" who were defending the bourgeois régime. In that sense the offensive of reaction could have been contained much earlier. It was *not* inevitable that the Generals should have had the initiative. But it is vital to understand that once the United States had decided to overthrow the elected government of Salvador Allende (and this is an indisputable fact, admitted before the Senate Committee by Henry Kissinger and former CIA chief, Richard Helms), the only way to prevent a defeat was to go on the offensive.

The Communist Parties argue that the *coup* could have been avoided if more concessions had been made to the right. This view was also expressed in *Pravda,* which attempted to pin the blame on the moves towards a *coup* on the far left. *Soviet News* of August 21, 1973 (the fifth anniversary, incidentally, of the Soviet invasion of Czechoslovakia) carried an English-language translation of an article which appeared in *Pravda* and which was signed by a Vitaly Borovsky. He wrote:

"Reaction has tried hard to provoke a conflict between the army and the people. Ultra-left elements, who by their provocative actions have helped to set the military against the people, are, as always, playing a disgraceful part in this sinister affair.

"The plotters have tried to set the armed forces against the government and to transform the military men from being defenders of their country's interests into tools upholding the narrow and selfish interests of a handful of exploiters."

This bizarre attempt to portray the Chilean army as a neutral force being egged on by reactionaries on one hand and provoked by ultra-lefts on the other was certainly an innovation for an analyst speaking in the name of Marxism. Borovsky not only completely revised the classical Marxist position on the State, he also slandered the only groups in Chile, such as the MIR who, despite all their other political weaknesses or deficiencies, were nonetheless aware of the danger of an impending *coup* and had actually attempted to distribute propaganda

81

to that effect to the people who could have helped to defeat it: the ordinary soldiers and sailors.

Jack Woddis, a leading analyst of the British Communist Party, argued that the major problem was that the Popular Unity needed more time. If they had been given a chance they would have won a "decisive majority" which would have had "its impact on the armed forces too". That may or may not be true. But surely the real point is the following: the main reason for Allende increasing his electoral support was because of the significant reforms carried out by his government. The standard of living of the peasants and the working class improved rapidly. They responded by voting for Popular Unity. However, many of these reforms were extremely unpopular with Chilean capitalists and landlords. A compromise with the Christian Democrats would have necessitated a curtailment of a number of important reforms. This might have won Allende more time, but only at the expense of seriously alienating the social base of Popular Unity. The dilemma which confronted Popular Unity was that it was a reformist workers' government which found itself faced with the dialectic of the permanent revolution. It started a process which, to be concluded, needed a set of decisive blows to the head of the enemy, not friendly remonstrations, and certainly not concessions.

Woddis further states that:

> "Whatever their intentions, the ultra-left groups outside Popular Unity, such as the MIR, and those sections supporting them in the Socialist Party and in MAPU (two of the Popular Unity coalition parties) acted in such a way as played into the hands of reaction."

This social-democratic whining is intended to conceal the fact that reaction was on the offensive from the autumn of 1972 onwards. Instead of grappling with the real problems which confront a reformist workers' government dependent on the apparatus of the capitalist state, Woddis and his friends try, by a political sleight-of-hand, to obscure the debate by focussing attention on the actions of the far left. The fact that what they say about the far left is also inaccurate is not, strictly speaking, relevant.

On one question amongst others the far left was consistently

82

correct. It pointed out that the fascist group Fatherland and Liberty and fascist paramilitary organisations such as the Rolando Matus Commandos, were involved in regular acts of sabotage and terrorism. They demanded that these groups be outlawed. They were not. These were to be the ideological outriders of Pinochet's gangsters. In an interview with London Weekend Television on January 12, 1977, Luis Corvalan, the Chilean Communist leader released from prison in exchange for the Russian dissident Bukovsky, made this implicit self-criticism:

Question: Would the Fascist Party be legal? [in the event of a restoration of Chilean democracy and a new government — TA].
Answer: No. We are in favour of eradicating fascism, of pro-scribing it in public life. . . . To do otherwise would show that we had learned nothing from these lessons which are so tragic for the Chileans. I do not believe that democracy consists in giving freedom of action to the fascists.

This brings us to the heart of the debate between revolu-tionaries and reformists. It is often assumed by reformists that revolutionaries are opposed in principle to participation in elections or interventions in the domain of bourgeois politics. This is totally false. On the contrary, revolutionaries must par-ticipate in a whole number of institutions which exist under a bourgeois democracy, including parliament and local coun-cils. This participation, of course, has a goal, which is to strengthen and multiply the extra-parliamentary mobilisations of the working class and other oppressed people, with the aim of developing new and more democratic organs of power. The Bolsheviks in Tsarist Russia participated in the Constituent Assembly, but they always attached more importance to *soviets* or popular representative councils. The success of the Russian Revolution in 1917 was determined by the fact that the Bolsheviks were winning majority support in representative institutions which were more democratic than the Assembly and where fluctuations in mass moods were reflected more immediately and accurately.

The elementary revolutionary lesson of how communists intervene in bourgeois parliaments has been completely inverted by the Communist Parties in bourgeois democratic countries.

In Western Europe, Japan, India and in pre-*coup* Chile, these parties used extra-parliamentary mobilisations to focus the attention of the masses exclusively on the bourgeois parliament. They trained and educated their members in this direction.

Thus the inability of the Popular Unity to resist the *coup* was not an historical accident, a chance mistake — it was a direct reflection of the fundamental flaw which characterises reformist politics: a failure to understand that the state in capitalist societies is ultimately a coercive apparatus designed to protect and defend the interests of the indigenous ruling classes. A total failure on the part of the Popular Unity government to grapple with or even understand this problem reverberates throughout the three years it was in office. Time and time again both Allende and Corvalan reiterated their complete faith in the armed forces. The most favourable interpretation of their line is that they hoped that by constantly stressing that the armed forces were "neutral" they would actually transpose their hopes on to the consciousness of the officers and the latter would ultimately come to believe that they *were* "neutral". Soon after he assumed power in 1970 Allende established the Popular Unity line on the armed forces:

"I have repeatedly pointed out the pure patriotic tradition, democratic and professional, of our armed forces and have stated my purpose of fulfilling the national obligation by facilitating their technical improvement and by respecting their specific function, so that their mission of guarding the sovereignty and territorial integrity of the country should be more effective."

In order to reinforce the loyalty of Popular Unity towards the armed forces, the Communist Party leader, Luis Corvalan, wrote in his book, *Chile: The People Take Over*:

"The Popular Unity parties came to power not as a result of grappling with the armed forces or any part of them. . . . When the people triumphed, with the National Congress confirming their victory, the armed forces publicly recognised the government. They retained their spirit of professionalism, their respect for the Constitution and the Law. . . ."

In July 1973 Corvalan claimed that the attempted *coup* of June 29 had been defeated because of the "loyalty of the

84

armed forces and the police" and he spoke of marching towards socialism without "civil war". His speech was printed in the theoretical journal of the British Communist Party in September 1973, a few days before the Generals disproved the reformist view of the state. The cost was the lives of between 30,000 and 50,000 workers, peasants, trades unionists, members of left-wing political parties, etc. The "peaceful" road to socialism had led to enormous loss in life and liberties. The entire strategy of the Allende government had been based on the belief that the state was "neutral". Because of this, it was argued, socialism could be achieved without bloodshed. Salvador Allende said as much in his important speech to the peasants in Linares on May 28, 1971:

"I have pointed out that this process of change is possible, because the armed forces and the Carabineers (armed police) have a professional conscience. They respect the laws and the Constitution, which is not the case in the majority of Latin American countries, and this constitutes an exception in this and even in other countries."

Given this wrong assessment the Popular Unity tackled the problem of the bourgeois army in the worst possible fashion. Instead of appealing to the conscript base of the army and navy it concentrated its attention on the military and naval high command. Thus they tended to substitute psychology for political analysis. Instead of seeing the army and its overall function in class terms they saw it in categories of good and bad generals. This proved to be the Achilles heel of the Popular Unity.

If from 1971 onwards the Popular Unity and its constituent parties had directed their attention to the base of the armed forces, they could have won a new audience for their views which could have proved decisive at the crucial moment. Democratic rights enjoyed by other citizens should have been extended (by Presidential decree if necessary) to soldiers and sailors. They should have been granted the right to form trades unions, to join political parties, to produce their own newspapers. If the army top brass had physically attempted to prevent these rights from being exercised it would have provided the Popular Unity with an extremely useful basis from which it could isolate the officers from the ranks. The integration of elected soldiers' delegates into the JAPS and the industrial cordons would have been the next step and would have provided an institutional basis for weakening and splitting the army.

While propaganda directed at the soldiers, coupled with the granting of democratic rights, would have been an important step forward it would, on its own, not have been sufficient. The creation of workers' militias, of committees to defend Popular Unity against the Army, could have been decisive in persuading the soldiers and sailors to participate in a resistance and help in creating the embryo of an alternative, democratic and popular army. The absence of all these factors virtually excluded a generalised resistance. The Popular Unity parties had no armed detachments of their own; the MIR was too small, though it did have its armed units, many of which did organise a resistance after the *coup,* but were rapidly crushed. The success of the *coup* was not inevitable, but was made possible by the failure of the Popular Unity to *politically* arm the masses.

One of the novel lessons of Chile was that we were able to perceive the functioning of a workers' government within a bourgeois régime. With the French and Italian communists on the threshold of entering governments and the undoubted electoral support of the majority of workers for the Socialist and Communist parties in Portugal and Spain, the Chilean experience acquires a far greater significance.

The existence of a workers' government within a bourgeois state unleashes a more far-reaching *extra*-parliamentary mobilisation of all classes than does a strategy of *direct* moves to dual power, short-circuiting the bourgeois-democratic régime. Thus the *cordones,* the occupation of over 1000 factories, the networks of local supply committees, were more advanced than anything seen in other parts of Latin America, where guerrilla warfare was used instead. The situation was far more precarious than France in May 1968; the extra-parliamentary mobilisation of the bourgeoisie was much greater. The bourgeoisie understood how grave the force of developing working-class consciousness really was for the bourgeois order. It is this that makes the strategic errors of the workers' parties all the more reprehensible and tragic. 30,000 trade unionists, socialists and communists paid the price with their lives. Those who attack the "ultra-left" just because it believes that the state is not neutral should ponder the losses in life suffered by the masses and the economic "genocide" to which they are still subjected.

The reason Marxists oppose the bourgeois state is because it maintains the class division of society. Within its framework the majority of the people can never exercise real power. Any political party which attempts to implement structural reforms which damage the interests of capitalism finds itself confronting the coercive powers of the state. For while the bourgeois democratic state is based on the partial consent of the masses, if this consent is withdrawn then coercion becomes the only means of maintaining the capitalist order.

There is, however, another way of looking at Chile as we have already indicated above. This is to reduce the problem to one of tempo. If Allende had not proceeded so fast . . . if the nationalisation measures had been delayed . . . if . . . if . . . if. . . . What these *ifs* ignore is the independent capacity of the proletarian masses to mobilise themselves and demand various measures. The Italian Communist Party believes that it can prevent another Chile by adapting to the capitalist state. This, of course, depends on the goals of the party in power. If Allende had attempted to confront the masses and repress them in the interests of Chilean capital it is possible that there would not have been a *coup*. But the workers' parties would have been electorally defeated and demoralised. But then if socialism is not possible either through struggle or through parliament and is a utopia for the distant, ever-receding future, why bother to maintain a workers' party? Why not institutionalise the situation by merging with the main bourgeois party? This dilemma will continue to haunt the new reformists of the "Eurocommunist" parties of Western Europe. Up until now they have argued that socialism is possible by winning a majority in parliament and using that majority to politically overwhelm reaction. Chile shows that this is an unlikely scenario. The answer of the Eurocommunists is then to put socialism on the shelf indefinitely and to retreat further into a reformist problematic. This pessimism, in effect, reveals a distrust of the masses and, despite their distance from Moscow, this fundamental characteristic of Stalinism still defines the Communist parties throughout the world.

87

If bourgeois democracy, even in a truncated form, is restored in Chile in the coming period all the problems we have already discussed will return to the foreground. The struggle for democratic rights is the crucial one today, but to link this exclusively to a return to an unspecified "Chilean democracy" is to leave important questions unanswered. It *was* Chilean bourgeois democrats who agreed to the decision of their ruling class to change the form of its rule to a semi-fascist military dictatorship. A return to bourgeois democracy would obviously be better for the working class than Pinochet. The point is whether it is enough. In that sense the experience of Chile over the last decade is very important, for it has prefigured, in its own way, the debates in Western Europe which will become more heated with the advent of left governments in France and Italy.

5. The Portuguese Laboratory

"What, generally speaking, are the symptoms of a revolutionary situation? We shall certainly not be mistaken if we indicate the following three major symptoms: (1) when it is impossible for the ruling classes to maintain their rule without any change; when there is a crisis, in one form or another, among the 'upper classes', a crisis in the policy of the ruling class, leading to a fissure through which the discontent and indignation of the oppressed classes burst forth. For a revolution to take place, it is usually insufficient for 'the lower classes not to want' to live in the old way; it is also necessary that 'the upper classes should be unable' to live in the old way; (2) when the suffering and want of the oppressed classes have grown more acute than usual; (3) when, as a consequence of the above causes, there is a considerable increase in the activity of the masses who uncomplainingly allow themselves to be robbed in 'peacetime', but, in turbulent times are drawn both by all the circumstances of the crisis *and by the 'upper classes' themselves* into independent historical action.

"Without these objective changes, which are independent of the will, not only of individual groups and parties but even of individual classes, a revolution, as a general rule, is impossible. The totality of all these objective changes is called a revolutionary situation."

V. I. Lenin: *The Collapse Of The Second International,* 1915

On April 25, 1974, a military revolt overthrew the decaying fascist régime of the Portuguese dictator Caetano. The rapidity of the overthrow shocked the entire world. The originality of the historical process took everyone by surprise. Was it really the case that the oldest and most tenacious of fascist régimes had been displaced or were we merely witnessing a "palace *coup*", a change of personnel which would preserve intact all the institutions and structures of Salazarism? The events which shook Portugal in 1974-75 were remarkable on many counts. Italian fascism (1923-44), German fascism (1933-45) and

Japanese fascism (1934-45) had all been overthrown by the intervention of outside armies. Portuguese fascism (1926-74) was overthrown by an internal revolt, itself precipitated by a set of costly colonial wars in Africa and a deteriorating economic situation at home.

The colonial wars had been going on for over thirteen years. Portugal, the weakest of all the old colonial powers, was also the most tenacious. Marcello Caetano had proclaimed in the thirties that:

> "Africa is more than a land to be exploited . . . Africa is for us a moral justification and a *raison d'être* as a power. Without it we would be a small nation; with it we are a great power."

The African colonies began their revolt with an urban insurrection in Angola in 1961 and with guerrilla warfare in Guinea-Bissau in 1963 and Mozambique in the following year. Unable and unwilling to follow the British model of de-colonisation (political independence to the local ruling élite and intimate economic links), the Portuguese rulers now paid the price for their short-sightedness. Between 1964 and 1974 they sustained 60,000 casualties. By 1969 the expenditure on defence was forty-two per cent of the entire state budget and by 1971 the amount increased to fifty-eight per cent of the total. Add to this the fact that Portugal's population is 9 million. Sustaining a colonial army of 200,000 with such a small population cannot but be a crippling exercise. The "civilisers" of Africa had an adult illiteracy rate of forty per cent at home. Furthermore, Portugal had the highest rate of infant mortality in Europe.

The size of the army led to an increase in the length of conscription. Many of the conscripted junior officers were university students. The impact of the war (i.e. the fact that they were losing it) coupled with the fact that the Portuguese secret police, PIDE, had no authority inside the army, meant that the flow of radical literature was smoother inside the army than in the rest of society. While some of the works of John F. Kennedy were banned in bookshops, the "Communist Manifesto" and various other Marxist texts circulated inside the army. Furthermore soldiers and officers on their way to Africa were officially supplied with handbooks on guerrilla war by authors such as Mao Tse Tung, Vo Nguyen Giap and Che Guevara, in order that they might understand the mind of the enemy. In many cases the handbooks actually succeeded in radicalising their Portuguese readers. One such reader was a young officer named Otelo Saraivo de Carvalho.

On the home front the Salazar régime had been compelled to accept the internationalist logic of capital and abandon their protectionist economic policies. Restrictions on foreign capital were removed in the early sixties. These restraints had enabled indigenous capitalism to accumulate its strength, and a number of consortiums dominated the economy. The largest of these was the CUF (Companhia Uniao Fabril), which owned over a tenth of the country's industry including the chemical and textile industries. The weakness of Portuguese capitalism prevented the State from helping the further development of these companies. The turn to foreign investment was thus not an optional extra, but a necessity.

Familiar names were soon to be seen on billboards in Portugal: ITT, Timex, Ford, Grundig, Renault, British Leyland and Plessey. These companies found Portugal a paradise: colonies, low wages and a corporate state. From 1.5 per cent in 1960 the scale of foreign investments rose to 27 per cent in 1970. The impact of this foreign-financed industrialisation process increased the size of the urban working class from 25 per cent of the total adult population in 1950 to 35.8 per cent in 1970. The proportion of the population employed on the land fell from 47 per cent in 1950 to 30 per cent in 1970. Those who could not be absorbed into the internal labour market went to Western Europe: by 1973 there were nearly 2 million Portuguese workers outside the country, an important transmission belt for new and, in certain cases, radical ideas. The population increased in the predominantly urban provinces of Lisbon, Setubal and Oporto.

In the countryside there was a division between the large landed estates in the south and the *minifundia* in the north. The former were mechanised and employed agricultural labourers. The small farmers in the north were racked by debts and dominated by the Church. The north-south division was to be consistently reflected in the country's politics after the overthrow of Caetano and the dismantling of fascism.

The increase in the size of the urban working class after the entry of foreign capital brought its own "diseases". Infla-

91

tion hit Portugal with a surprising intensity, reaching a rate of twenty-one per cent in 1973. At the same time a strike by transportation workers in July 1968 signalled the emergence of strength within a working class exploited and repressed by fascism for over three decades. As the recession developed in the rest of Western Europe, many migrant workers began going home, swelling the ranks of the unemployed, but bringing with them a whiff of what it was like in the rest of the continent in terms of politics and trades unionism. In 1973 a number of strikes broke out in the engineering and car industries: Ford, General Motors and the Lisnave shipyards (the largest in the world, owned by the CUF in partnership with Dutch and Swedish companies), ITT, and finally in the air transport services. This pattern was continued in the following year. The strikes were by no means generalised. Their character was fragmentary, but they nonetheless reflected an important and growing class-consciousness in the urban centres of Portugal.

The external and internal problems confronting the Salazarist state produced growing divisions within the ruling class. Internally, some of them favoured political relaxation and integration within the European Community. As far as the guerrilla wars in Portugal were concerned, the divisions were even more pronounced and, because of the importance of what was at stake, more serious. On February 28, 1974 a book was published in Lisbon, entitled *The Future of Portugal,* by the former military commander of the expeditionary force in Guinea-Bassau, General Spinola. The theme of the book was to propose a Gaullist-type solution, granting autonomy to the former colonies within a federation including Portugal. Spinola argued that: "If we do not achieve this solution, we will inevitably drift towards disintegration, losing our African territories one after the other."

These relatively moderate proposals produced a furious backlash from the diehard colonialists ensconced in the upper reaches of the governmental and state apparatus. They discussed the replacement of Caetano for permitting the publication of the book, and the political police seized large numbers of copies from bookshops throughout the country. The Spinola book exposed the simmering discontent within the government and the army: junior officers and NCOs demanded a set of reforms; the infantry company of Caldas Da Rainha, fifty-five miles away from Lisbon, threatened a march on Lisbon. The hardliners struck on March 13, 1974. They removed Generals Spinola and Costa Gomez from their posts, instituted repressive measures against dissident soldiers and attempted to stabilise the situation. But they were too late, for within the army there already existed an organisation of officers who were not prepared to wait any longer for the reforms which they felt were necessary to put Portugal on the right track. This was the Armed Forces Movement (MFA). It had been organised in 1973 to oppose a Caetano decree granting equal rights to conscript officers, but they soon transcended this narrow professional issue. Indeed, given that conscript officers joined the MFA several months later, it would appear that the initial point of dispute could well have been a pretext to organise meetings within the army.

In January 1974 the MFA circulated a document amongst its supporters entitled: "The Movement, the Armed Forces and the Nation". It was the first real sign that a major reformist opposition to Salazarism existed within the army. The document spoke of the colonial wars as "the gravest question which underlies the general crisis of the régime" even though it called for a "political solution which safeguards national honour and dignity", a clear sign that the more radical officers were anxious to prevent any premature break with the supporters of the monocled General Spinola. However, the document refuted the "myth that our armed forces are politically neutral" and accused the army of sustaining a régime of repression in Portugal itself. This was a remarkable development foreseen by no political analyst. It was a direct reflection of the tensions which existed in society as a whole inside a conscript army. The fact that all opposition parties and currents were underground, that the student movement had suffered heavy repression and that there was no freedom of the media resulted in the desire of the majority of the masses for democratic rights being channelled through an unlikely source: a section of the officer caste of the Portuguese army. The character of this caste had somewhat altered over the preceding decade. The progeny of traditional "martial families" were finding increasingly unattractive their careers in an army fighting three wars and sustaining heavy casualties. Furthermore the opening up of Portugal to foreign capital provided alternative employment on the managerial level for the children of the wealthy. The result was dramatic: in 1961-62 there had been 257 admissions to the élite military academy. In 1971-72 when the army needed more officers than ever before the figure was down to seventy-two. The vacuum was filled by conscript and non-commissioned officers drawn largely from university graduates. At the same time the conscription period was increased from two to four years. The influx of new ex-student officers, many of whom had been radicalised by the post-1962 wave of student agitation in Portugal, was to have an important impact inside the army: many of the students were sympathetic to the politics of the Socialist and Communist parties, while others were more in tune with the aspirations of the far left.

The MFA leadership followed the discussions on its initial document and formulated a draft programme, the task of which was to codify the aims and demands of the movement. Thus the programme contained demands for overthrowing the Caetano régime, organising a large-scale *saneamento* (purge) to cleanse the army and the police of fascist influences, the immediate dissolution of the hated political police and the convocation within twelve months of an elected constituent assembly. As far as the economy was concerned the draft programme sketched out a schematic "anti-monopoly strategy" and called for measures which would have "the essential objective of defending the interests of the working classes". As far as Africa was concerned the programme was extremely muted, restricting itself to calling for a "political" rather than a military solution and pledging "an overseas policy which leads to peace". There was no mention of a withdrawal from Africa. The programme as a whole was left-reformist in tone. The fact that it could only be implemented by a forcible overthrow of the corporatist régime gave it a force which was beyond the control of its initiators.

On April 25, 1974 Caetano was deposed by a well-executed military *coup*: the officer who played a leading role in co-ordinating the work necessary was Carvalho. The takeover in Lisbon proceeded smoothly, enabling the MFA to consolidate its national position. Later, Carvalho admitted in an interview that they were all surprised by the extent of popular support inside the army itself for the overthrow of the Caetano régime.

There were some units, commanded by right-wing officers who were prepared to resist. In order to prevent an outbreak of violence the MFA leaders concluded an agreement with Spinola. This haughty figure refused to talk to any officer of the MFA below the rank of a colonel. Caetano formally handed over power to Spinola. A Portuguese civil servant described the Spinola-Caetano encounter as "a meeting of two gentlemen, of two friends who respect each other and who share a great sense of honour and responsibility". Caetano was provided with a military plane to leave for Brazil, where he was welcomed by the military dictatorship and appointed Professor of Comparative Law at the country's leading university. It was a fitting appointment for a fascist in a country where the only law that prevailed was despotic and barbaric.

Spinola appeared on television on April 26 and promised free elections and democratic rights. The statement he read out was clearly a compromise and the Junta of National Salvation over which he presided was composed exclusively of generals and admirals, who had had long tours of duty in Africa. The masses demonstrated their joy at the overthrow of the régime without inhibition or restraint. They secured the release of all political prisoners within a week. Almost overnight they transformed a society marked by fifty years of fascist rule and decay into one where everyone could speak his or her own mind. The fascist regulated press found itself taken over by its employees. A campaign was immediately launched in the liberated press for the abolition of reactionary religious edicts which prohibited divorce for those unfortunate enough to be married in a Portuguese church! Education began to be reorganised. The night of ignorance, of repression, of a clerico-fascist morality, had come to an end. Many wondered whether it was all a dream. The reactionary members of the ruling junta, including Spinola, regarded these events as a nightmare. Their military minds found the breakdown of traditional law and order repugnant. While Spinola's position as Head of State protected the reactionary officers in the army from the wrath of the *saneamanto* the navy was not immune to anti-fascist measures. Several hundred officers proclaimed their support for the MFA and demanded the removal of eighty-two admirals and vice-admirals because of their intimacy with the Salazar régime. Their demands were met.

The first Provisional Government sworn in by Spinola reflected the political crisis confronting a collapsing state. Apart from reactionary military men there were two ministers each from the Communist and Socialist parties. This attempt to contain the working-class movement by tying the two workers' parties to the State was, however, unable to limit the mass upsurge. If anything, it discredited the Communist Party in the eyes of the workers. A Communist, Aveliono Pachecho Goncalves, was the Minister of Labour, and the Communist Party waged a ferocious ideological campaign against strikes. It was a display of extremely short-sighted opportunism in a country which had, only a few weeks previously, been under a fascist government, where official ideology had strongly disapproved of any form of strike action. May Day 1974 was an historic event in the calendar of the Portuguese working class: it was the first occasion in half a century that they had been able freely to commemorate this day. A massive wave of strikes shook Portugal after May 1, 1974. They were a novel combination of everyday economic demands fused with struggles against the fascist apparatus and its representatives. In addition strikes which had been repressed in 1973 were now resumed with an additional demand: all workers dismissed for leading the strikes in the preceding year be immediately rehabilitated. In the construction industry workers of most of the major companies went on strike and organised flying pickets to defend their struggle. On May 13 the workers in the Ponasquiere iron mines unleashed a strike which lasted a week until their demands — which included a guaranteed minimum monthly wage of 6000 escudos, an extra month's pay every year, one month's free holiday and free medical aid — were granted. The following week saw the chemical, automobile and related industries paralysed by a series of strikes. Although the official trades unions had been state-controlled, democratic forms of organisation emerged in many factories, jealously guarding their autonomy against all encroachments.

In many cases the workers won major demands, but the mobilisations receded towards the end of May. The movement had not been consciously unified: the two mass parties of the workers were in government, though it is unlikely that they would have attempted a general strike had they been out of office. The Portuguese Communist Party in the first phase after the overthrow of Caetano acted not unlike the French Communist Party in May 1968. It was desperate to preserve "order" at all costs. It attacked those on its left, who were aiding and helping to organise the strikes as: ". . . consciously or unconsciously acting in favour of reaction". They were described as ultra-lefts taking undue advantage "of an inexperienced politically very young working class that could be plunged into adventure". The Communist-organised demonstration on May 30, 1974 to pledge support for the party's anti-strike crusade was a miserable flop: 6000 people marched behind the Communist Minister for Labour, singing the old national anthem and carrying portraits of General Spinola! "Social peace" was the main slogan of Mr Cunhal's party in the period after April 25, 1974. The "politically very young working class", however, continued to ignore the advice of the leaders of the Communist Party, mature though they were in the ancient art of class-collaboration. The postal workers' strike which erupted in June 1974 became an important test for the workers' parties. It was the first national strike after April 25. The ideological offensive against the postal workers was orchestrated and led by the Portuguese Communist Party. Jose Vitoriano, a member of the Central Committee, was reported in the French Communist Party's daily paper, *l'Humanité* of June 21 as saying: "Today it is the fascists and reactionaries of all stripes who want more strikes. Yesterday they repressed them with blood and iron. Today they are the principal promoters." It was hardly surprising that the *Financial Times* of June 18 saw fit to note that: "The Minister of Labour, Avelino Goncalves, nevertheless works hard at settling conflicts that seriously affect production, and it is extremely important to note that it is nearly only the Communists who are counselling caution in the use of the strike weapon at this time." The notion that it was the fascists and reactionaries who were promoting the strikes, was, of course, ludicrous. It was a slander that bore all the hallmarks of the Stalinist school of falsification. It should be stressed that throughout this period of the First Provisional Government the policies and tactics of the Portuguese Communist Party were to the right of the Socialist Party, in fact many Socialist Party cadres were more sympathetic to the strikers and their demands at this time. The postal workers' strike, supported incidentally by ninety-seven per cent of the workers,

97

was defeated by a military occupation of the post offices and repression against sections of the media which backed the strike. Military officers who refused to occupy the post offices were suspended, and newspapers reporting the suspension were penalised. None of this met with opposition from the Portuguese Communist Party. It is vital to remember the role played by the PCP in this phase for evaluating its electoral standing and its inability to resist the ideological offensive of social-democracy in the following year.

The Junta had been able to inflict a defeat on the postal workers, but it soon discovered that it was impossible to repeat the process in the African arena. The Junta was now confronted with a pincer movement. On the one hand it confronted the African liberation movements and at its right flank were the reactionary, colonialist, Portuguese settlers, opposed to any concessions. The federal solution envisaged by Spinola, Costa Gomes and the military High Command was a non-starter. The African guerrillas refused to agree to a ceasefire if all they were offered in return was a pan-Portuguese fantasy. In Portugal itself virtually the entire far-left was beginning to agitate for immediate and complete independence. A Maoist newspaper *Luta Popular* was suppressed and its editor imprisoned for inciting troops to refuse to fight in Africa. Under growing pressure both the Socialist and the Communist parties demanded that negotiations with the liberation movements commence without a prior cease-fire. The Portuguese right wing attempted to boost Spinola's reputation in the country, comparing him to de Gaulle. But there was no analogy between post-Caetano Portugal and the French Fourth Republic. Spinola's primitive anti-communism was not enough to guarantee his victory against the left and the masses. The Portuguese had just got rid of fascism. They were not keen on embarking on a course which turned out to be a modified version of the *Estado Novo,* with a monocled Bonaparte at its head. The failure of the Communist and Socialist Party to contain the working-class upsurge in the summer of 1974 had clearly alarmed sections of the ruling class, and they were now prepared to consider a strong state led by a strong President ruling by decrees confirmed by occasional plebiscites. But proposals to put some of these ideas into practice were firmly rejected by the Council of State, a body not known for its radicalism. The Council was obviously more aware of the deep divisions inside the army than a number of left-wing commentators writing in the revolutionary press in Western Europe and North America. The impasse in which the supporters of Spinola now found themselves led to the fall of the Government. Spinola tried to reconstitute it by appointing Colonel Firmino Miguel, one of his trusted aides, as the new Prime Minister, but the MFA leadership blocked this and insisted that Vasco Goncalves, a member of the MFA Coordinating Committee, become the new head of government. Four important leaders of the MFA were brought into the Second Provisional Government, including Costa Martins, Melo Antunes and Vitor Alves. At the same time Vitor Crespo and Vice-Admiral Coutinho, two officers trusted by the MFA leaders, were despatched post-haste to Mozambique and Angola respectively. It was now obvious that the MFA had decided to disregard Spinola's supporters in the army, ditch the federalist dream and begin negotiations to end the war and organise a Portuguese withdrawal. Melo Antunes and Mario Soares were authorised to carry out such a plan. The decolonisation proposals of the MFA and its governmental strength represented a serious setback for General Spinola's political project. The right wing within the army decided to accept defeat for the moment, but there is considerable evidence to suggest that it began plotting a *coup* to defeat the MFA and impose a strong Presidential form of government.

For its part the MFA utilised the advent of the Second Provisional Government to put into practice a number of the proposals contained in its draft programme. A *saneamento* was carried out in the fields of education and local administration. Though in regard to the latter it should be mentioned that the eagerness of the PCP to fill the places of the sacked fascists without any recourse to mass opinion was to have damaging effects at a later stage. As censorship was now almost totally abandoned the hunger of the masses for socialist ideas and texts could be fully assuaged. A hundred flowers bloomed in the real sense of the phrase. Marxist literature could be found everywhere; pamphlets by Lenin were displayed in the smallest shops; revolutionary and socialist ideas were discussed regularly in the mass media; Eisenstein's classic film, *Battleship Potemkin,* was seen by huge audiences in Lisbon. The ideological mechanisms of the old order were in a state of virtual collapse. The Portuguese ruling class had still not found effective new channels for reasserting its hegemony. Some of the demonstrations which took place in Portugal in 1974, and even more in 1975, reflected the dramatic changes which had taken place. Who could have predicted that the spectre of Petrograd would appear for the first time in post-war Europe in the streets of Lisbon rather than Milan or Paris or Barcelona? The demonstrations of soldiers, sailors, workers and students marching with linked arms on the streets of Portugal sent a tremor of fear through the capitalists in the West.

The summer of 1974 saw further developments in the country, which resulted in the further isolation of reaction and ultimately to a confrontation from which the latter rapidly retreated. In Africa the two emissaries of the Second Provisional Government, Mario Soares and Melo Antunes, negotiated the independence of Guinea-Bissau and Mozambique in September. A white settler revolt in the Mozambique capital was suppressed by a joint expedition of Portuguese troops and African guerrillas. This came as a serious blow to Spinola and the right wing, as it effectively ended their dream of a Greater Portugal. At the same time the MFA leaders postponed a purge of fascist army officers but organised a military unit known as COPCON (Continental Operations Command) with responsibility for defending the authority of the government. COPCON's commander was Otelo Saraiva de Carvalho, who was promoted to the rank of brigadier and also given charge of the military district of Lisbon. This was clearly a move by the MFA radicals to institutionalise the semi-dual power structure which existed in the Army. COPCON was used to "solve" industrial disputes and persuade workers to end occupations, but it did not open fire on any banned demonstration. Meanwhile the workers of the giant Lisnave shipyards demanded a more thoroughgoing *saneamento* and issued a communiqué. This declaration symbolised the new mood of the Portuguese working class. It indicated that the advanced workers had, at any rate, understood that what was taking place in the country was not simply a process of democratisation, but that it posed more fundamental questions. For that reason the short communiqué is reproduced in full:

"In struggling to rid the Lisnave management of its fascists, the workers have become aware they are not only fighting for the downfall of the fascist structure inside Lisnave, but also against the whole of the exploiting ruling class.

"In this way the workers of Lisnave are joining with the brave fight of TAP, of *Jornal do Commercio,* of Siderurgia, of Texmalhas, backing all the struggles from North to South, and leaving the narrow walls of the factory to come onto the streets and show:

"That our fight to rid ourselves of fascists is not a secondary fight, it is a principal struggle because it is part of the permanent fight against all the forms of fascism being constantly generated by monopoly capitalism.

"That where there is initiative and organised struggle by the oppressed classes, the forces of reaction retreat. Where there is lack of vigilance on the part of the people, the counter-revolutionary forces advance and wipe out the freedoms already achieved.

"That we support all the laws and measures of the Provisional Government which help to increase the freedom of the workers, and of the peoples exploited and oppressed by Portuguese Colonialism.

"That we do not back the Government when it comes out with anti-working class laws which undermine the struggles of workers against capitalist exploitation.

"That we shall actively fight the strike the 'strike law' because it is a big blow to the freedom of the workers.

"That we reject the 'lock-out law' as a law against the workers and for the protection of the capitalists, granting to the bosses the freedom to starve thousands of workers.

"Because we know that the 120 million escudos, are not, as claim the Melos, Champalimauds, Quinas & Company, to create 120 thousand jobs, but to create better conditions under which to exploit the workers.

"That we reject all attempts, no matter from where they come, to sabotage and divide the working masses in their fight against fascism and capitalism.

"That we support the Armed Forces so long as they support the struggles of the oppressed and exploited classes against the oppressing and exploiting classes.

LISNAVE WORKERS PURGE FASCISTS
DEATH TO PIDE — DEATH TO FASCISM
RIGHT TO STRIKE — YES!
LOCK OUT — NO!
SOLIDARITY WITH THE COMRADES ON STRIKE"

101

The Lisnave workers organised a one-day strike on September 12, 1974 and organised a demonstration outside the Ministry of Labour. Despite the fact that the march was banned it did take place. The COPCON units moved aside to let the workers march to their destination where they handed in their communiqué. It was an extremely important indication of the mood inside sections of the army. It was also regarded as a provocation by Portuguese reaction, which had been viewing the deteriorating situation inside the army with growing unease. The twin processes of decolonisation abroad and democratisation at home (especially the energy of the latter) were seen by Spinola and the right wing as developments which had to be stopped. In the northern part of the country the old members of the fascist organisations had been regrouping under new names, intended to deceive, but which fooled no one. A COPCON raid on the offices of the so-called Progressive Party in Oporto revealed an armoury and fascist personnel. On September 10, Spinola broadcast a speech appealing against "anarchy" and calling on the "silent majority" to oppose "extremism". This was clearly not a spontaneous decision by the would be Bonaparte. It had been taken in consultation with the right wing in the army and sections of the ruling class. Spinola's speech was welcomed by all the forces opposed to the "hasty" decolonisation and democratisation which was taking place. A demonstration by the "silent majority" was called for on September 28, setting the stage for some form of confrontation.

The workers' parties and the trades unions were alarmed by this move. They saw in it an attempt by the displaced forces of Salazarism to try and reverse, or at worst modify, the relationship of forces which had developed in Portuguese society. On September 26, the Communist and Socialist parties and Intersindical issued a joint communiqué describing the proposed "March on Lisbon" as a fascist attempt to strangle democracy and they organised the formation of militias to resist all attempts at a presidential putsch. The transport workers decided that they would not man the specially booked trains and coaches. On the morning of September 27, the liberated Radio Renascenca called on workers to organise "picnics in the evening" on all the main roads which led to Lisbon. The workers' militia organised armed roadblocks throughout the city. These militias consisted of members of the SP, the PCP and a whole range of far-left groups. It was a united front *par excellence*. It created extreme tension inside the Presidential Palace. Spinola was alarmed by these developments much more than by the open fascist intrigues leading to the demonstration. Once again, there were moves by armed force to break the roadblocks and barricades of the workers' movement. Vasco Goncalves and Carvalho were summoned to the Presidential Palace and, in effect, placed under arrest. The COPCON units were contacted by Spinola's aides, but refused to take orders from anyone but Carvalho. Once again it was the divisions in the army which foiled the attempts of reaction to carry out a *coup*. On the morning of the proposed demonstration no newspapers were published on Spinola's orders. The General and his aides were fearful lest the availability of information further inflame the masses. They also ordered a radio silence except for official broadcasts. This was broken at 8.30 on the morning of September 28 by an MFA communiqué stressing its determination to carry out the measures stated in its programme and asking the masses to remain on guard against the intrigues and movements of reaction. COPCON commandos joined the workers on the barricades. At midday a mass demonstration assembled in the centre of Lisbon to block the "silent majority". In its vanguard were the workers of Lisnave and TAP, the Portuguese airlines. Within the next two hours Spinola banned the reactionary march. His capitulation swelled the size of the workers' demonstration which transformed itself into a celebration of a victory. Two days later, on September 30, the inevitable happened: Spinola resigned after delivering a speech attacking decolonisation in Africa and "the inversion of authority" at home. The MFA leaders thought that this victory was sufficient. They did not make a reply to Spinola detailing the manoeuvres of reaction in the preceding months. It was a grave political error reflecting the lack of a determination to be able to go on the offensive. In an interview with *Diario de Lisboa* after the overthrow of Spinola the best-known radical inside the MFA leadership said:

"I knew I was not fighting against Spinola. That was never my intention and it never occurred to me to go against him or to

103

make some sort of *coup d'état* to remove him from power. It was he who was convinced of this."

If Carvalho was not speaking in such a fashion to maintain the unity of the army (in itself a utopian desire) then all one can say is that it reflected the utter political confusion that dominated the High Command of the MFA, a confusion which compelled it to be permanently on the defensive. If you have no clear conception as to how your own programme is to be implemented you tend to *react* to events instead of shaping them. Thus the fall of Spinola was treated by the MFA as a routine event. In Cuba Fidel Castro by contrast had used the counter-revolution to his advantage: he had patiently explained what reaction was plotting and had educated the masses in such a way that the final stage of the Cuban revolution was an enormously popular occasion with mass participation. The failure of the MFA to teach the masses was not a surprise. The MFA was in itself a hybrid and heterogenous movement which contained within it most of the colours of the rainbow. Nonetheless the left did exercise considerable influence and could have deflected the movement, provided it had understood what was at stake.

But if one cannot expect a worked-out strategy from an organisation which inhabits a vital section of the State apparatus and acts under its constraint, the role of the Communist and Socialist parties in helping the masses assimilate the lessons of what is going on is virtually nil. Both parties tended to support the MFA and they tended to treat the MFA as a uniform and cohesive political bloc, they did not put forward any alternative line of action for the masses for fear of weakening it. The one occasion on which they carried out an independent political act of significance was the setting-up of barricades in September 1974. But here too, their aims were to provide mass backing for the MFA against Spinola and his right-wing supporters. The independent *political* capacity of the Portuguese working class was limited because of its inexperience and the straitjacket imposed on it by decades of fascist rule. Once Spinola was ejected the two parties went back to business as usual. The working class was learning fast, but it was conscious of its limitations. The barricades of September showed the strength of the masses and its parties. They also

104

revealed that the mobilisation had a sufficiently strong impact on the MFA to pressure it to remove Spinola. The mistake was that it regarded this as a victory.

Spinola was replaced by Costa Gomes, a veteran from the same milieu, but more able and prepared to compromise, when necessary, with the MFA. The Lisbon daily, *Diario de Noticias,* remarked on the changeover that "between Generals Spinola and Costa Gomes there is all the difference between an emotive and an intellectual. Two men, two styles but the objectives remain the same. . . . This excludes all alarmist hypothesis". The removal of Spinola ensured that the country's first general elections in fifty years would be held on schedule as promised. The ruling class was not pleased by the imminence of the elections; they had not been able to create a political instrument which could win a mass base and ensure stable bourgeois rule. Post-war Italy had seen the formation of the Christian Democratic Party. Backed by the United States, Italian capitalists and the Vatican, this party still rules Italy. In ideal circumstances the Portuguese ruling class would have attempted the post-war Italian solution, but they were confronted by a world which had considerably changed. The United States had suffered a severe defeat in Indo-China, its internal credibility was dented by Nixon and the growing Watergate crisis. In Western Europe the post-war euphoria fed by the economic boom had given way to recession and unemployment. In addition there had appeared a new group of militants to the left of the traditional workers' parties which was sympathetic to revolutionary ideas and strategies. The Portuguese ruling class was uneasy about the outcome of the elections promised for 1975 because it feared that the Socialist and Communist parties would gain an overall majority, which could increase rather than put an end to political instability. It was this anxiety which prompted sections of the army in league with the deposed General Spinola to attempt a right-wing *coup* on March 11, 1974. The attempt proved to be abortive. The plotters found little support and the ranks of the army remained loyal to the central leadership of the MFA. Spinola and his aides fled, after a short stay in Spain, to Brazil. This defeat did mark a serious setback for the whole bourgeois order in Portugal, but the mass mobilisations which greeted the defeat of the *coup* saw the spectre of Petrograd raising its head in Lisbon once again. Soldiers and sailors fraternised with the workers. Red flags were flown on a number of tanks. The mass movement lurched forward and demanded in its slogans and chants more radical measures to deal with the growing economic crisis.

Once again the PCP played an important part in the anti-Spinolist agitation. But it preferred to act in liaison with its faction inside the MFA. For the truth is that the PCP, while talking at great length about the "unity of the MFA", had built its support around Goncalves and the Fifth Division. It now exercised control over a section of the MFA apparatus which was far from democratic. They systematically weeded out from central commands those unsympathetic to them; not only right-wingers and reactionaries, but also social-democrats and socialists. The formation of the "Group of Nine" at a later stage was partially in response to the attempted "colonisation" of the state apparatus by the Goncalves/PCP faction.

The March 11 *coup* was, in many respects, a pathetic affair. Within a matter of hours the Goncalves faction had used it to consolidate their grip on the MFA council and to marginalise Melo Antunes and his supporters. At the same time the PCP-dominated bank workers' unions took over the main banks. Official nationalisation was announced a few days later.

Over the preceding year, the rate of inflation in the country had risen to thirty-five per cent. A quarter of a million workers were unemployed. At the same time there was economic sabotage, investment strikes by Portuguese monopolists and by multinationals, restriction and suppression of credit to small and medium-size enterprises and the flight of capital. The left alleged that the United States was intervening through its favourite "destabilising" apparatus, the Central Intelligence Agency. Memories of Chile were still strong throughout Western Europe. It was alleged that the American Ambassador to Portugal was a high-powered officer of the Agency. This was denied at the time, but it is worth recalling that Frank Carlucci, appointed Ambassador to Portugal by Henry Kissinger in January 1975, was made Deputy Director of the Central Intelligence Agency in December 1977. Jonathan Steele reporting from Washington in *The Guardian* on December 23, 1977 wrote in relation to US involvement in Portugal in 1975:

106

"American officials have conceded that large sums of money were being channelled to anti-Communist parties and trade unions at that time through the CIA. West European intelligence services, and political parties, particularly the West German SPD. After the abortive right-wing putsch within the army in March 1975, which led to General Spinola's exile from Lisbon, some officers accused Mr Carlucci of involvement. The US State Department denied the charges."

The economic sabotage and the response of the mass movement prompted the government to embark on a project of large-scale nationalisations. The Military Revolutionary Council assumed open control of the government and passed a decree nationalising the banks, insurance companies and a number of other industrial concerns. Sixty per cent of the country's economy was soon nationalised. The only major monopoly to escape was the CUF enterprise, but even its workers were agitating for it to be taken over. Several dozen factories were occupied by the workers and a form of workers' control existed. In the large estates in the Alentejo in the southern tip of the country agricultural workers seized estates and established collectives, while empty buildings, luxury homes and hotels were taken over by homeless people.

It was in this atmosphere and these conditions that the country's first elections for half a century took place. Members were elected to a Constituent Assembly on April 25, 1975. The result was a victory for the workers' parties. The combined vote of the Socialist Party (thirty-eight per cent), the Communist Party (thirteen per cent) and the MDP/CDE (a CP front) (five per cent) was fifty-six per cent. Antonio De Figueiredo, a social-democratic observer, commented: ". . . a new Portugal may be able to achieve, if not a revolution, at least a process of accelerated evolution capable of achieving socialism in the context of a freer society". In other words the Portuguese political situation was ripening into a pre-revolutionary crisis. The election results were a striking proof that the workers wanted their own government, a workers' government which would bring about some form of socialist democracy. They were to find themselves disillusioned extremely rapidly.

The combined impact of the elections and the deteriorating political and economic situation brought about further splits in the army, which were reflected within the MFA. On one side a rapid process of radicalisation was taking place at the level of rank and file soldiers, and this had played a decisive part in defeating the *coup* of March 11. Soldiers of several key regiments had refused to obey orders. In addition specially convoked soldiers' assemblies were removing reactionary officers from the army. The imposition of a *saneamento* from below clearly worried the moderate sections of the MFA High Command. Some of them obviously wondered whether the whole process would end with the election of officers! There were even instances of soldiers and revolutionary officers providing military training for workers in a number of proletarian districts in Lisbon.

In these conditions the elections to the Constituent Assembly were utilised by Portuguese capitalists and their backers to try and disrupt the process of radicalisation. Having failed to bring about a stabilisation of the system through the extra-parliamentary channels of a rightist military *coup,* they now attempted to create a polarisation between the extra-parliamentary mass mobilisations and the Constituent Assembly. The problems which allowed the ruling class to go on the offensive were not unrelated to the fact that the MFA left wing, the Portuguese Communist Party and the overwhelming majority of the far-left also made such a counterposition from the other side. An understanding of what happened in the summer of 1975 is impossible unless one studies closely the strategy and aims of both the ruling-class formations and the working-class parties.

The outcome of the elections to the Constituent Assembly were not regarded by the masses as irrelevant. Given that they were the first elections based on universal adult franchise in fifty years it is hardly surprising that they had an overall national impact. Following the elections the Socialist Party leaders were triumphant and on the offensive. Their organisation had emerged as the largest single party in the Assembly. If they chose to form a government with Communist participation, they could do so with an overall majority. Soares did not want an SP-CP government, but mass pressure from below could well have forced him to create one. Instead the Communist Party, nursing its wounded pride at being defeated by the Socialist Party, refused, on its part, to countenance any such compromise. Instead they chose to strengthen their links with their supporters within the MFA and, in effect, preferred an MFA government under the Prime Ministership of Vasco Goncalves rather than a government representing the will of the people. This "will" was the result of a bourgeois democratic election. The point was that there was at that time no other way in which the *masses* could determine who should represent them and who should form the government. Thus Soares, aided and abetted by the German SPD, and financed from diverse sources, embarked on a campaign against the Fifth Provisional Government of Vasco Goncalves. He also aided objectively by the bureaucratic and manipulative strategy of the Communist Party and by the infantile leftism of the most important groups of the revolutionary left. In a developing pre-revolutionary state there was no organisation which attempted to come to grips with the central strategic problem which confronted all Portuguese revolutionaries: how could the masses be won over to revolution. The vanguard, the workers, students and soldiers in Lisbon and Oporto were clearly ready for a socialist revolution. How could their views and new consciousness be utilised to win over the masses? This remained the unsolved dilemma of the Portuguese Revolution. In Portugal, as in Chile (albeit in very different circumstances) the revolutionary left failed to find the road to the masses, whereas the Communist Party demonstrated once again its refusal to trust the masses.

The summer of 1975 opened up a decisive new period for the Portuguese revolutionary process. Up till then the revolution had advanced. Every date since April 25, 1974 had taken the mass movement forward. September 28, 1974 and March 11, 1975 had seen serious setbacks for the ruling class and its projects. In a despondent state the main political party of the ruling class, the Popular Democratic Party (PPD) had accepted after September 28 the role of the MFA as the central arbiter in Portuguese political and economic life. It clearly hoped that the Spinolist remnants within the MFA would be able to maintain control until the elections rocketed them (the PPD) into a governmental coalition. The elections to the Constituent Assembly, however, provided an overall majority to the SP and the CP. The failure of the CP and the far left to intervene in the crisis of the Socialist Party by implementing the tactic

109

of the united front allowed Soares to mount an offensive against socialism in the name of democracy.

Given the chorus of black propaganda throughout the Western European press in the summer of 1975, a campaign orchestrated, incidentally, by the Central Intelligence Agency, and directed against the "breakdown of law and order", "anarchy", etc., it is important to get the facts straight. While the MFA were not pleased with idea of holding elections at that stage (for a mixture of confused and ultra-left reasons) they had no option but to authorise them. At the same time they appealed to the people to cast blank votes in order to show their approval for the MFA which was, in the words of Admiral Coutinho, attempting to construct a "third political force" in the middle of the CP and the SP. It was an unrealistic and inane attempt to solve the dispute between the SP and the CP for the simple reason that it stressed the irrelevancy of politics. But it was politics for which the masses were thirsting. Ninety-two per cent of those eligible to vote went to the polls and only seven per cent cast blank votes. Before the elections the MFA had signed a pact with all the political parties whereby the latter agreed that the task of the Constituent Assembly was to frame a constitution and that the results would not be binding on the selection of a new coalition government, but would merely provide some form of guidance for restructuring the same. Soares was a signatory to this pact which accepted the dominant role of the MFA after the elections.

Vasco Goncalves proclaimed after the election that he was not dissatisfied with the results as "the election will not decisively influence the revolutionary process". What Goncalves did not realise was that without mass support the revolutionary process cannot be completed. It is possible that he harboured illusions that socialism could be brought about behind the backs of the majority of the population and with the support of an active and dynamic minority of workers. If he was suffering from these delusions it was because his military training had not alerted him to appreciate the uneven development of mass consciousness. Furthermore he was being backed to the hilt by the Portuguese Communist Party: some of its activities in this period created the impression that Cunhal and his Central Committee actually harboured hopes that an alliance with Goncalves and a section of the army could catapult it into power thus neatly avoiding the dilemma of the election result. In other words the Communist Party hoped that through its alliance with Goncalves it could leap over the masses and then manipulate them into line. It was a bureaucratic conception and it was doomed to fail. However, for the immediate post-election period it suited both the Goncalves faction within the MFA and the Communist Party.

The May Day rally organised in 1975 was held under the auspices of Intersindical, the CP-dominated trade union federation. The chief guest was the Prime Minister, Vasco Goncalves, and he was joined on the platform of the May First Stadium by leaders of the Communist Party. This was the first major rally since the elections. Its ostensible purpose was to celebrate international workers' day. In reality it was a manipulated occasion designed to exclude the Socialist Party and indicate that the elections were irrelevant. It was yet another attempt by the Communist Party to somehow circumvent the tricky problem of devising a strategy to win over the masses. The Communist Party throughout underestimated the independent political capacity of the Portuguese working class. This resulted in a bureaucratic and manipulative approach to politics. It was in its own way an admission that the masses would not respond to the politics of Portuguese Communist Party. When Mario Soares and thousands of Socialist Party workers entered the stadium to join the rally the slogan they were chanting was: "The People have voted. The Socialists have won." The reply which a revolutionary Marxist would have made to such a slogan would have been along the following lines: "What you say is true. Let us now discuss how to set up a workers' government consisting of all workers' organisations. In our opinion such a government should be based on working-class institutions. In order to carry through socialist measures we must mobilise the enormous potential of the working people themselves. Let us therefore extend and institutionalise the already existing organs of popular power so that the voice of the entire working class can be heard through them. Are Soares and the Socialist Party leaders prepared to work towards such a government? We certainly are because it best reflects at the present time the interests and desires of the Portuguese working class." An appeal of this sort would have opened up a dialogue and put Soares on the defensive, in a

111

position where he would be forced to explain to his own working-class supporters why he was opposed to forming a workers' government. The reply of Cunhal and Vasco Goncalves to the chant of the SP workers was to prevent Soares from addressing the rally and finally to instruct soldiers to escort him from the stadium. Actions of this sort merely helped to fuel the forces of reaction. The question was not that they would have remained inactive or passive if the PCP and the Fifth Provisional government had *not* made these mistakes. The point is that they could have been marginalised and defeated by a workers' and soldiers' united front.

On the heels of the short-sighted and sectarian exclusion of the Socialist Party from the May Day rally came the episode centred on the newspaper *Republica*. Under the Salazarist régime, *Republica* had been kept alive by money from various liberals and social-democrats and so it had reflected their views. Its proprietor, Paul Rego, was a leading member of the Socialist Party and after the events of April 25, Rego served for a period in the coalition government which actually penalised *Republica* for defying censorship laws. Rego at that time made no protests against censorship, nor did Soares wage a campaign for unfettered democracy. In the period following the Constituent Assembly elections and after a growing split between the CP and the SP, *Republica* emerged as a strong supporter of Soares and was widely regarded as an SP paper. Rego decided to dismiss two printing workers and replace them with two supporters of the Socialist Party. The printworkers went on strike, occupied the plant and demanded Rego's dismissal. The paper was closed down and COPCON troops were stationed outside its offices. When it reopened after five weeks the workers remained adamant and produced the paper themselves, forming it into a weapon of the class struggle. The Socialist Party left the coalition government in protest and Soares spoke at meetings throughout the country to defend "democracy". The incident was presented in the entire Western press as an attempt by the Communist Party and its supporters in the MFA to deny the Socialist Party the right to publish its own newspaper. The hue and cry over *Republica* was used by forces well to the right of Soares to unleash a counter-revolutionary offensive in the north of the country. In reality the Communist Party had little to do with the takeover of *Repub-*

lica. It was the decision of the printworkers, many of whom were sympathisers and supporters of a semi-Maoist far-left group which was extremely hostile to the Portuguese Communist Party. That the group in question was ultra-left is beyond dispute. It should have certainly opposed the sacking of two printers, but it was politically incorrect to deny Rego, and indirectly the SP, the right to publish *Republica.* For whatever the motives, it created the impression that the country's largest political party (in terms of electoral representation) was being denied the right to produce a newspaper. Despite the CP's manipulation of the media, Soares was *not* prevented from appearing on television to air his views. So the campaign of the SP leaders was quite calculated: it was intended to polarise the working class against the revolution by raising the banner of democracy. It was a tragic and unnecessary polarisation. And the far left paid the price in the months that followed for not understanding that the question of socialist *democracy* was not an irrelevant abstraction which could be ignored.

Soares now went on the offensive. A massive campaign against the radical officers, the CP, the far left and workers occupying factories was unleashed in the name of "democracy". It is now known that the CIA alerted its agents and friends throughout Western Europe for the occasion. The problem lay in the fact that the CP and the far left (with the partial exception of the Trotskyist International Communist League — LCI) found themselves still unable to respond to the SP on the question of "democracy". Now was the time to work out the tactics necessary to isolate the SP leaders from their base. A concerted attempt to unite the working class was desperately needed. Instead the CP and some far-left groups attempted physically to prevent the SP from marching in Oporto and Lisbon. The attempt to set up barricades to prevent the Socialist Party organising mass demonstrations was easily defeated by the presence of large numbers of pro-SP workers, but it made increasingly difficult any united front to counter the threat of a bourgeois offensive. Furthermore it enabled Soares to move the party to the right without meeting any massive opposition from within his ranks.

Soares had become of key importance for the Portuguese ruling class by this stage. The right-wing parties were heavily compromised by their collaboration with the fascist régime.

113

In fact many of the old fascist notables were finding themselves a new home in the CDS and the PPD (the self-proclaimed Centre-Democrats and Social-Democrats respectively). Thus an anti-working class offensive, led by Carneiro for the right-wing parties, would have been more logical, and would have met a united working-class resistance. Soares had succeeded in building a party from a handful of individuals. True, he had been helped directly, and indirectly, by the Communist Party. But he had proved to be a skilful demagogue and a leader capable of understanding the importance of timing in politics. In its early days after the overthrow of Caetano, the Socialist Party had engaged in a display of leftist rhetoric. Its original statement of aims was well to the left of the Spanish, Italian and British Communist Parties. It spoke a language which drew it closer to the mood of a growing number of workers:

"The Socialist Party fights the capitalist system and bourgeois domination. . . . The Socialist Party is implementing a new conception of life that can only be brought about through the construction of workers' power. . . .
"The struggle against fascism and colonialism will only be achieved by the destruction of capitalist society and the construction of socialism. . . . The Socialist Party refutes those who say they are social democrats but continue to preserve the status quo, the structures of capitalism and the interests of imperialism."

The fact that a social-democratic party had to construct a working-class base speaking a militant language is, in itself, a reflection of the overall political situation which developed after the overthrow of fascism in Portugal. Language such as this was precisely the pétard on which the revolutionary workers and soldiers could have hoisted Soares and his friends. That they failed to do so was to become a tragedy for the Portuguese Revolution. Having carved out a base for the Socialist Party inside the working class, Soares then participated in the April 1975 elections as the leader of a party which offered both socialism and democracy. His victory gave him the necessary confidence to act as a national leader and he began increasingly to posture as the "saviour of the nation" — he was the leader who offered the ruling class an end to "anarchy" in the factories and the countryside and a stabilisation of the status quo. The leader he resembled was not so much the German social-democratic Noske, who drowned the workers' vanguard in blood, but Mitterand, the suave spokesman of French social-democracy.

What cannot be doubted is that those who wanted a bloody counter-revolution — groups like the fascist ELP based in neighbouring Spain — made full use of Soares' campaign and in the name of "democracy" in July and August started a campaign of terror and violence in the northern part of the country. The Archbishop of Braga, an ardent supporter of Portuguese fascist dictators, used democracy as an excuse to come out on to the streets and bless those about to perpetrate acts of violence against the left. While trade unions and far-left groups were attacked as well, the main brunt of this wave of counter-revolutionary violence was borne by the Portuguese Communist Party. Its headquarters were completely devastated by bomb attacks in twenty-five centres while another twelve were severely damaged. In northern towns Communist militants were confronted by large lynch mobs who had been blessed by the Catholic Church and egged on by the right-wing parties. In the face of this assault the Portuguese Communist Party found itself virtually paralysed. Its Central Committee meeting held on August 10 to discuss the danger in the north came up with no specific proposals to meet the threat. The most concrete measure the party decided on was to set up a fund to rebuild the headquarters which had been destroyed.

The Portuguese Communist Party was the strongest working-class party after the fall of Caetano and it had a record of struggle against the dictatorship. Its leaders and militants had suffered torture, harassment, death and long prison sentences. Its prestige was extremely high as was demonstrated by the reception awarded to Cunhal on his return to Lisbon from exile. Its membership when Caetano was overthrown was 5000. Within a year party membership jumped to 50,000. The majority were the more politically conscious workers in the urban centres. Many of them joined the party not to break strikes or support censorship, but to move towards socialism. More to the point these workers had not been subjected to decades of Stalinist propaganda vilifying the far-left. As a result many of them remained responsive to the initiatives of the far-left groups.

115

The failure of the Communist Party to use its strong working-class base to unite the working class against its enemies was not accidental: it was the direct product of the PCP's basic ideas on the character of the struggle taking place in Portugal. It did not believe that socialism was on the agenda. In that sense it was more true to its real beliefs than Soares. Furthermore its actions throughout the first phase after the overthrow of fascism were designed to establish a capitalist democracy. It opposed strikes, it defended press censorship and it tried to contain the mass upsurges which were shaking the country. In 1931 Trotsky had described the strike movement, which followed the overthrow of the Spanish monarchy, in a fashion which was apposite to the Portuguese working class in 1974:

"The overwhelming majority of the Spanish proletariat does not know what organisation means. During the time the dictatorship lasted, a new generation of workers grew up, lacking in independent political experience. The revolution awakens — and in this lies its force — the most backward, downtrodden, the most oppressed toiling masses. The strike is the form of their awakening. By means of the strike, various strata and groups of the proletariat announce themselves, signal to one another, verify their own strength and the strength of their foe. One layer awakens and infects another. All this together makes the present strike wave absolutely inevitable. Least of all do the communists have to be afraid of it, for this is the very expression of the creative force of the revolution. Only through these strikes, with all their mistakes, with all their 'excesses' and 'exaggerations', does the proletariat rise to its feet, assemble itself as a unit, begin to feel and to conceive itself as a living historical force."

(Leon Trotsky, "The Role of Strikes in a Revolution",
The Spanish Revolution, New York 1974)

But the Portuguese communist leaders were afraid of the strike movement and attempted to put an end to it, without much success. It was at this time that the leftist demagogy of the Socialist Party enabled it to outdistance Cunhal's party. The Communist Party believed in a "national and democratic revolution" in alliance with small and medium-size capitalists and farmers. However, the tempo of the situation was such that these formulas and tactics designed to implement them were soon outpaced by events. After the victory of September 28,

116

1974 — the Night of the Barricades — the PCP realised that strike-breaking was a recipe for political suicide. It stopped concentrating on its alliance with the Socialist Party and with the Popular Democrats within the government and pushed hard instead to try and establish an alliance with the MFA. The latter was now in control of the State, it had overthrown Caetano and it enjoyed a certain prestige in the country as a whole. The PCP put forward the notion of the "People-MFA alliance". In this alliance the PCP was to be the main representative of the mass of working people. Together they could prevent Portugal from making a deal with imperialists and attempt to carve out a "third way" forward. The PCP thus shifted its positions and started a frenetic, sectarian and manipulative campaign to ensure that its members held important posts in the unions, the local councils, the State machinery and the mass media. The result was growing friction with the Socialist Party, which could portray the PCP as a power-mad and Stalinist party which manipulated the masses.

The reactionary offensive in the north found the PCP paralysed. It had by now thrown most of its eggs into the MFA basket, but the MFA as such could not help defend it against reaction. Furthermore the polarisations in society were being reflected more and more within the MFA and there were growing demands for the dismissal of Vasco Goncalves because of his close links with the PCP. Certainly the fact that the newspapers dominated by the PCP, including the *Diario de Noticias* (the Portuguese equivalent of *The Times*), insisted on presenting Goncalves as if he were the leader of an Eastern European state and at the same time publishing articles on the joys of Bulgarian collectivisation, did not advance the cause of either Goncalves or the PCP. If anything it turned sections of the masses *away* from the PCP. The best way to defeat the manoeuvres of reaction was to try and establish democratic organs of popular power. But the PCP was frightened by the prospect of giving real power to the masses. At the same time it failed completely to immobilise the peasant base of the Catholic Church in the north by a wide-ranging decree of reforms. In an area of abject poverty and mass illiteracy (sixty per cent of the people could neither read nor write) the Catholic Church was strong, playing on the superstitions of the peasants. The government did not write off their debts to landlords or banks.

No serious attempt was made to provide subsidies and loans without interest, though in some areas a start was made on improving education and social facilities. So far as the northern peasants were concerned the "People-MFA" alliance had not particularly benefited *their* people.

The failure to mobilise the masses and encourage their initiatives went hand-in-glove with another weakness: in their eagerness to cement an alliance with the MFA, the PCP failed during the early stages to appreciate that there was a growing crisis in the army. This provided an unexpected turn to Portuguese events after the July-August days, which were described in the *Daily Telegraph* of August 14 as "the most heartening thing to have happened in Europe for years". Communists were being physically attacked, their headquarters were being subjected to terrorist attacks and the *Daily Telegraph* and most of the British press were standing by and applauding, not to mention misreporting these events. The only European bourgeois paper which managed to preserve a certain balance was the French daily *Le Monde.* The July/August days came to an end with the resignation of Goncalves, brought about by moderate forces within the MFA who were in league with Soares. The new Prime Minister was Admiral Pinheiro de Azveida, who took over on August 29, 1975 and on September 19 organised the Sixth Provisional Government. Within eighteen months, Portugal had witnessed the rise and fall of six governments. No one could deny that there was a severe political crisis in the country.

However, any hopes on the part of the ruling class that the fall of Goncalves would mean stability were soon shown to be completely illusory. The objective force of the workers' struggles was leading more and more towards dual power in the factories. The strikes-occupation-workers' control pattern had spread beyond the massive industrial combines in Lisbon and was extending to middle-sized firms, and the distribution sector. Similar actions had already led to the nationalisations of the banks and the insurance companies, the first capitalist country in Western Europe where these crucially important sectors had been taken over by the State. The rapid development of workers' and tenants' committees linked the factories to the neighbourhoods and the communities. However, the fact that in some of these commissions the influence of the far left was so strong led some groups to imagine that it represented an indication of the overall relationship of forces. This was a serious error as it led to underestimating the strength of the Socialist Party and overestimating the implantation of the far left. Nonetheless the continued activity of the working class, while uneven and suffering from a lack of centralisation and political focus, was nonetheless seriously hampering the efficient operation of the Portuguese economy. To the political and economic crisis there was now to be added another dimension, far more serious in character as it threatened the cohesion of the state apparatus itself.

The army constitutes the spinal chord of every State apparatus. If damaged it adversely affects every other organ and induces a state of paralysis. Even in the bourgeois parliamentary states of Western Europe, North America, Japan and India, it is in the last analysis the coercive force on which the State rests, to be used only in cases of emergency. Engels' definition of the State as "armed bodies of men" retains its essential validity. The army and its structures are thus of vital importance for both the oppressor and the oppressed. No revolution can be successful unless these structures are weakened, pierced and ultimately destroyed. Every successful revolution, starting from the Russian, has had to confront this problem. For revolutionaries in the West today it poses a very real problem, for clearly the idea that the armies of capital in the West will be weakened by inter-imperialist wars as in 1914 or even in 1945 is ludicrous. The Portuguese experience was therefore of tremendous importance as it was the first post-war occasion where a growing political awareness was taking place in the army. The causes of this can only be explained by seeing world politics as an interrelated process. The liberation struggle of oppressed African peasants, city-dwellers and workers had played an important part in the overthrow of fascism in Portugal, almost inverting the process which followed the liberation struggle in Algeria. There a war pursued by a Socialist Party government and not opposed by the Communist Party had been lost as well, but had resulted in the overthrow of the Fourth Republic; and the emergence of a right-wing, Bonapartist military saviour. His seizure of power had taken place without being challenged by any political strikes by the French working class. In Portugal the situation was completely the opposite.

119

The polarisation of the Portuguese working class as a result of the 1975 elections saw a similar development within the upper reaches of the MFA. The two positions were polarised around documents prepared by different factions within the MFA. The first document was drafted by Melo Antunes and Vitor Alves. It was signed by seven other MFA officers, including the two regional commanders, Charais in Coimbra and Correia in Evora. The growing breakdown of discipline in the army had led to soldiers refusing to obey orders and beginning a *saneamenato* within the most hallowed institution of the Portuguese state. A number of reactionary officers had been dismissed. In early August Jaime Neves, the Colonel commanding the Amadora commandos, near Lisbon, was removed, but managed to get himself reinstated with the help of COPCON and Carvalho! Antunes and Alves decided that things had gone too far. Their document reflected their social-democratic preoccupations. The "Group of Nine", as they came to be known, were aligned politically with Soares, though some of them probably felt that he had carried his anti-leftist offensive too far. The "Group of Nine" were the Gorondins of the Portuguese revolutionary process. They felt that the revolution had achieved a great deal and should now be subordinated to the electoral results. Antunes and his comrades believed in bourgeois and not socialist democracy. Their document was fairly explicit in what it wanted:

> ". . . things have moved too fast to avoid tearing the existing social and cultural fabric. The social and economic organisation of the small and medium bourgeoisie quickly disintegrated, without new structures being created to guarantee the management of production and distribution units and to maintain a minimum of morality in the relationships among all Portuguese.
> "Hand in hand with this, we have witnessed a progressive deterioration of the state machinery. Wild and anarchistic forms of management have appeared everywhere, even within the MFA itself. Well-organised partisan organisations eager to seize the various power centres have tried to profit from the disorder. . . .
> "The country is profoundly shaken. . . ."

The document went on to demand the removal of the Goncalves government and attacked the crude manipulation of the Fifth Division, which was in charge of propaganda. Interestingly enough while attacking the "bureaucratic and totalitarian model" of Eastern Europe, the Nine also stated that Western-style social-democracy was not sufficient and what was needed was a peaceful, national transition to "socialism". In other words the authors of the document wanted to stop the revolutionary process, but not through a counter-revolution. Rather, they wanted to institutionalise or freeze the *existing* relationship of class forces through creating and strengthening bourgeois democratic institutions.

Four days later, on August 13, another document appeared, published by a group of COPCON officers and entitled "A Working Proposal for a Political Programme". It was a populist text, but it called for strengthening the organs of popular power and the creation of a Popular Assembly. It attacked Goncalves and the PCP from the left, thus objectively isolating the Fifth Provisional Government by constituting the second half of the pincer. However the COPCON document attacked all political parties, while laying stress on the "MFA-People Alliance" and calling for ending all dependence on imperialism. The COPCON document also called for the election of officers and argued that this was the only way in which discipline could be maintained. Many of the individual demands of the COPCON document were correct, but its utopian and populist character meant that it could not be seen as a realistic strategic alternative to the Antunes manifesto. The Girondins of the Portuguese Revolution had a more coherent approach than its Jacobins. The key weakness of the COPCON programme was its conception of organs of popular power moving forward on the one hand and the MFA guaranteeing their success on the other. What this left out of account was *politics*. Political parties do not exist as abstract entities hanging in mid-air. They reflect the divisions between and within different social classes. They cannot be wished away. If the embryonic organisms of dual power had developed and been extended it would have been utterly bureaucratic to prevent different political currents or parties from speaking or arguing for their political positions. Similarly the whole notion of the "MFA-People Alliance" was both populist and apolitical. Real political differences existed inside the MFA. The COPCON document itself was an

121

oblique response to the Group of Nine. The question which was raised was simple: what section of the people should align with which section of the MFA? And, it could be added, on what political basis?

However, the fact that two politically counterposed documents were produced by military officers and circulated within the MFA was in itself a unique historic occasion. Here was the officer caste of a bourgeois army debating its differences on paper. Of course both sides were aware that the only other method of conducting debates within the military was with tanks and heavy artillery and neither wanted that for obvious reasons. The two documents were soon circulating throughout the Portuguese Army and being discussed in a fairly democratic fashion. More important, soldiers' assemblies were putting them to a vote after discussions. A clear political polarisation was taking place within the army and around written documents. The result was a sharp acceleration in the political maturity within the army. This created a further differentiation and led in early September to the announcement of a new organisation. This was the Soldados Unidos Vencerao (SUV — Soldiers United To Win). It was the first organisation of rank-and-file uniformed soldiers and represented the extreme left wing of the radicalisation in the army. It was the answer from below to the MFA, which was throughout restricted to the officers.

SUV made its first appearance in the northern city of Oporto. Its first statement was issued on September 8 and explained that it was organising soldiers to fight against reactionary officers in the barracks:

"For more than six weeks it has been clear that reaction is raising its head in the barracks. Many facts show this: the purge of left-wing soldiers . . . the attacks on comrades who struggled for popular power in the barracks, the fact that the ADUs (Democratic Unit Assemblies) are being turned into disciplinary instruments which condemn comrades instead of being what they should be: organs which discuss and struggle for the interests of the workers in uniform, for pay increases, free transport, purging of reactionary elements in the barracks, links with the base organisations. . . ."

122

The formation of SUV presented the State with a serious challenge to its authority. It soon spread from the north to the centre and the south of Portugal. Its manifesto and appeal (printed as an Appendix at the end of this chapter) was a conscious break with all past ambiguities, and a mass expression of the class struggle inside the army. It organised its own demonstrations. Soldiers regularly defied their officers to attend these occasions, which turned out to be large affairs, swelled as they were by workers and the left groups. "Portugal will not be the Chile of Europe" was the most popular chant of the soldiers. Coming from their mouths it had a somewhat different impact than when it was shouted by the far left.

The Sixth Provisional Government was confronted with increasing opposition. Within the army the SUV was growing, and naval ratings were also beginning to join its ranks. The Government responded by disbanding regiments, transferring leftist officers and limiting repression. On a number of occasions these measures backfired. The Government had set itself a primary task, namely, "to re-establish order, authority and discipline" in the army, the factories and the media. It was a Government dominated by supporters of the Group of Nine. Its aim was to contain the working-class upsurge and its main backer inside the working-class movement was the Socialist Party. In fact as the early attempts of the Sixth Provisional Government to take over the workers' radio stations collapsed because soldiers who had been sent to clear out occupying workers instead *sided* with them, it was obvious that tensions were increasing inside the Socialist Party. During the summer it had been in opposition to the Government. Now, in the autumn, it was backing the Azveido government, and Soares speeches were concentrating on preaching "order" and attacking "anarchy". The Socialist Party had drifted rapidly to the right. A non-Marxist commentator, Tony Banks, wrote in the official organ of the British Labour Party, *Labour Weekly,* on September 12, 1975:

"Since the April election, when the SP won thirty-eight per cent of the votes, Dr Soares has led his party towards the right. There is mounting dissent within the SP about the party programme and the personal leadership of Soares.

"There have been many expulsions of those expressing their

discontent, and although the SP campaigned on a Socialist programme, its growing denunciations of nationalisation measures carried out by the MFA seem to indicate a readiness on the part of the SP to stand aside from attempts to construct a popular front and to indulge in the sort of inflammatory anti-communism that has given rise to violence in the North. . . .

"My own feeling is that the SP is now being used by the old ruling class to give it respectability and to thwart any real progress towards socialism."

The autumn of 1975 provided yet another opportunity to unite the Portuguese workers' movement against the reactionary offensive in the north and those who wished to extend it to the south. In the first few weeks of October the crisis had advanced further and the decomposition of the army appeared to be gathering speed. Sixteen out of twenty military units in Lisbon now had elected representatives who met regularly to discuss a common policy. Supplies of arms to reactionary troops from the Bairolas arsenal were blocked by left-wing soldiers. Strikes by steelworkers and agricultural workers supported the soldiers. If a civil war had been unleashed by the right at this stage it is obvious that Lisbon and the south would have fought with the left and the Socialist Party would have experienced a rift in its ranks if it had attempted to do otherwise. But the right did not launch a civil war for just that purpose. They were aware that if there was a straight left-right split, there would be massive pressure on the moderates in the MFA either to remain aloof or back the workers. As the Azveido government re-enlisted and re-armed the demobilised "élite troops" it also passed decrees calling on the workers' militias to disarm. An innocent observer in Lisbon in October could well have imagined that he/she was in a country on the verge of a semi-spontaneous seizure of power by a working class led by the far left and a rank-and-file soldiers' movement. The observer could be forgiven for dreaming, but far left groups aspiring to lead the Portuguese masses could not be taken too seriously for believing the same. Since the events which unfolded in November saw the far left at the centre of the stage in Lisbon it is useful to discuss the various groups to the left of the Communist Party.

A dominant feature of left-wing politics since May 1968 has been the emergence of a vanguard of workers and students who have either outgrown the political tutelage of the traditional social-democratic and Stalinist apparatuses within the European workers' movement or have never been attracted to them. It is this group on which the far left is based in Europe and North America. Portugal was no exception, but here the rapid pace at which the political crisis developed saw also the growth of the far left groups. The traditions to which they aligned themselves were Maoism, Trotskyism, syndicalism or, in some cases, a mixture of all three. The dominant characteristic of MES (Left Socialist Movement), the largest far left group, was its centrism: a constant vacillation between reformist and revolutionary positions. The MES was composed essentially of three different layers. Its origins were in radical Catholicism and its leadership was predominantly from this milieu. It had an important base among the textile and engineering workers and it had a fair sprinkling of Marxist intellectuals. While it participated in most local far left demonstrations there was a strong tendency on the part of the national leadership to adapt to the Communist Party, particularly during the period of the Fifth Provisional Government of Vasco Goncalves. The two far left groups which emerged from "armed struggle" against the Caetano régime were the LUAR, led by the legendary "bandit" Palma Ignacio and the Revolutionary Party of the Proletariat (Revolutionary Brigades) — PRP-BR. The latter produced a regular weekly paper, *Revolucao*. Its politics were a combination of populism and syndicalism and its strategic thrust was more often than not ultra-left. It had some working-class support in the south and inside COPCON. It also had illusions in the MFA and idolised Otelo Carvalho. It also for a while believed in building revolutionary unions, thus isolating itself from the mass of workers.

The Maoists were divided into four groups, the most influential amongst them being the Popular Democratic Union (UDP). It did not raise the slogan of workers' power but, like the PCP (which it denounced as "socialist-fascist") it raised "national democratic" demands. It had an important following within the working class. The other dominant group was the MRPP, which consisted largely of university students and the children of old Salazarist functionaries. Its demented political line led it to isolate the Portuguese Communist Party as the main internal enemy and the "Soviet social-imperialists" as the dominant external threat. As a result it participated in the anti-communist mobilisations of reaction in the north.

The smallest of the far left groups was the Trotskyist International Communist League (LCI). Its political line, especially, in relation to the masses, was the most refined and it was not, except for a limited period, afflicted with the disease which characterised the entire far left in Portugal: anti-parliamentary cretinism. But the LCI was small, with a weak foothold in the working class and therefore somewhat susceptible to being overwhelmed by the rest of the non-Maoist far left. It was in addition hampered by the lack of a regular weekly newspaper. As the Portuguese section of the Fourth International, it received support from its comrades elsewhere in the continent, but the failure of the latter to insist on the *political* necessity of a weekly revolutionary Marxist paper clearly adversely affected the enormous potential which the LCI possessed. The LCI understood the importance of elections to the Constituent Assembly, while the rest of the major groups tended to underestimate the importance of national politics. In 1931, Trotsky had sharply criticised the Soviet Communist Party newspaper *Pravda* for a similar blindness:

"By speaking *only* of the seven-hour day, of factory committees and arming the workers, by ignoring 'politics' and by not having a single word to say in all its articles about elections to the Cortes, *Pravda* goes all the way to meet anarcho-syndicalism, fosters it, covers up for it . . . To counter-pose the slogan of *arming the workers* to the reality of the political processes that grip the masses at their vitals means to isolate oneself from the masses — and the masses from arms."

(LT, "The Spanish Revolution and the dangers threatening it", *op cit*)

A similar error was made by the MES and the PRP(BR) in the important period opened up by the fall of the Goncalves government. The non-Maoist far left groups had certainly understood the need for unity, but they sought to unite the proletarian vanguard based in the south and not the masses. On August 25, 1975 the Revolutionary United Front (FUR) was introduced at a press conference. The significant feature of this Front was that it included the Portuguese Communist Party and a leftist branch of the Socialist Party, the FSP, in addition to the PRP,

126

MES, LUAR and the LCI. The main reason why the CP entered the Front was to use it to drum up some last-minute support for the faltering government of Vasco Goncalves. Indeed the weak political basis of the FUR was strongly criticised by the Secretariat of the Fourth International. It made five cogent points of criticism, which effectively summed up the weaknesses of the FUR:

(a) The accord in effect sanctioned the CP's policy of supporting the Government and maintaining the unity of the MFA, precisely at the moment that the MFA was being ripped apart by the pressure of antagonistic class forces.

(b) The accord mentioned no concrete objective that would permit the unification of the working class and the actual stimulation of workers' self-defence and self-organisation.

(c) Because of this absence, and because of the lack of proposals to the SP (a party that currently groups together nearly half of the proletariat), the accord sanctioned the present division of the workers' movement and did not contribute to surmounting this major obstacle to the development of the revolutionary process.

(d) Furthemore, the "unitary accord" envisaged the formation of a "front" in which the MFA is included on the same footing as the autonomous organs, parties, and revolutionary organisations of the workers' movement. This not only appeared as a stamp of approval of the CP's project of creating a "democratic and socialist popular front", but also fell within the framework of the perspective of integrating the autonomous organs in opposition to their real independence of the institutions of the bourgeois state.

(e) Thus, the accord could easily serve the objective of the CP (as it did during the August 27 demonstration), which is to utilise the weight of the workers' vanguard to negotiate compromises on the level of the state apparatus, the government, the army, and the MFA under the best possible conditions.

Now, the relationship of forces permitted revolutionaries to seize this opportunity to lead the CP to take a position on the implementation of the essential tasks necessary for the progress of the revolution. Here, again, the lack of concrete objectives and the concessions made to the CP's political orientation prevented the lessons of the policy of the CP leadership and the rupture of the "front" from being clearly drawn before the masses.

127

Once again the Portuguese far left, hypnotised by the situation in the army, ignored the crucial question of winning the masses. Lisbon and its enclaves were naturally of key importance, but they were not Portugal. The FUR was an organisation which reflected the chauvinism of the vanguard (the Portuguese Communist Party withdrew from it after a week of "unity") and an inability to construct a real united front, which was urgently needed. In the face of an offensive by capital, revolutionaries propose a united front of *all* workers' organisations, including the most moderate and those with right-wing, class-collaborationist leaders. The FUR's failure even to appreciate this problem was shown at one of its demonstrations where the main chant was: "Down with the Constituent Assembly".

October and November saw a growing opposition to the Sixth Government within the working class. Land occupations increased rapidly and 600,000 hectares were occupied in a month alone. Workers occupied the Ministry of Social Security in protest against the presence of a former PIDE official. On November 16 there was a demonstration of 100,000 workers. Coming on the heels of the victory of the construction workers the most popular slogans were those directed against Azveido and his government. The bakers were threatening to follow the construction workers if the Ministry of Labour did not meet their demands.

At the same time talks of *coups* and counter-*coups* dominated the press. Soares alleged that a left-wing *coup* was being prepared. The left-wing soldiers and SUV countered with similar charges of a right-wing *coup*. The PRP and the MES, excited by these developments, talked in terms of seizing power. There were still no proper representative organs of dual power. On November 8, the PRP made a public declaration on the question which was clearly preoccupying the minds of its leaders:

"The PRP defends armed insurrection . . . The objective conditions for a victorious armed rising exist today in Portugal. Knowing the devotion to the revolutionary process of a great many officers of the army and navy, and knowing also the positions which they hold at the level of unit commands, it is easy to think of a scheme based on a sortie by these troops, in an operation of the type of April 25."

128

This was, presumably, an elaboration of their statement of September 30 when they had stated that: "It is now time for the revolutionary forces and the workers to pose the question of an insurrection." The sentiments were repeated on November 10. Not only was this a fantasy, but it was supposed to be carried out by army and navy officers. The friends of the PRP in Britain, with whom the latter was in close touch, were the Socialist Workers' Party (then the International Socialists). Tony Cliff, the SWP's central theoretician, attempted to give some fraternal, though belated, advice to the PRP and warn them against premature insurrections. The advice was ignored. The internal régime of the PRP was, like its politics, commandist, and differences were not tolerated or encouraged.

Carvalho had refused to use COPCON against the construction workers. He had tolerated, and on occasions even encouraged, the fraternisation of soldiers and workers. He had made a number of pronouncements, some of them thoroughly confused, but nonetheless in favour of socialism. He was, and this is the important factor, seen by tens of thousands of workers and soldiers as the only coherent alternative to the Group of Nine. In reality his alternative in so far that it existed was extremely sentimental and subjectivist and his view of the revolutionary process was tinged with romanticism. Sometimes he sided with the far left (especially the PRP, which in its turn referred to him in glowing terms: "We underline the courage of this soldier, who is always ready to advance without fear," wrote *Revolucao* on May 8, 1975); on other occasions he flirted with the PCP; then again there were the constant attempts to reach an accommodation with Melo Antunes and the Group of Nine. It is possible that all these reflected a sincere desire to unite these differing forces against reaction, but it was a confused sincerity as it ignored the primacy of *politics*. Carvalho had been one of the central organisers of April 25, 1974. He had operated with Jacobin skill and succeeded, but he had not been able to move politically beyond that experience in any clearcut and cohesive fashion.

The Portuguese revolution was, in many ways, a combination of old, very old and new. The French Revolution was mingled with the Russian, though while there were Girondins and Jacobins and Mensheviks in plenty, the number of Bolsheviks (real, not imitation models) was small and not limited to a single

129

organisation. But there were also problems which had not faced the Bolsheviks: the stranglehold of bourgeois democracy in Western Europe and the contrast this offered to Stalinism in the East. This division had been emphasised by the right-Menshevik Soares:

"What divides us is not Marx or the construction of a classless society . . . what divides us is Stalin, the totalitarian concept of the state, the all-powerful single party, the rights of man (sic), and the problems of freedom. What divides us is not 'nationalisations' or 'agrarian reform' but how these are to be controlled — by a bureaucracy dependent on centralised power, or by the democratic control of the workers wherever it spontaneously emerges. What divides us is not the neighbourhood committee or other forms of direct democracy (these are included in our programme) but the question of their democratic representation . . ."

This is what the Portuguese Kerensky said, but he received no adequate response from the Stalinist Cunhal nor, it should be added, from the main far left groups.

Carvalho's reply was to declare that direct democracy and the MFA were "good" and political parties were "bad". Throughout the upsurge, Carvalho's actions were determined by the relationship of forces. If the workers' strikes were strong he would side with them. If Goncalves was weakening, then he would help to topple him. If the Group of Nine was gaining ground in the upper reaches of the MFA he would submit to their pressures. A good man? Yes. A well-meaning and brave man? Certainly! But a revolutionary leader of the masses? No, alas not. Like his most ardent admirers in Britain and France he could say, in the words of T. S. Eliot:

"No! I am not Prince Hamlet, nor was meant to be;
Am an attendant lord, one that will do
To swell a progress, start a scene or two,
Advise the prince; no doubt an easy tool,
Deferential, glad to be of use,
Politic, cautious, and meticulous;
Full of high sentence, but a bit obtuse;
At times, indeed, almost ridiculous —
Almost, at times, the Fool."

(*The Love Song of J. Alfred Prufrock*)

But none of this detracted from his popularity within the van-guard of Portuguese working class and the army. "Otelo is with us" was a common sentiment and within limits it was true, for though Carvalho was unable to provide any real leader-ship for taking the mass struggle forward, he was uncompro-misingly against any repression against the workers or the soldiers. In that sense his presence in the apparatus was of some importance and for that reason the basis of his popularity was not irrational.

While the PRP was the far left group most in favour of the armed insurrection, the other major grouping, MES, was not far behind them. In its weekly paper, *Poder Popular*, of November 5-11 the MES leaders gave their considered views of the political situation:

"The military, political and economic conditions exist for the development of a popular offensive. From the military point of view, the right does not possess the soldiers to carry out a *coup*; from the economic point of view, the rising cost of living, unemployment and the satisfaction of the most immediate needs are problems that cannot be resolved without a revolutionary régime; from the political point of view, illusions in bourgeois democracy, illusions in the reformists, are beginning to be clearly overcome and the workers finally understand that it will not be the politicians who will make the revolution in their name; only the masses through their organisation and their struggle will be able to make the socialist revolution triumph."

The same issue of the newspaper which contained this simplis-tic nonsense contained an even worse theoretical atrocity. After linking the Socialist Party of Soares to fascism the MES weekly went on to declare: ". . . consequently we cannot separate our slogan 'Death to the ELP (fascist "Portuguese Liberation Army") and those who support it' from the slogan 'Down With Social Democracy'. That, comrades, is why the MES says — and this is ever more correct and appears ever more clearly — that the Social Democracy is a phase in the transition to fascism." This delirious ultra leftism showed the far left at its weakest and most vulnerable, but it was only the strongest expression of a political line that had been in operation from the spring of 1975.

It was Carvalho's removal as the military commander of

131

Lisbon by the military High Command, now in the grip of the Group of Nine, that precipitated the crisis of November 25. This date marked the end of the most dynamic phase of the unfinished Portuguese revolution. Lourenco, the officer who replaced Carvalho, was reluctant to play the role. He changed his mind at least once, but was persuaded by his political mentors. The Army High Command, under the control of the moderates and the right, was determined to start a purge of leftist officers and soldiers from the army and navy. On November 23 Lourenco's appointment was confirmed. It was obvious that those opposed to the left were prepared for some sort of a reaction. Many leftist officers were convinced that a right-wing *coup* was being prepared. In any case given the general rhetoric of the far left and the provocations of the right, the paratroopers at Tancos (the latest converts to a radical solution in the country), revolted and occupied their base in solidarity with Carvalho. The right-wing officers had been gathering at the military base at Amadora from where they were preparing to quell any insurrections in favour of Carvalho. According to a statement from the latter on the November events, Eanes and Neves were expecting the Artillery Regiment (RALIS) and the COPCON units to protest on the streets, but were surprised by the Tancos reaction. The COPCON and RALIS remained disciplined and while they took some important positions in the city, they were not instructed to go on the offensive. The Amadora commandos led by Jaime Neves, numbering 800, moved into Lisbon and reoccupied the positions held by RALIS. A number of left-wing officers and activists were arrested, and the media under the control of the far left was retaken. It was a *political* rather than a military defeat. And it was a defeat for infantile and ultra-left political predictions and analysis. Many left-wing soldiers clearly believed the far left propaganda which proclaimed that most workers were ready for a seizure of power. The soldiers, acting alone, responded in the only way they knew: militarily. They were easily contained and a State of Emergency was declared. This premature action by the Tancos paratroopers provided the pretext for putting in operation a plan which Soares and the Group of Nine had long been preparing and which involved stabilising the army and the economy. Within twenty-four hours the moderates were in complete control. There was no general strike, no mass de-

132

monstration. No Lisbon Commune either and just as well. It would have been a short-lived and messy affair.

The quotation from Lenin at the head of this chapter retains all its validity. *Without the independent activity of the masses there can be no revolution.* That there was a developing pre-revolutionary mood in Portugal is undeniable, but for that to be transformed into a revolutionary situation needed the masses. Their radicalisation would have been decisive in aiding the decomposition within the army. The correct response to Carvalho's dismissal would have been to organise assemblies of his soldiers to discuss the issue. If they opposed it, as he maintains, and the army still insisted on replacing him, then a call for solidarity from the workers should have been made and a general strike organised. But even here the only force capable of calling a proper strike was the PCP and not the far left, despite illusions to the contrary. And for the PCP to call a general strike which would have involved a show of independent mass actions was almost inconceivable.

The Portuguese laboratory finally exploded on November 25, 1974. The wrong combination of ingredients was responsible for its sudden end. The only way in which the legitimacy of the Constituent Assembly (and the Soares leadership plus the Group of Nine) could have been challenged was through the emergence of centralised organs of dual power which organised the *masses.* These did not exist. What did exist were popular committees, which organised the most advanced sectors of the masses, but which were manipulated by the PCP and the far left.

The legitimacy of the Soares project would have been challenged immediately after the Constituent Assembly elections. Given the scope of the PSP's official programme the correct strategy would have been to take it at face value and demand its *implementation.* The PCP should have proposed that Soares become Prime Minister of a Provisional Government and Goncalves the Chief of Staff, after the April 1975 elections. The formation of a workers' government, committed to socialist policies, would have accelerated the mass radicalisation and enabled the formation of factory committees and popular committees to implement these policies. The character of these committees would have been strengthened when Soares renegued on his pledges or if reaction had unleashed an armed counter-revolutionary offensive. In that sense 1917 is not irrelevant when discussing Portugal in 1975. Kerensky was, for a period, defended by the Bolsheviks, who demanded the dismissal of the bourgeois ministers. The Constituent Assembly in Russia could only have been dispersed once the fully-fledged soviets had conquered power!

It is an interesting paradox that while the French Communist Party derailed the general strike of May 1968 by subordinating it to elections, the Portuguese Communist Party showed its contempt for the masses by attempting to bypass the much *more* democratic procedures for a Constituent Assembly in favour of bureaucratic manipulation of sections of a weakened state apparatus. In Portugal the Constituent Assembly was, for a period, a more accurate reflection of the overall relationship of forces than in Russia in 1917. It focussed the hopes of the majority of Portuguese after decades of fascism. It produced a constitution that claimed to be both democratic and socialist. A development like this could not be bypassed. The development of soviets would have to be geared into the contradictions present in the Constituent Assembly and the "unfinished" character of the upheaval that overthrew Caetano. The PCP was remarkably blind to this fact. Most of the far left was intoxicated with the scent of insurrection. A Marxist political strategy was to be developed with the benefit of hindsight.

November 25 marked the beginning of a new phase, but the governments which followed did not engage in large-scale denationalisations *à la* Pinochet, nor could they dismantle workers' control bodies in a number of industries. In the first four months of the next year nearly 400 factories went on strike against the austere new policies. What was ended was the situation in the army and on the estates, where a new law was passed prohibiting any further seizures. Bourgeois democracy was partially stabilised, despite the disappointment of many on the extreme right and the far left, and elections were organised in April 1976 for a legislative assembly. These produced a clear majority for all the workers' organisations: the SP, CP and far left received a combined vote of fifty-three per cent, thus expressing the overall relationship of social forces which November 25 was unable to destroy. The SP and the CP captured the south with large majorities (sixty per cent in Lisbon,

134

seventy-six per cent in Setubal, seventy-five per cent in Beja, seventy-three per cent in Evora) and the PPD and CDS captured the northern provinces (sixty-one per cent in Braganca, fifty-three per cent in Braga, sixty-three per cent in Viseu, fifty-seven per cent in V Real), thus demonstrating the inability of the SP and CP to win over the peasants. However Soares formed a minority government and refused to ally himself with either the PCP or the PPD. In December 1977 he was brought down by a *bloc* of the PCP and the right on the question of his readiness to accept all the conditions of the International Monetary Fund before it bailed out the ailing capitalist economy. November 25 represented a severe setback, but not a defeat for the masses. To recover all the lost ground it will be necessary to assimilate all the lessons of the Portugal experience and incorporate them in a revolutionary strategy which can win over the masses. The revolutionary left failed the test in Portugal. Whether it can meet the challenge likely to be thrown up in France and Spain will depend on its willingness to learn from its errors in Portugal.

Appendix 1

The SUV Manifesto

1. The SUV (Soldiers United Will Win) is a united anti-capitalist and anti-imperialist front that arises at a time when fascist reaction is organising again, making use of the hesitations and divisions introduced among the workers as well as the policies of governments that are neither willing nor able to defend the just demands raised in the struggles of the workers and peasants, of whom we, soldiers, are a part.
2. Already on several occasions we have made concessions to the bourgeoisie, particularly by subordinating our struggle to the alliance with the MFA (Armed Forces Movement), a movement of officers which, because of its contradictions and hesitations in the past, serves a counter revolutionary policy today. This has cost us not only the abandonment and hostility of important layers of the population (notably among our peasant brothers) but also the demoralisation of many fighters in our

own ranks and has resulted in sluggishness in face of the reactionary offensive inside and outside the barracks.

The SUV sets itself the task of unleashing an independent offensive on a class basis:

— To struggle for a democratic life in the barracks by imposing the election and democratic functioning of the ADUs (Assemblies of Unit Delegates), the free circulation of the workers' and people's press and propaganda, and the holding of general assemblies of soldiers each time that we call for them;

— To struggle for the formation of soldiers' commissions.

— organs of power of the workers in uniform in the barracks — elected and recallable at any time by general assemblies of soldiers;

— To stimulate and deepen the liaison with organs of popular power (workers' commissions, village councils, tenants' commissions) strengthening the power of the exploited through Popular Assemblies.

— For the expulsion of reactionary officers;

— Against all attempts to purge progressive military men;

— For the improvement of the living conditions of the soldiers (against the poor pay, for free transport, for common quarters and mess halls, against militarist discipline).

3. The SUV struggles with all the workers for the preparation of conditions that will permit the destruction of the bourgeois army and the creation of the armed forces of the workers' power: the revolutionary people's army.

ALWAYS, ALWAYS AT THE SIDES OF THE PEOPLE; THAT IS OUR WATCHWORD!

WORKERS, PEASANTS, SOLDIERS, AND SAILORS, UNITED WE WILL WIN!

Appendix 2

SUV Appeal to Workers and Soldiers of Europe

We Portuguese proletarians are now going through some particularly difficult moments in our revolutionary struggle against the bourgeoisie, capitalism, and imperialism.

A year and a half after the fall of the fascist dictatorship, capitalist reaction is redoubling its attacks in the factories, the fields, the neighbourhoods, and the barracks, utilising either insidious demagogy or open terrorist violence, but always with the same goal: to stop the progress of the alliance of workers, peasants, soldiers and sailors, an alliance leading to the establishment of workers' power; to prevent at any price the abolition of the class privileges it has won through exploitation and oppression; to prevent its disappearance as a ruling class.

The bourgeoisie and the capitalists still have powerful weapons; two of these are especially threatening, unless we are able to fight back in time. The first is our disunity, our inability to push our independent offensive through to the end on a real class basis. On many occasions we have made this concession to the class enemy, notably by subordinating our struggle to the alliance with the MFA (Armed Forces Movement), a movement of officers whose contradictions and hesitations have cost us the abandonment and hostility of important layers of the population (especially the rural population), the demoralisation of many fighters in our own ranks, and sluggishness in face of the reactionary offensive inside and outside the barracks.

We have to be able to counter this danger with our own class organisation by breaking down the militarist hierarchy and raising an overall challenge to the power of the state apparatus of the bourgeoisie, of which the army is an integral part. The creation of the SUV and the demonstration the SUV organised on September 10 represent important steps in this direction, especially when it is recalled that this formidable response of 50,000 workers (among them 1500 soldiers and sailors who marched in uniform in spite of the escalation of militarist manoeuvres and repression) took place in a region that has been the centre of the terrorist offensive and of reactionary demagogy.

The second powerful weapon in the hands of our class enemies is undoubtedly the broad international support from which it benefits. That is the result of the common interests that link the exploiters throughout the world. Recent history shows us how powerful and terrible this weapon is, this counter-revolutionary potential of imperialism. It is up to us, proletarians of Europe, to determine the forms of battle, which can be waged only through our class solidarity, through the organisation of our national struggles into a single international

137

battle to make sure that any attack by imperialism receives the response it deserves: the indestructible force of the entire international workers' and people's movement.

Today it is Portugal. Tomorrow it will be Spain, France, Italy, and others. Difficult battles are approaching. Against the common enemy our common solidarity is urgent and necessary; it is for this that we address you.

LONG LIVE MILITANT AND COMBATIVE PROLETARIAN INTERNATIONALISM!

PORTUGAL SHALL NOT BE THE CHILE OF EUROPE!

WORKERS, PEASANTS, SOLDIERS, AND SAILORS, UNITED WE WILL WIN!

Soldados Unidos Vencerâo (Soldiers United Will Win) September 12, 1975.

6. The Critical Condition of British Socialism

"What political lessons have you learnt from the occupation?"

"All the socialist press have been asking that question. The left-wing movement felt that we were politically motivated, but if they talk to the lads they find they are not. The only political motive is the feeling that this government has to go whether it's over the Common Market or unemployment or the Industrial Relations Bill — it must be brought down. Its policies are totally against the working class. But the majority of the men don't like politics. Just look at that Union Jack out there. Someone brought in a Red Flag and about fifty said they would walk out if we put that up. It's their upbringing through the *Express* and the *Record* that men get frightened of Communism and nationalisation and things like that — of the words I mean. They are doing what the socialists say, but they don't want to be politically involved."

Jack Gray, Convenor of occupied Plessey factory in Scotland interviewed in *The Red Mole,* October 20, 1971

An important feature of recent British politics has been that the Labour Party has held office for much longer than the Conservative and Unionist Party, which was considered until recently the "traditional ruling party". All the repercussions of this development have still to be felt. The next General Election will have been crucially important in determining whether a new pattern has been established — in which case it could have important effects within the Labour movement as a whole — or whether the last two Labour governments merely represented the transition to a startling transformation of the British political map.

The 1968-74 period was an extremely important one for both

139

British workers and capitalists. It revealed the strengths and weaknesses of both social classes and the lessons of that period are only now beginning to be understood and assimilated by sections of the British left. The struggles which characterised the period began with the last year of Wilson's second Labour administration in 1969 and ended with the fall of Heath in 1974. In five years the British working class showed its capacity for unleashing struggles on a scale which had not been witnessed in Britain since the twenties — struggles which had their own specific character and limitations. There was no British May 1968: one reason for this lies in the fact that Marxism as a mass political current has never existed in Britain. Working-class politics has been the preserve of a bourgeois social-democratic workers' party, the Labour Party, whose ideology — Labourism — has rigidly separated political struggles (confined to parliament) from economic struggles (confined to factories). This party, resting for its support on a politically undivided trade union movement, has constituted, together with the bureaucratic caste which dominates the latter, an extremely important pillar of the British system of bourgeois-democracy.

Before developing this theme further, we shall illustrate it by briefly recounting the developments of 1968-74 and their overall impact. It will then become easier to understand the central weaknesses of all sections of the British left, ranging from the left wing of the Labour Party and the Communist Party down to the organisations of the revolutionary left.

The Labour Government elected in 1966 had won an impressive majority in the House of Commons. It had received the second largest popular vote in its entire history and had won 363 seats, only thirty less than in 1945, so it had a "safe" majority. The question arose: "safe" to do what? The Labour left had argued in 1964-66 that radical reforms were hampered by the small size of the Labour majority. They had pleaded with party activists that the "boat should not be rocked" until Labour had a larger majority. They unscrupulously used the bogey of a Tory return. In the event, Labour's 1966 victory resulted in reinforcing Wilson's set of policies which were cynically described by the *Financial Times* as "bombing the communists in Vietnam, bashing the trades unions and keeping the blacks out of Britain". There was no concerted left opposition to these policies within the parliamentary party. The decision

140

of the Labour Government to enforce an incomes policy had been accepted, with protests, by the trade unions. It was only when Labour attempted to institutionalise the situation and permanently weaken the trade unions by putting legislation on the statute book that the unions protested. Barbara Castle's proposals on the matter were embodied in a White Paper entitled *In Place of Strife*.

Action against the document initially emerged from below. In February 1969 the Liaison Committee for the Defence of Trades Unions (LCDTU), in which the Communist Party was a dominant force, organised a strike involving 150,000 workers. A few months later, the LCDTU called out 250,000 workers in protest against the Labour government. At the same time the TUC leaders, sensing the mood of the rank and file, made it clear to the Labour government that they would resist the bill. A number of leaders warned Labour ministers that unless the White Paper was withdrawn there was the possibility of a national strike. TUC opposition split the Labour Cabinet. Within that body James Callaghan led a group of ministers to oppose the Wilson-Castle plan. Mounting opposition within the mainstream of the Labour movement left Wilson with no option but to suffer a humiliating defeat: the White Paper was withdrawn. Soon after wage controls were relaxed and substantial increases were won by large sections of workers. The opinion polls showed a resurgence of popularity for Labour. Wilson foolishly announced a snap election, only to discover that the Tories were back in office on the strength of Labour abstentions. Labourism's political formulas had proved bankrupt as far as its traditional social base was concerned. The year before the election had been a dress rehearsal: it had shown the inability of Labour to integrate the working class and tie it to the bourgeois state. How else could the capitulation of *In Place of Strife* be explained? At the same time it had paved the way for a strong Tory government committed to "taming the unions".

On Thursday, June 18, 1970, a Conservative government under Edward Heath took office. Its main obsession was to take Britain into the Common Market. Heath had understood that the key to the European Community lay in Paris and it would need a shift in Britain's post-war subservience to the Atlantic alliance: a posture which now would have to be altered to make way for a new balance of forces on an international scale. At a series of lectures given at Harvard University in 1967, Heath had spelled out his ideas on the question in the following way:

"On the Twelfth of December 1826 George Canning, then Her Majesty's principal Secretary of State for Foreign Affairs, spoke these memorable words in the House of Commons: 'I called the New World into existence to redress the balance of the Old.' He was defending the support England had given to the people of South America rebelling against the authority of a Spanish Empire that had itself come under the domination of France. Now, just over 140 years later, my theme reverses the old proposition. It is that the Old World must be brought together to redress the balance of the New, that we must try to create a wider unity between the ancient nation states of Europe, of which Britain must be a part, so that together we can provide the basis for a better balance with our friends and allies on this side of the Atlantic."

In the same set of lectures Heath also mentioned the possibility of a European defence force which included nuclear weapons under the joint trusteeship of the British and French states. Here he was clearly reflecting both the pressure of Gaullism and a way of avenging the lost honour of the Tory Party. For the Suez adventure had been a débâcle mainly because the United States had rapped both Britain and France on the knuckles and withdrawn support. Heath had been a firm supporter of Anthony Eden and he must have felt some pain at the fact that the French learned different lessons from the episode than the British. While the latter gracefully accepted Britain's subservient international status and became loyal camp followers of the State Department, their French collaborators decided that it was necessary to build European strength in order to preserve a relative independence from the United States. Thus the Common Market for Heath was also an occasion to settle old scores.

His obsession with entering the European Community and his personal knowledge of what that would entail was not matched by an understanding of the British trade union movement. It was not without reason that Cecil King wrote in his diaries after learning of the appointments to Heath's cabinet that they "have filled me with alarm and despondency. The membership suggests that Heath is mainly concerned (a) with entering the Common Market and (b) with containing Powell. But his most important and immediate problem is labour relations and the trades unions." It was the only perceptive entry in an otherwise banal diary — an incidental indication of the growing intellectual decline of the British ruling classes.

On the domestic front Heath thought that a simple repetition of the ruling-class strategy of the late twenties and thirties would be sufficient to stem the tide. In those two turbulent decades of this century the British ruling classes and their chosen political instruments had arrested the decline of British capitalism by an aggressive frontal assault on the British working class. Churchill regarded the 1926 general strike — unlike the generals who were leading the strike — as a war which had to be won. He was an exceptionally ruthless bourgeois politician who excelled in periods of turmoil. On the heels of the defeated strike, the Labour Party was split with the defection of Ramsay Macdonald and under a peacetime national government the working class was further attacked through mass unemployment. The result was a massive decline in living standards and an increase in the rate of profit. Heath, as a Tory leader not impervious to historical experience, clearly felt that the British workers' movement had to be dealt with in a similar way for the decline in the rate of profit to be reversed. He embarked on a strategy of frontal confrontations. What he had forgotten was that the British workers' movement, in terms of its position in the economy, its level of trade unionisation and overall confidence was stronger than it had ever been. A new generation of workers had grown up since the war. They had not experienced the defeats of the pre-war decades and their consciousness was not marled with the traumas which had inflicted their parents and grandparents. This was the new breed confronting a Tory government bent upon war.

Within its first twelve months of office the Conservative government carried out a massive escalation in the class war. They cut off credit to the Upper Clyde Shipbuilders (UCS), a firm which had been formed under the aegis of the Labour government, the result of an amalgamation of several smaller yards with subsidies from the State. Most commentators agreed that it had the potential of being profitable by 1971, but in the

October of the preceding year, John Davies, the Tory Minister for Trade and Industry, cut off its credits, raising the spectre of mass unemployment in a region where the dole queues were already far too long. The Scottish workers were now confronted by the collective historical memory of their class: the images of the thirties, stories they had heard from their past now seemed a contemporary reality. They occupied the shipyards, began to run them under the control of the shop stewards, and used the occupation to mount an offensive against unemployment. A wave of other factory occupations soon followed, including the one at Plessey. It was a new tactic for British workers and it won support from the local population. Its weakness was that those who led it decided consciously to restrict it to the factories in question. There were no serious efforts made to coordinate the occupations nor to take them beyond the factories and into the neighbourhoods. The main concern of the shop stewards of UCS, for instance, was to show that they were "reasonable", "moderate" men of goodwill, who merely wanted to save jobs. That was tactically correct, but on its own not sufficient to defeat unemployment. Of course, as the interviewer with the Plessey convenor quoted at the beginning of this chapter indicates, the shop stewards in many cases were in advance of the mass of workers. The point was that as the struggle continued many workers were assimilating politics through their own experiences. It was at this stage that an attempt to broaden the struggle beyond populist and Labour demands *could* have had a wider impact, had it been attempted. The result of the occupations were mixed and, in most cases, they succeeded only in delaying and reducing rather than preventing redundancies.

At the same time the Heath government had succeeded in defeating the postal workers' strike. The postal workers' union was a weak union, which had never had a national strike. It had not participated in the 1926 General Strike and it had only recently established a strike fund. It had refused to lend support to a strike by post office engineers and the latter now continued to operate the telephone system, effectively sabotaging the strike. Furthermore, the UPW leadership made a virtue out of its isolation and refusal to appeal for broad support. While well over ninety per cent of its members wanted to strike the union leaders decided after eight weeks to go back to work.

144

Heath regarded this as a major victory in his offensive against the unions. The latter, for their part, also saw it as such and a widespread resentment spread amongst ordinary, rank and file trades unionists.

As part of his overall project for defeating the unions, Heath had approved the draft of an Industrial Relations Act, which seriously affected the powers of trades unions and made them accountable to courts: the National Industrial Relations Court was to be set up specifically to adjudicate over trade union disputes. Twenty months elapsed before this Act became law. In the House of Commons it was opposed by Labour, while outside trades unionists began to mobilise support against the Tories. A massive demonstration of 150,000 trades unionists marched against the Act in February 1971 from Hyde Park to Trafalgar Square under the slogan of "Kill The Bill", though more radical chants in favour of a General Strike to bring down the Tories also excited a certain response. At the meeting in Trafalgar Square the TUC leaders pledged not to rest until the Bill was defeated. Of special interest was the fact that no leader of the Labour Party was represented on the platform. The wounds of *In Place of Strife* were too recent to be forgotten. The feeling amongst the organised sections of the working class was that they owed this government nothing. More importantly, it was a Tory government and therefore the struggle to prevent a decline in their living standards took precedence over all else. But despite growing anti-Tory sentiments the working class failed to unite to defend either the postal workers in 1971, nor the power workers in the same year, and the UCS battle, too, was essentially lost. Towards the end of 1971 the Engineering Union accepted defeat on its national claim and the General and Municipal Workers' Union accepted the government's pay norm. By the end of 1971, the Heath Cabinet was jubilant. It had been relatively successful in containing the trade unions. Cecil King recorded on December 16, 1971: "We attended a carol party at No 10 last night. Ted exuded optimism."

It had reckoned without the National Union of Mineworkers, which now submitted a large pay claim. It was duly rejected and the miners went on strike during the second week of January 1972.

The miners represent the conscience of the British working

class. The last national miners' strike had been in 1926. They had fought alone after the TUC decision to call off the General Strike. They had been humiliated and defeated by a triumphant and vindictive ruling class. The memory of the beleaguered miners resisting until the tragic finale had haunted the British workers' movement ever since. Furthermore, the mining communities were very different from ordinary council estates in the industrial towns of England, Scotland and Wales. The unity and cohesion of these communities is well-known. It was only natural that in a strike the miners received massive support from their families. The ability of the national press to divide the strikers from their families was severely restricted. Over the preceding fourteen years the closing down of mines and other "rationalisations" had resulted in over half a million miners being made redundant. While their *per capita* productivity had risen by eighty per cent over the last decade inflation had resulted in a decline in real wages. At the same time the Coal Board chief, Lord Robens (a former Labour supporter) and Will Paynter, a Communist Party miners' leader, had collaborated to prevent all unofficial strikes. In his memoirs, *Ten Year Stint,* Robens acknowledges the sterling role of Paynter in helping to "eliminate strikes" in the coal industry. This was achieved by eliminating piece-rates and insisting on a national rate. Ironically, it was this measure, designed largely to end the possibility of local miners' strikes, which also provided the objective basis for uniting the miners on a national level.* In 1969 the Yorkshire miners broke the pattern and organised a strike for an eight-hour day. Lord Robens resisted their demands and attempted to isolate the miners. They received no official support, no strike pay, no solidarity from the Labour Party. The strike was ended by the leaders of the Yorkshire miners only after they obtained an assurance than an eight-hour day would be conceded for surface workers. The very fact that the miners were having to fight for an eight-hour day in *1969* is a revealing commentary on the method whereby nationalised industries have been administered under Labour and Tories alike in post-war Britain. The

*In 1977-78, the Labour government of James Callaghan and the majority of the NUM executive realised the problems that had been caused and reverted to a system of local "incentive schemes", once again dividing the miners.

146

result of the 1969 dispute was the emergence of a massive grassroots pressure to change the rules of the Union. Previously a 66⅔ per cent majority was necessary for a strike. By 1971 the rules had been altered, permitting national strike action by the NUM with a fifty-five per cent majority. In the same year most of the miners voted for industrial action, and, beginning with an overtime ban, the NUM escalated the action into a national strike.

But Heath was not alone in "exuding optimism". Even sober and intelligent ruling-class newspapers, such as the *Financial Times,* hypnotised by Heath's successes, were unable to perceive the dangers that lay ahead. On January 7, 1972 the *Financial Times* light-heartedly commented: "It is extremely difficult to see what the miners hope to gain out of the national strike they are bent on starting this weekend."

The miners suffered no such doubts. They were fighting a struggle to earn a decent wage for an extremely taxing job and cruel working conditions. They were not prepared to accept the Tory wage freeze. As the strike continued, the miners began to find increasing support from the general public as well as the organised core of the trades union movement. They launched a new tactic: the miners flying picket left the mining towns and went to the industrial centres to picket the coke depots. The Government declared a State of Emergency and introduced power cuts. Heath still hoped that the miners could be defeated; Maudling proposed the use of troops — a measure rejected by the Tory Cabinet because of its likely counter-productive impact. The battle over picketing centred round a coke depot — one of the largest in the country — in the Saltley district of Birmingham. There had been a battle between the police and the miners, and the miners did not succeed in closing the gates of the Saltley depot despite the size of their picket (4000). The miners' leader in charge of operations was the tough and uncompromising Yorkshireman, Arthur Scargill. It was his initiative, backed by the miners, to appeal to the rank-and-file trades unionists of Birmingham that proved to be decisive. Scargill appealed to the Birmingham Trades Council for support to close the Saltley gates, which had now come to symbolise the nationwide strike. The Trades Council, including its moderates, responded favourably. More important, the District Committee of the Engineering Union decided to

147

call their members out on strike to strengthen the picket. Other unions soon followed suit.

On February 10, 1972 the city of Birmingham witnessed a massive display of working-class solidarity. Arthur Scargill described it three years later in a remarkably frank interview with *New Left Review*:

"The time was about ten o'clock and there was a hush over the Saltley area. 3000 miners altogether, Welsh miners singing, Yorkshire miners, Nottinghamshire miners, Midlands miners. And yet nothing happened. You could see apprehension on the faces of the police. Here we had a situation where miners were tired, physically and mentally, desperately weary. They had gone through nearly six weeks' strike action, they had gone through a three months' overtime ban, they had gone through the worst battling encountered in strike action in any time in recent years. Their comrades had been arrested, one of them had been kicked to bits and yet they were still battling on. I readily concede that some of the lads were feeling the effects and were a bit dispirited that no reinforcements were coming. And then over this hill came a banner and I've never seen in my life as many people following a banner.

"As far as the eye could see it was just a mass of people marching towards Saltley. There was a huge roar and from the other side of the hill they were coming the other way. They were coming from five directions, there were five approaches to Saltley; it was in a hollow, they were arriving from every direction. And our lads were just jumping in the air with emotion — a fantastic situation.

"I heard the police talking — Sir Derek Capper was one, Donaldson his deputy — the tactic was simple: get the pickets coming from the east to go through to the west and get the pickets from the west — the striking engineers — to go through to the east. East to west, west to east, past each other. I got this megaphone and I'm yelling like hell: 'When you get to the picket line, Stop! Stop!!' They were trying to tell me to shut up and I said: 'You try today, no bloody shutting up today. These boys are coming to our picket line.' And they were piling up like sandwich cake, as far as the eye could see they were just pouring in. Saltley, the area of Saltley, was now just a mass of human beings, arriving from all over, with banners. The only time this crowd opened was when a delegation of girls from a women's factory came along all dressed in bright white dresses. They plunged through and one of the lads shouts:

148

'Go on officer, tell them they can't come. Try and hold them.' And no police officer moved, you know. Who'd have dared to try and stop those girls coming into that square? Nobody. The crowd was absolutely dense by this time. We were in the centre of it and everybody was chanting something different; some were chanting 'Heath Out', 'Tories Out', 'Support the Miners', 'General Strike', a hundred slogans were being chanted. I got hold of the megaphone and I started to chant through it: 'Close the Gates! Close the Gates!' and it was taken up, just like a football crowd. It was booming through Saltley: 'Close the Gates'. It reverberated right across this hollow and each time they shouted this slogan they moved and the police, who were four deep, couldn't help it, they were getting moved in. And Capper, the Chief Constable of Birmingham, took a swift decision. He said 'Close the Gates' and they swung them to. Hats were in the air, you've never seen anything like it in your life. Absolute delirium on the part of the people who were there. Because the Birmingham working class had become involved — not as observers but as participants. The whole of the East District of the Birmingham AUEW were out on strike, 100,000 were out on strike, you know. It was tremendous. And they were still marching in from Coventry and other places, still advancing into Saltley. It was estimated that there were 20,000 in this area. Maudling, who said that the gates wouldn't close, suddenly found that they were bloody closed and locked. The Chief Constable said: 'That's it. I'm not risking any more here, those gates stay closed.' He then turned to me — this is absolutely factual — and said: 'Will you please do us a favour? Will you please disperse the crowd?' And I said on two conditions: firstly that I can make a speech to the crowd. He said, 'Agreed.' And secondly that I can use your equipment, because mine's knackered. He said: 'Agreed.' Then I spoke from the urinal in Birmingham, with this police equipment. I gave a political speech to that mass of people and told them that it was the greatest victory of the working class, certainly in my lifetime. The lads who were there were overcome with emotion, emotion in the best possible way. Here had been displayed all that's good in the working-class movement. Here had been displayed what for years had been on a banner but had never been transferred from the banner into reality. You know the words: 'Unity is Strength'; 'Workers of the World Unite', 'Man to Man Brother Be'. They're big words. Sometimes they'd been ridiculed. Through all that ridicule, all that sneering, they survived. Here was the living proof that the working class had only to flex its muscles and it could bring governments, employers, society to a total standstill. I know the fear of Birmingham on the part of the ruling class. The fear was that what happened in Birmingham could happen in every city in Britain. Had that occurred in every city in Britain — and what happened later in Sheffield showed that it could — that would have produced a whole new concept in what was after all a wage battle as far as the miners were concerned. I reckon when the ins and outs are written about Saltley, the telephone-calls, the intrigues, the manoeuvres on the part of the right, the plans of the Tories, the decisions taken in Birmingham, it will make a most remarkable book."

The fact that Arthur Scargill could retain and express the excitement of the occasion two years after it had occurred gives one an idea of what was considered to be at stake in those days. The Saltley gates were closed and that victory determined the fate of the strike. The British ruling class always likes to portray a defeat in terms of a concession it willingly made after due consideration. A Court of Enquiry under the stewardship of Lord Wilberforce was duly set up. They began deliberations on a Sunday, studied the details of the strike on Monday, heard evidence on Tuesday and Wednesday, dictated their report on Thursday and it appeared in print on Friday! He awarded them twenty per cent. Much to his surprise the NUM executive rejected the offer by one vote. Further concessions were offered and finally accepted by the miners. Heath had offered seven per cent at the beginning; at the conclusion of the strike the miners won an award which added up to nearly thirty per cent. As the *Financial Times* gloomily remarked:

"It will be some time before we shall be able to assess even the direct costs of the coal strike to the country. . . . But this immediate cost pales to insignificance compared to the potential long-term damage done not merely to the economy, but to the country as such. Most important in this context is that the authority of Government has been damaged. . . . In war — and that is what the miners' dispute turned out to be — the active support of the community as a whole is essential. The Government failed to obtain it. That is why it lost."

Almost to the day the miners' strike was permanently called off, the controversial Industrial Relations Bill became the Industrial Relations Act. The first blow against it was administered by the non-militant National Union of Railwaymen. They organised a national ballot under the terms of the act before any strike action. The railway unions wanted a fourteen per cent wage rise. The most they were offered, after arbitration, was twelve and a half per cent. The result of the ballot was a six to one verdict against the government. British Rail settled without a strike.

The second use of the IR Act was even more disastrous. It was used against the dockers who were picketing a container depot against fellow workers. The latter took the dockers to the NIRC, which summoned the dockers to appear before it. They refused and were supported by 55,000 other dockers who now went on strike. The dockers said on television that they would continue to defy the law. The NIRC retreated on the grounds that there was *not* enough evidence to prove that they were picketing: it was an extremely lame excuse for retreating. Heath appealed to the House of Lords, but in the six weeks which elapsed before the Law Lords could give a ruling the crisis escalated further. A firm named Midland Cold Storage (painted by Heath as a small enterprise threatened by trade union power, but in reality owned by the giant meat company, Vesteys), was using cheap, non-dock labour and enticing work from the dockland storage centres. The dockers who were picketing it and persuading lorry drivers to black the outfit were taken to court. The dockers refused to obey the NIRC and they were imprisoned. Reginald Maudling had been sacked for opposing Heath and arguing for a consensus policy in a letter to *The Times*. The pretext for his sacking was real enough: Maudling's links with financial scandals had been the talk of Fleet Street for some time. The satirical magazine *Private Eye* had waged an effective campaign against the Tory deputy leader and discredited him thoroughly. Heath's problems were far from over. He now discovered that the Government could not manipulate the IR Act at will. It had a force of its own and employers were not over-sensitive to the political problems facing the Tory government. Heath found himself, as during the miners' strike, a prisoner of events. The jailed dockers began to receive mass support. Unofficial strikes began to shut down factories in London as workers marched to Pentonville prison to demonstrate their support

151

for their comrades. Ruling-class opinion was shocked by Heath's inability to control the situation. Their early admiration for the ruthless determination of the Tory leader to deal with the unions had begun to turn sour. Characteristically it was *The Times* that hurled the first dagger. In an editorial on July 22, 1972 — in the middle of the fiercest class struggle since the twenties — it openly speculated whether or not a replacement could be found for Heath within the existing ranks of the Tory Party. Its opinion of Heath was severe:

"The Prime Minister is a remote and unintelligible figure to the great majority of the public, to many of his colleagues in Parliament and no doubt to even some of his colleagues in the Cabinet. He takes discussion for criticism, criticism for disloyalty and disloyalty for high treason. In his administration he has lost able men through misfortune and gained mediocrities through choice."

But Heath stayed on and within the next week the strike movement in support of the dockers grew. What was clearly developing was a general strike. In order to capture this discontent the TUC leaders threatened a *one-day* general strike to gain the release of the dockers. In the meantime the Law Lords ruled that the Transport Union — not the five dockers — should pay the fine. An antiquated legal figure, the "Official Solicitor", stepped into the fray and organised the release of the five dockers, who were carried back to the docks on the shoulders of their comrades. The workers had won yet another victory. If the miners had destroyed the incomes policy the dockers now made the IR Act virtually ineffective. Heath embarked on a set of negotiations with the TUC leaders and the Confederation of British Industry. The talks collapsed as the unions were not prepared to accept the deal offered by Heath in return for a wage freeze. Heath unilaterally imposed a wage freeze and established a set of guidelines and restraints as far as wage agreements were concerned. He had argued during the elections that the Tories would abandon restrictions on prices and incomes. The Government had attempted to do this by shackling the unions via the IR Act. Once this exploded they were back to square one, and prices and incomes machinery was once again set into motion.

Once again the Tory government's insistence on having a rigid set of pay policies brought it into conflict with the miners. The left-wing leaders of the NUM are convinced that the confrontation was unnecessary as their case was a powerful one, but that Heath was determined to "teach the miners a lesson" and was keen on a confrontation to settle accounts with an old adversary. Towards the end of 1973 negotiations had broken down and the miners were considering strike action. By February 1974 the strike was in full swing. The power stations had been well prepared for this eventuality, but the miners' pickets succeeded in crippling a complex of steel works throughout the country. Other unions refused to cross the miners' picket line, except on rare occasions, and the Anchor steel works in Scunthorpe and the roller steel plants in Sheffield were on the verge of complete standstill. A plan to import coal from Europe was sabotaged by dockers who refused to handle the contraband coal. Once again the Conservative Cabinet was confronted with a severe dilemma. This time they decided to call a snap General Election. What was at stake was the right of workers to defend their standards of living by withdrawing their labour. The Labour leaders avoided the miners' strike during the election. They sent their supporters into battle with both hands tied behind their backs. In the midst of an unprecedented class confrontation in post-war British history, Labour fought a traditional electoral campaign. The only way Labour could have won a convincing victory would have been to make the miners' strike the crux of their campaign. But such an approach was quite alien to Labour's whole electoralist and reformist conception of politics. It preferred the tried and tested ground of cringing class collaboration. The miners refused to call off their strike despite the election call — in sharp contrast, incidentally, to the French workers in May-June 1968 — and at one stage Mick McGahey, the Communist miners' leader, stated that the miners were out to bring down the Tory government. Even though McGahey later denied these remarks, under the pressure of a witch-hunt in the media, they were perfectly true. What is more to the point the miners *did* defeat Heath. That he was replaced by Wilson was a fact of political life, though Labour received its lowest popular electoral vote since 1935: 11,654,726 in contrast to the Tories' 11,963,207. Labour emerged as the

153

largest single party and formed a weak government dependent on the tacit support of the Liberals and the nationalists.

The strategic project embodied by the Heath government remains vitally important for the British State. The fact that it had to be modified in the face of a working-class offensive does not, in any way, detract from its importance.

Heath was very aware of the inadequacy of the political leadership of the British ruling class after the Second World War. He suggested a break with the fundamental beliefs of his predecessors and argued that such a reorientation was essential to get to grips with the developing social and economic crises. The only serious Marxist analysis of the Heath government appeared in an article by Robin Blackburn in *New Left Review* (November 1971) entitled: "The Heath Government: A New Course for British Capitalism". The central thesis of the Blackburn text was that Heath would use the *political* strength of the ruling class to defeat the *economic* strength of the working class. In other words, the political weaknesses of the British workers' movement would prevent them from launching an effective counter-offensive although Heath's provocations could well result in a sharp radicalisation amongst a minority of workers thereby increasing the influence of revolutionaries in industry. Blackburn aptly summarised Heath's intentions when he wrote: "In formulating a strategy for restoring the fortunes of British capitalism, he intends to jettison the backwardness of British bourgeois politics — its sentimentalism about old friends and customs — and to exploit the backwardness of the British working class — its parliamentarism and economism."

However, what he underestimated was that the politics of the British Labour movement, embodied in the weak and flabby formulas of Labourism, were nonetheless extremely resistant to Toryism and a Tory Party on the offensive. In other words the Tories are regarded as the traditional political enemy by the organised sections of the working class. Their undoubted addiction to parliamentarism presents no insoluble contradiction, for the political focus in anti-Tory struggle has hitherto been the return of a Labour Government, even if it is led by a Wilson or a Callaghan. Thus it would be inaccurate to say that the wave of struggles which shook Britain in the period when Heath was in office had no political aim. This may not have been expressed in an explicit fashion, but it was there, lurking in the background of every major confrontation. Certainly there was a developing mood that Heath might have to be brought down by a generalised strike, but only to return Labour to power so that it could repeal the hated Industrial Relations Act. This was the main goal of the mass of trades unionists in the period.

Heath underestimated both the economic strength of the unions and their political opposition to Toryism, particularly the new aggressive brand, which was resulting in high unemployment and which dispensed with the consensus formulas of preceding governments. This fact did not go unnoticed in the upper echelons of the Conservative Party. During the 1971 Conservative Party Conference an anonymous senior Tory wrote an article for *The Times* entitled "A Warning to Tory Gravediggers". The article advised the government not to forget that "the memories of the older working generation and their children, who may not have experienced privations themselves as adults, but can well remember times when the future seemed a bleak desert and the possibility of a well-paid job and a well-kept home were things about which they dare not hope." The article criticised the element of ruthlessness in Tory policy which was supported by those who were "motivated more by love of money than by patriotism, yet setting their faces against the very processes that had raised them. . . . In themselves they were despised by radical Conservatives such as Macmillan and by the landed and aristocratic families. . . . To say that there is now a group of the party which is identical to the 'hard-faced men' of the twenties is perhaps an exaggeration. But there is a group of their godsons who seem to relish the beliefs that unemployment is something that must be accepted, that efficiency must come first at any price, as contentedly as they accept that things will not be put right without great industries falling to the ground, which they argue is desirable. Of course there is logic in what they say, but what is wrong is the way they say it and if at the coming conference too many voices speak in these terms they will greatly add to the Prime Minister's difficulties. . . ."

By the time Heath had absorbed these lessons and was prepared to return to the consensus method of administering Britain, the measures on which he had embarked had already begun to exact their toll. The final casualty was to be Heath

155

himself, initially rejected by the electorate and consequently by his own party, which is not known for its generosity towards unsuccessful leaders. Heath had not been a leader in the mould of either Stanley Baldwin or Harold Macmillan. He had been, if anything, attempting to model himself on the Conservative leaders on the Continent. Unlike Wilson, who at times became a sub-Churchillian parody, Heath was a great admirer of Pompidou and other Gaullist politicians. However, he overextended himself and chose to ignore the sage advice of Walter Bagehot that "the higher classes . . . must avoid, not only evil but every appearance of evil; while they still have the power they must remove, not only every actual grievance, but where it is possible, every seeming grievance too; they must willingly concede every claim which they can safely concede, in order that they may not have to concede unwillingly some claim which would impair the safety of the country." Naturally Bagehot's prescriptions became a bit difficult to accept in conditions of capitalist decline in a post-Empire Britain, but to stand them on their head, which is what Heath attempted, was equally impossible.

The main problem confronting Heath was the existence and continual growth of mass unionism in Britain. During the period of the Heath government, trade union membership had exceeded 11 million, making it the most powerful labour movement in the advanced capitalist countries of Western Europe. Furthermore it was a united movement, not divided on political or religious lines as it is on the Continent, particularly in France and Italy. To weaken this movement, without at the same time weakening the Labourist ideology that sustained it, was a near impossible task. Added to these existing features is the fact that the British trade union movement was supported by a backbone of 300,000 shop stewards throughout industry and the public sector. These shop stewards are elected by the work-force and only a tiny proportion of them work full-time in this capacity. Most members are workers. It is this peculiarity of mass unionism in Britain that has been the focus of critical attention from the State and trade union officialdom alike. A Royal Commission established by the Labour government under the chairmanship of Lord Donovan to investigate the unions stressed this fact more than once to explain the state of industrial relations in Britain, exemplified by a rash of unofficial strikes at regular intervals in particular industries. Attempts to strengthen the trade union officials at the expense of the shop stewards by the Wilson government of 1966 did not meet with much success. They were defeated by a combined trade union opposition.

The expansion of trade union membership is remarkable. In the thirties economic recession and heavy unemployment had led to a sharp decline in the number of trades unionists, though, it should be pointed out, this was also the cumulative impact of the defeat of 1926. By contrast the sixties and seventies have seen a rapid rise in membership, despite the economic and social context of British society. Even before the 1974 recession, employment was receding: in comparison to 23.3 million employed in 1966, there were 22 million in 1971. The same period saw a rise in trade union membership of over a million, half of whom were women. While the heavy industrial unions increased their base and further developed their organisation, a new feature was the explosion of public sector unionism. The membership of the largest non-manual union in the public sector (National Association of Local Government Officers — NALGO) increased by twenty-nine per cent or 100,000 members from 1968-71. The largest civil service union (CPSA) increased by twenty-four per cent or 36,000 in the same period. By 1976 NALGO membership stood at 625,000, the CPSA at 220,000 and the National Union of Public Employees at 600,000 members. There was a similar growth in the non-manual, white-collar unions orientated towards the private sector. The combined membership of ASTMS, APEX, NUBE, AUEW(Tech) doubled in the period from 1966-71. The expansion of education in the fifties and sixties also saw the rapid growth of the National Union of Teachers, which after 1968, was to receive an influx of radicalised teachers. Following the collapse of Wilson and Barbara Castle's anti-trade union measures in 1969 the process of collective bargaining saw a strike offensive by sectors which had never struck before: women cleaners, nurses, hospital attendants, dustmen, farmworkers and teachers all came out on strike. In many cases they won substantial concessions from their employers.

The failure of Heath to curb the power of the unions certainly represented a setback for the Tory Party. It did not, and this difference is important, create a profound crisis for the institutions of British bourgeois democracy. The closest these came to being challenged was when the miners disregarded the call for the February 1974 general election and continued their strike. If the minority Labour government which resulted from that election had decided, at that stage, to try and defeat the miners, it could have triggered off a major political crisis. In fact it settled the dispute fairly amicably, before it embarked on its task of proving to the City of London that only Labour could preserve social peace in Britain.

The election of two successive Labour governments in the spring and autumn of 1974 could well turn out to be extremely decisive events in the political calendar of the post-1968 period. The reason for this is not so much for what they represent in themselves as for what they herald for the future of British politics. Virtually ever section of British society, except the central core of the Labour and TUC leadership, was taken by surprise at the turn taken by the 1974 Labour government.

It should be pointed out that the Labour Party, in opposition, had as usual moved somewhat to the left in an attempt to recuperate its base inside the trade unions. Its leaders had pledged that incomes policies were disastrous and would not be imposed by Labour ever again. The Labour left, in particular Tony Benn, had attempted to give old social-democratic reformism a new radical flavour by talking about nationalisations and industrial democracy, and the constituency parties had registered a sharp left turn. As a result, the ruling class was slightly uneasy at the prospect of a weak Labour government in power in the midst of the most powerful working-class upsurge since the twenties. When Harold Wilson appointed Michael Foot to the Cabinet there was alarm in some quarters, illusion in others and hopeful prophecies from *The Economist* which commented on March 9, 1974 that: "There are not many, even in the Labour Party, who believe he will stay for long whatever the life of the Labour government. It is expected that one whiff of incomes policy and Mr Foot will be off rather quicker than Mr Frank Cousins was in the first Wilson government." The same journal had, a month earlier, given its readers its considered views on the likely evolution of another left social-democratic leader, Tony Benn: "A Labour government in office usually moves towards the right. Would-be leaders of the left then tend to stalk out of it with ill-timed resignations which are supposed to cause crises but actually cause widespread relief. Mr Tony Benn seems typecast for the part." A third prediction from the same journal contained some advice for the employers: "In 1974-9 employers will need to show greater willingness to sack contract breakers, use blacklegs, resist pickets, import coal." In the event, with the partial exception of George Ward of Grunwick, all these prognostications turned out to be inaccurate. In other words the rightward drift of the Labour government, including the left social-democrats in the Cabinet, took everyone by surprise. The resignation of Wilson as party leader and his replacement by Callaghan turned out to be, in terms of real-politik, an extremely shrewd changeover. Callaghan's links with the union leaders were closer than those of Wilson. Furthermore the image he presented was that of a bluff and genial paternalist, a lumpen country squire. In him Labour appeared to have discovered its Stanley Baldwin, a politician who successfully smothered class differences in the name of the "national interest".

The measure of Callaghan's success, even if it is only temporary, should not be underestimated. He developed Wilson's policies of subordinating Labour to capital in a blunt, no-nonsense fashion. He has pressed through an incomes policy and refused to tolerate any "special cases" as far as the public sector unions are concerned. He was praised for his handling of the firemen's strike in 1977 by every leading ruling-class newspaper and journal. In fact what ensured the success of Callaghan's austerity measures was the fulsome support he received from the two most important trade union leaders in the country, Jack Jones and Hugh Scanlon. They represented the two largest industrial unions and their support for Labour's policies ensured the passivity of the TUC as a whole.

After a period of sustained industrial struggles against the Heath government the British trade unions meekly accepted the policies of the Labour government, which had as its aim the regeneration of British capitalism. How does one explain this paradox? The theses advanced by Robin Blackburn in relation to the Heath administration need to be slightly modified in order to understand the situation in which the British workers' movement finds itself today. A determined Labour

159

government can use its political hold over the working class to defeat its economic strength, and this is what the 1974 Labour government succeeded in doing far more effectively than the Tories. Callaghan's message to the British bourgeoisie is simple and effective: they do not need either a Tory or a National Government. Labour can do the job. What he underestimates is the extent of working-class demoralisation and despair and the resulting nationalist fervour in Scotland and Wales. These factors could indeed change the face of British politics for a long time.

The present crisis therefore needs some reflections on the future of Labourist politics in Britain. From its inception the British Labour Party has been a party of reform. It has had no truck with Marxism. Its principles were stated by the Fabian ideologue Sidney Webb years ago. In his Presidential address to the Labour Party Conference in 1923, Webb declared:

"Let me insist on what our opponents habitually ignore, and indeed, what they seem intellectually incapable of understanding, namely the *inevitable gradualness* of our scheme of change. For the Labour Party, it must be plain, Socialism is rooted in Democracy. . . . Thus even if we aimed at revolutionising everything at once, we should necessarily be compelled to make each particular change only at the time, and to the extent, and in the manner which ten or fifteen million electors, in all sorts of conditions, of all sorts of temperaments, from Land's End to the Orkneys, could be brought to consent to it. . . . Once we face the necessity of putting our principles first into bills, to be fought through Committee clause by clause; and then into the appropriate machinery for carrying them into execution from one end of the Kingdom to the other — that is what the Labour Party has done with its socialism — the *inevitability of gradualness* cannot fail to be appreciated."

The only change since Sidney Webb's display of characteristic Fabian arrogance and philistinism has been that few, if any, of Labour supporters really believe that the Labour Party is moving inexorably towards a fundamental transformation of the capitalist system. And yet despite the fact that no Labour leader of note still talks about the gradual and inevitable *replacement* of capitalism, many left social-democrats cling to this theory. To abandon it would leave them totally denuded

160

of any political rationale and the fact that a number of Communist Parties in Western Europe have begun to utilise a similar rhetoric — though they misuse the authority of Gramsci to render Webb more profound — has given these ideas a new lease of life in Britain.

For many decades the time-honoured justification for the failures of the Labour Party was the fact that it had in the pre-Second World War period never governed with a majority The traumas of the defection of Ramsay Macdonald had further demoralised the party. So the argument which stated that a *majority* in parliament would be a decisive test still commanded the sympathy and understanding of many Labour supporters. It was, after all, only a question of time as the Labour vote was constantly climbing. Within the first ten years of its existence (1900-10) the Labour vote jumped from 62,698 to 2,244,945. Its second decade saw the vote doubled once again to 4,348,379 and the party took office as a minority government with Liberal support. In the 1935 elections the Labour vote had crossed the 8 million mark. In the next election, ten years later, Labour won a landslide majority with 11,992,292 votes and over the next three years its popular vote increased still further. When it lost to the Tories in 1951, its actual popular vote was higher than that of the Tories at 13,948,385. In the two general elections which followed, Labour retained over 12 million votes. Thus arguments which use the period of full-employment and "affluence" to explain the Labour Party's decline of popularity and its growing weakness are somewhat inaccurate. Labour preserved its base in the working class throughout the years of the economic boom.

1945 gave it a massive majority. The insipid and colourless figure of Attlee replaced the prestige-laden Winston Churchill as Prime Minister of Britain. Ten years of unemployment, recession and a failure to prevent the rise of fascism had brought about the defeat of the Tories. The 1945 Labour Government carried out a number of important social reforms. Any post-war government would have been obliged to offer the British masses a "new deal", and naturally a reformist party did so with more enthusiasm. In the foreign sphere Labour accepted the Indian clamour for independence, which was conceded in August 1947. The creation of the National Health Service — the jewel in the crown of British social-democracy — and the independence of India were presented as the two major achievements of the Attlee government. Many Labour supporters in the country were satisfied, as some progress was being achieved. After its first set of reforms, the Attlee government (which, incidentally was thoroughly conservative in its foreign policy) found itself at an impasse. It could have soldiered on in 1950, but in the words of Richard Crossman it suffered from a "loss of nerve". He went on to write that: "In the history of the British Left, there can seldom have been an administration so conservative in its solicitude for the stuffier constitutional conventions, so instinctively suspicious of all suggestions for popular participation in decision-taking and workers' control, and so determined to damp down the fiery demands for a new social order that had won them the election." In effect, Attlee's government was killed by Labourism. But though the limits of British reformism were clearly demonstrated in the 1945-51 period, the thirteen years of Conservative rule which followed permitted the nurturing of myths and illusions. 1945 has become enshrined in Labour mythology as the finest period in the history of the British Labour movement. Certainly in the sense that there was a clear material basis — aided by the Marshall Plan — for reforms, the Attlee government carried out the most elementary tasks expected from it, but it went no further. Nonetheless those tasks, compared to the failures of the fifties and sixties, seemed Herculean by comparison. The fact that the restrained reformism of Attlee, Morrison and Cripps is now seen as the heroic period of British social-democracy is in itself an indictment of its weak and sickly ideology — Labourism.

The change which has taken place over the last decade is of some significance. It is that Labour has, in the period 1964-78, become a party of government. It has been in office four times in contrast to the single spell in office by the Tories. That in itself is an important change, but what makes it even more dramatic is the fact that in the same period Britain has experienced a severe economic and social crisis. It is the combination of these two features of contemporary British politics that imparts a novelty to the present situation. There were two basic causes for this crisis. In the first place it was inserted in a context of a generalised recession in the advanced capitalist world, which inhibited British capital from indirect profits in the world market. Secondly the decline of British imperial power drastically reduced British hegemony, initially on a global scale and finally in Europe, South Asia, Africa and the Mediterranean. It was outstripped economically by the United States, Japan and West Germany and, in terms of political influence and prestige, was overtaken by the French Fifth Republic.

The decline in the economic and political power of British capital could no longer be obscured from view when Wilson took office in 1964. Over the next five years its effects became obvious: a decline in the rate of profit, the decline in Britain's share of world exports, the decline of sterling as an international currency and a decline in wages in comparison to several other capitalist countries. This crisis was symbolised within the first few weeks of Wilson taking office in 1964. An attempt to force devaluation of the pound by international speculators gave the Labour government a difficult choice. Devaluation was avoided on that occasion by a massive loan by the leading state banks of international finance capital, including the US Federal Reserve System. In return Wilson did an about-turn on every foreign policy promised by the Labour government. He was soon to become the weakest of European leaders in backing the war in Vietnam. In addition he decided to carry through the Tory decision to sell Buccaneer planes to the racist Verwoerd régime in South Africa, a decision criticised from the left by *The Economist*! He extended the use of Ascension Island by the United States and Belgian government for troops to be sent to crush the Stanleyville régime in the Congo and he refused to stop the construction of nuclear Polaris submarines as part of a special NATO fleet. This was Wilson's *quid pro quo* with Capital in the first six weeks after taking office.

The stability of British bourgeois democracy was founded on two centuries of solid hegemony over the capitalist world. This enabled the British ruling class to avoid large-scale social explosions at home, and also explained the special characteristics of British social-democratic ideology and a deep influence of patriotism and chauvinism inside the working class itself. The four Labour governments which were elected in the 1964-74 period carried out an extremely important task for the ruling class. On every possible occasion they blatantly defended capitalism inside the trade union movement and attempted to get a whole series of austerity measures accepted by the organised working class. With the notable exception of 1969 the Labour leaders have been successful in carrying out their tasks. Naturally what has aided them is the entire structure of the British workers' movement. While the Labour Party is the strongest social-democratic party in Western Europe it is also the weakest. Its strength lies in its power over an undivided trade union movement. Its weakness lies in the fact that most of its membership is not just inactive, but "dead". The proportion of actual members of the constituency Labour parties in relation to the collective membership of the trades union is 6 : 1 in the latter's favour. Thus the trade union block vote determines the fate of a Labour Party conference. The undemocratic nature of British trade unionism is thus transported ready-made into the heart of the Labour Party. A tiny delegation of trade union officials casts millions and millions of votes. It is what Tom Nairn has characterised as "the crushing weight of the dead souls, the purely nominal voices which theoretically govern the destiny of the Labour Party, and sometimes of Britain as a whole". The votes of the "dead souls" can cancel even a unanimous vote by party activists, the members who service every need of the party during local and national elections. Thus the strongest social-democratic party in the West is structurally extremely dependent on all the agencies of the bourgeois state. It is so well integrated into the functioning of the system that it does not even feel the need to have its own daily paper. Its ideas are presented through a relatively new publication, *Labour Weekly*, and the views of the "Left" in the Cabinet are presented through the dilapidated left social-democratic weekly *Tribune,* which has little fight left in its pages. More to the point the combined sales and readership of the two weeklies is less than that of the press and publications of the Communist Party and the far left groups. Its publications are meant for party activists and close supporters; there is nothing for the masses. The *Daily Mirror* supports Labour, certainly, but the terms of this support are determined by the overall needs of the system. In other words the *Mirror* is read by large numbers of workers, but despite its correct stance on a few questions, it cannot be characterised as a *working-class* paper. It essentially transmits, often in a mediated form, bourgeois ideology and bourgeois values. In other words the British Labour movement has, ever since the demise of the *Daily Herald,* left its members at the mercy of the ideas which reflect the views of those who rule and control the real levers of power in British society. This enormous gap between Labour's electoral strength and its nominal membership on the one hand, and political reality on the other, could create a severe crisis inside the British Labour Party in the near future. It is impossible that the crisis of British imperialism will not result, sooner or later, in a crisis of working-class reformism.

Some elements of this decline can already be seen. The long spell in office has begun to have an impact, and the popular vote gained by Labour in February 1974 was the smallest since 1935. Its share of the total poll was the lowest since 1931. In relative terms Labour gained a much higher vote during its year of opposition in the fifties than it did in 1974. Its actual popular vote — 11,654,726 — was less than that of the Tories. In October 1974 it overtook the Tories, but the popular vote declined to 11,468,136. The new "enemy" on the horizon was not the socialist left, but nationalism. The Scottish and Welsh nationalists increased their vote from 803,396 in February to 1,500,949 in October. In response to this supposedly "transient" intrusion the Labour government pledged to provide separate elected Assemblies for Scotland and Wales as part of their plan for devolution. These attempts were resisted by Labour MPs and sabotaged on a number of occasions. The nationalist turn was still in its early stages in 1974, but it reflected a growing dissatisfaction with traditional Westminster politics in the regions where unemployment was reviving memories of the thirties. Unemployment in the Clydeside areas was nearly twenty per cent! In addition, the total integration of the local Labour Party bureaucracy into the local governments in Scotland and Wales and the obvious exercise of patronage and the existence of large-scale corruption further alienated the people in these regions at a time of economic and social crisis. The turn to nationalist politics may never be completed. Scotland and Wales are old-established Labour strongholds. Without them Labour could not form a government at Westminster. In that sense if these areas decide to abandon their support for Labour, which they have *not* done so far, and move towards national-

165

ism, they could alter British politics for ever. For what would then be at stake is not just the hegemony of Labourism over the British working class, but the cohesion of the Great British State.

The first political columnist to draw attention in a serious way to the national question in relation to Scotland was George Orwell. He had a regular column, *As I Please,* in *Tribune.* On February 14, 1947, this prophetic writer noted:

"Up to date the Scottish Nationalist movement seems to have gone almost unnoticed in England. To take the nearest example to hand. I don't remember having seen it mentioned in *Tribune,* except occasionally in book reviews. It is true that it is a small movement, but it could grow, because there is a basis for it. In this country I don't think it is enough realised — that Scotland has a case against England. On economic grounds it may not be a very strong case. . . . The point is that many Scottish people, often quite moderate in outlook, are beginning to think about autonomy and to feel that they are pushed into an inferior position. They have a good deal of reason. In some areas, at any rate, Scotland is almost an occupied country. You have an English or anglicised upper class, and a Scottish working class which speaks with a markedly different accent, or even, part of the time, in a different language. . . ."

Three decades later Orwell's cudgels were taken up, sharpened, coated with a Marxist gloss and put into action by another gifted political columnist, Tom Nairn. He wrote a set of powerfully argued essays and columns in which he developed a thesis which, in some ways, overtook Orwell. Nairn described the inability of the British working class to effect a radical break with Labourism and challenge the structures of the British State. He developed the thesis that what "class" had been unable to achieve, the "nation" could accomplish. Nairn's declared enemy is the British State: almost anything that destroys the cohesion of this State can only be a step forward. The point here is not what socialists should do if the people of Scotland decide that they want independence. If the majority of Scots want their own State they should be allowed to have one as it is their democratic right. The same applies to Wales. The real question which is raised is whether this is a desirable development from the interests of the workers on this island

166

as a whole. In other words should Scottish Marxists become the cheerleaders for Scottish capitalists and create a Scottish Home Guard to defend the border and build a Scottish Navy to ensure that the royalties from North Sea Oil are despatched to Edinburgh rather than London? To these questions Tom Nairn provides no real answers. His polemic against the chauvinism of left social-democrats in the Labour Party is not totally misdirected, but suffers from an important weakness. He does not project any perspectives for either Scottish or English Marxists in this situation. What Nairn ignores is that the strength of nationalism is not decreed by the objective development of the world. It is the direct result of the failure of socialist revolutions in the West. The fact that the German working class was subordinated to Hitler — the most important victory of German Nationalism — does not mean that it had to be so. It was a failure of social-democratic and comintern political strategies, which delivered the German working class to Hitler. His rise to power was certainly not inevitable. Nairn does not say that it was, but there is a strong element of providing *post factum* rationalisations of accomplished facts, which pervades his writings on nationalism. The exception is, of course, his predictions regarding the likely break-up of the British State. The merit of Nairn's work lies in the fact that he raises important questions for Marxists and the fact that he does not always satisfactorily answer these should not act as a cover for ignoring the questions altogether. Like Orwell, Nairn is not frightened of challenging orthodoxies, regardless of the camp to which they might be attached.

The relationships built up between the classes in British society over many decades have now become an obstacle to the process of capitalist accumulation. The attempt to resolve that crisis through the Heath government failed. But because British monopoly capitalism rules, not through one party, but through the State, the defeat of Heath represented not a defeat of strategic proportions, but a setback to its immediate policies. What it sought to do after the Heath débâcle was to make full use of the fact that one of the central pillars of British bourgeois-democracy, the Labour Party, was interwoven with the British trades unions. What Heath could not achieve through parliamentary coercion, Callaghan is attempting through Labourist consent. The problem lies in the fact that even Callaghan or a Labour government will find it extremely difficult to institutionalise declining living standards without an eruption at some stage either within the industrial or the electoral arena. In political terms the British ruling class, despite some victories, is faced with a stalemate in the class war. The change of leaders in the Tory Party from an aloof, but intelligent ruling-class leader to someone who believes that a strident, petty-bourgeois vulgarity is what is needed at the present time does not inspire the possessing class with great confidence. In fact the decline in the quality of leadership of the Tory Party is another reflection of the changed fortunes of British capital. The party of Churchill, Butler, MacLeod, Macmillan is now reduced to Margaret Thatcher, Keith Joseph, Rhodes Boyson and Geoffrey Howe. The sophisticated research apparatus built with great care during the post-war period has been allowed to decline. The new speech-writers and advisers of Tory leaders are the National Association for Freedom (NAFF), an extreme right-wing pressure group which espouses a virulent anti-socialist ideology and whose central ideologue is the former *Economist* correspondent, Robert Moss, who won his spurs by defending the Pinochet *coup d'état* in Chile. The word "freedom" presumably means freedom from those with whom we disagree.

Thus British society, a decade after 1968, presents a gloomy picture. Its crisis is unresolved. Bourgeois nationalism threatens the unity of the working-class movement in Scotland and Wales. A particularly nasty nationalism has gained ground in England as well. This is the old fascism of Oswald Moseley presented today in a new garb by the National Front. If any organisation has made a thorough and unscrupulous use of the decline of the British Empire it has been the fascist leaders of the National Front. Like their departed forebears in Weimar Germany, they play on the politics of fear. Their scapegoat is not primarily the Jews, but the blacks. It would appear that all the old imperialist chickens are coming home to roost. The black immigrants who come to Britain are those whose countries were colonised and plundered by British imperialism over the last two centuries. The same process systematically added racism to the arsenal of ruling-class ideology. It was a necessary ideological concomitant. The complicity of the British Labour Party in the process meant that there was never any consistent, mass propaganda against racist and imperialist ideology. The results of both processes can be seen now in clashes in a number of cities and the votes obtained by the fascists in Leicester and other town in the Midlands. The development of modern British fascism has been depicted in a serious and intelligent fashion by the socialist playwright David Edgar in his play *Destiny*. Initially destined for production at the Aldwych Theatre in London, the play was later adapted for and shown on BBC television at peak viewing-time: an indication that the threat posed by unchallenged fascist propaganda had to be shown to a mass audience.

And yet racism was not simply exploited by the fascist or semi-fascist currents in British political life. A whole range of Conservative Members of Parliament have shown no desire to combat the disease. At the beginning of 1978 a number of important speeches by Tory leaders on the question of "immigration control" (a synonym for keeping blacks out of Britain) suggested that a desperate leadership, worried by the temporary success of Callaghan's conservative economic and social policies, was seriously considering the option of playing the "black card". Of course if they decided to make racism a central issue in subsequent general elections the effects could be catastrophic. I am referring not to the plight of large numbers of black people in this country, who live as second-class citizens, suffering from regular legal harassment, racial discrimination and, increasingly, physical attacks at the hands of white racist gangs. Their lives are not of great interest to most Westminster politicians. No, the results would be catastrophic in terms of those whom it would aid. It would not be the Tories who would benefit from a blatant racist campaign, but the forces well to the right of them, organisations such as the National Front, the National Party and the British Movement.

Britain in 1978 has seen a sharp drift to the right in varying aspects of national life. In a broad sense this is the outcome of a period in which Labour had presided over the biggest decline in living standards since the thirties. The cuts in social expenditure, lying on the desks of the Whitehall bureaucracy as pages of statistics, were in fact creating increasing misery in the deprived areas of Britain's largest centres. The fact that all this happened under a Labour government has led to apathy, demoralisation and a turn to the right. There exists no mass

169

left-wing alternative to Labour which could attract the dispirited victims of Labourism, the "dead souls" who now realise that leaving it all to their leaders is totally useless in sorting out their everyday problems.

If the Labour Party is in a critical state, its adversary is not much healthier. The polarisation in British society has so far been of greater assistance to the forces of the extreme right than to the Marxist left. There is an objective reason for this development, and it is embedded in the fact that the British working class has for decades been a prisoner of ruling-class ideologies, the most tenacious of which has been Labourism. British society is increasingly polarised into two social classes. There is no peasantry, nor a significant middle layer of urban petty bourgeois on whom the ruling class can rely for mass mobilisations. Thus *ideology* and *institutions* are probably more important in Britain than in any other European country. This is what explains the extreme reluctance of the British ruling class to carry out a real change in its democratic structure. The British judiciary, civil service and parliament all reflect the degeneration of a bourgeois revolution which was economically advanced and politically backward, not a surprising fact given that they were established in the seventeenth century. Britain's political structures today continue to reflect this imbalance.

The attempt of chartism to rally the masses was thwarted by a range of concessions from above. These rendered inoperative a number of Chartist demands. Some of them, such as the demand for annual parliaments, still need to be taken up by the socialist left and inscribed in their platform of transitional and democratic demands. The success of bourgeois ideology in hegemonising the workers' movement was a cause of some irritation to the originators of scientific socialism. In a celebrated letter Engels wrote to Bebel, he noted that:

"... recently a lot of young people stemming from the bourgeoisie have appeared on the scene who, to the disgrace of the English workers it must be said, understand things better and take them up more enthusiastically than the workers themselves. ... Do not on any account whatever let yourself be bamboozled into thinking there is a real proletarian movement going on here. I know Liebknecht is trying to delude himself and the world about this, but it is not the case. The elements at present active may become important now that they have

170

accepted our theoretical programme and so acquired a basis, but only if a spontaneous movement breaks out here among the workers and they succeed in getting hold of it. Till then they will remain individual minds with a hodge-podge of confused sects, remnants of the great movements of the forties standing behind them, nothing more. And — apart from the unexpected — a really general workers' movement will come into existence here only when the workers feel that England's world monopoly is broken. Participation in the domination of the world market was and is the economic basis of the political nullity of the English workers."

Both Marx and Engels and their most celebrated follower, Lenin, were to pour scorn on those who persisted in "lending the economic struggle a political character".

In the preceding two decades a marked decline has taken place in Britain's global position. "England's world monopoly" of which Engels spoke, has been broken. Furthermore, the Marxist programme has been accepted by tens of thousands of radical students, women, white-collar and industrial workers, but there has been no real juncture of revolutionary politics and the British working class, and thus no revolutionary party has emerged in Britain. Nonetheless, important developments have and still are taking place to the left of the Labour Party, but the weaknesses of far left politics must be explained.

There have been two parallel developments in the British left since 1968, which have sometimes coincided but never fused. There has been an explosion of Marxist theory in the universities in virtually every discipline and there has been a considerable growth in the size and influence of the revolutionary left. At the same time the organisations which traditionally dominated and captured all developments on the left of the Labour Party — the Communist Party of Great Britain — is today in a state of decline. Despite the fact that its industrial base still dwarfs the far left groups in terms of political influence and political initiatives it has often been outdistanced by groups on its left. In sharp contrast to the thirties, when the British Communist Party dominated the militants and intellectuals to the left of the Labour Party and through them reached into the heart of Labour itself, the situation today is quite different. Despite the possibilities which exist, no socialist alternative, not even in an embryonic sense, has developed. It

171

could harness this potential and transform it into a revolutionary socialist organisation of several thousands and begin to offer a serious choice to the militants so dissatisfied with the state of the Labour Party. Neither the Communist Party nor the Socialist Workers Party (SWP), the largest of the far left groups, has developed a strategy for the construction of a significant socialist alternative in Britain today.

The British Communist Party is a shadow of its former self. It is trapped in the nexus of left social-democracy on the one hand and the legacy of Stalinism on the other. Both the Stalinist and the left social-democratic framework, however, are in the midst of a gigantic crisis of legitimacy. The Wilson and Callaghan governments have succeeded in integrating left social-democracy into the running of governments. Barbara Castle and Anthony Greenwood in the sixties and Michael Foot and Tony Benn in the seventies are the pathetic symbols of a wing of Labourism which in the thirties, forties and fifties did attempt to organise itself against the politics of the dominant leadership. The ultimate capitulation of Aneurin Bevan seemed to have set the seal on the collapse of his followers. For left social-democracy is only loosely organised in the House of Commons around the weekly journal *Tribune*. If Bevan represented, for three decades, the conscience of left-wing party activists in the Constituencies, his followers today are safely ensconced in the Cabinet. His biographer has, not surprisingly, become the most orthodox defender of all the eccentricities of the British parliamentary system. Tony Benn based himself on the left-wing leaders of the trade union movement. Unlike Bevan, who was constantly opposed and witch-hunted by the right-wing leaders who led the Transport Workers and Engineering Workers unions, Benn based his strategy on a link with the sympathetic trade union leaders of the seventies. When the latter decided to back the Labour Government's policies, the Benn opposition collapsed. No attempt was made by left social-democracy to organise mass campaigns against unemployment, racism and fascism, women's rights, civil liberties, etc. This abject collapse of the Labour left wing also posed a severe crisis of perspectives for the British Communist Party, whose theory of left advance was based on an alliance with the leftists in parliament and the trade unions. When both segments refused to organise any struggle against the Labour government, the Communist Party became a political orphan. Its dwindling vote in national and local elections — a result of its Stalinism and adaptations to left social-democratic politics made the prospect of a left government with the support of Communist MPs somewhat utopian. Sales of its national daily paper rapidly declined. Its half-hearted attempts to distance itself from the more appalling crimes of Stalin's heirs only succeeded in enabling a truculent, Brezhnevite wing in the Party to organise a breakaway faction which declared itself the New Communist Party and gained some support in the USSR and Eastern Europe.

Despite the fact that the Communist Party has hesitantly criticised the régimes in the USSR and Eastern Europe, it still supports the global politics of the Soviet leaders and its coverage of Eastern European politics remains biased towards the official positions. Nonetheless, the Eurocommunist developments in the rest of Western Europe, the uprisings in the East, and the monstrous bureaucratic crimes being perpetrated in the name of socialism in the USSR, have all left their mark on the party. A significant section of its leadership and most of its post-1968 membership would not defend Stalinist atrocities. If the permanent choice is to tail-end the political initiatives of left social-democrats, then many militants will begin to challenge the need to maintain a separate party, especially when it is as small as the British Communist Party, whose active membership is less than 10,000. One of the party's leading industrial militants, the Scottish shop steward, Jimmy Reid, took this logic to its ultimate conclusion, resigned from the CP and joined the Labour Party. There is a possibility, unless Labour totally collapses in Scotland, that he will one day become a left-wing Labour MP from Scotland! If the party had not lost its political nerve, and been capable of political flexibility, it could have carried out a left turn by revitalising its industrial arm and preparing to do battle against the social contract and its trade union companions who chose to honour its implementation. True, such a development could well have made the party membership vulnerable to the siren songs of the groups on its left, but the level of political discussion in most of these was less developed than inside the party. Furthermore, it is not inconceivable that a left turn by the party coupled with a distancing from the Soviet Union could well have won to its ranks some of the industrial militants in the far left. But the depths of the conservatism and mundanity exhibited by the gerontocracy in King Street proved to be too strong. The party could not offer any socialist alternative for militants looking for radical answers to the crisis of Labourism.

But if the Communist Party was incapable of action, what was the state of the revolutionary left? This had grown by leaps and bounds since the 1968 radicalisation. The Socialist Workers' Party (formerly the International Socialists) had acquired a modest working-class base by the early seventies. Its influence in the unions spread through its "rank and file" organisations. The Workers' Revolutionary Party started producing a daily newspaper, which despite its bizarre sectarianism was a better produced and more lively paper than the CP's *Morning Star*. The International Marxist Group, too, had grown in size and influence and within the Labour Party itself the moles of *The Militant* group were continuing to burrow away in much the same fashion as when they had started, a couple of decades earlier. And yet neither organisation was capable of producing anything vaguely resembling a socialist alternative for the advanced workers. *The Militant* rejected all independent activity outside the Labour Party. The WRP had developed sectarianism into such a fine art that anyone not as sectarian as they was instantly denounced as being an "objective aid" for the capitalist system. When some disgruntled writer defects from this organisation and writes a novel or a play about his/her experiences the comparison that will come to mind is with the Jesuit sects of the sixteenth century.

The dominant group was, without doubt, the SWP. They had the potential to unify the left and develop an alternative which would attract thousands of militants. What this needed was an understanding of the society for which the socialist revolution could fight. There is a collection of essays entitled *Party and Class,* by the central leaders of the SWP, Tony Cliff, Duncan Hallas and Chris Harman. While the latter's text was the most creative, all three writers strongly criticised the sects which postured as parties and explained how the party could never be a substitute for the working class. There was also the glimmer of an understanding that the revolutionary party which had to be constructed in the West could not be a monolithic formation. In fact monolithism was correctly de-

174

nounced as a Stalinist concept. A passage by Duncan Hallas explicitly states that a revolutionary party can not be built except "on a thoroughly democratic basis; unless, in its internal life, vigorous controversy is the rule and various tendencies and shades of opinion are represented, a socialist party cannot rise above the level of a sect. Internal democracy is not an optional extra. It is fundamental to the relationship between party members and those amongst whom they work."

These excellent sentiments, if properly implemented, would have formed an important pillar on which a revolutionary organisation could be constructed. Unfortunately this line of argument was soon abandoned. Tony Cliff's books on Lenin were written to demonstrate, amongst other more positive things, that modern Leninists need not fear unruly oppositions. The SWP now postured as the *only* organisation in Britain capable of building a party. In fact many of the criticisms in *Party and Class* against sects and sectarianism could now be applied to its own functioning. Inner-party debate was discouraged. Militant workers had no time to be "diverted" from the struggle by irrelevant debates. These errors were to damage seriously the SWP's standing within the far left and amongst those groups of individuals who were politically undecided between left social-democracy, the Communist Party and revolutionary politics.

On a more fundamental level, the major organisations of the British far left suffered from an impartial and faulty understanding of what constituted a revolutionary *political* orientation. In its own specific fashion, the British far left inverted the traditional social-democratic distinction between trade unionism and politics. British social-democracy deliberately confined its operation and politics within the framework of the bourgeois state by reducing politics to parliamentary and electoral activities. Everything else was considered trade unionism. Thus Labourism was extremely hostile to any notion of political strikes even when they obviously had a political motive, as in 1974 when the miners were determined to get rid of Heath, this could never be publicly stated. The far left did the exact opposite. The prime source of proletarian politics for them was the struggle at the point of production. All other activities were considered useless. Parliament and any form of consistent electoral activities were considered political death-traps. There

175

was no conception of a proletarian intervention into the bourgeois political arena. Discussions on bourgeois politics were conducted within the framework established by the bourgeoisie. Which party should we vote for? Once it had been agreed that one would cast ones vote for Labour, the matter of intervention was resolved and one could return to the serious business of acting as cheer-leaders for the next strike. Virtually every single strike was elevated by the far left press into an event of great importance. The crisis of local politics, the state of the local Labour Party, the strength of Toryism and its base were issues which were (and still are) rarely discussed in the Marxist press. There is a name for this disease: militant syndicalism or economism. And it has plagued the revolutionary left for a long time. While the SWP was the organisation which seemed to suffer the most, the IMG and other currents were not immune to its ravages. Its net result was that it led to a serious fragmentation of the political impact which the far left could have had from 1968 onwards. It prevented us from developing a practical intervention which related to the bourgeois government and State at every level. Such an orientation could have aided in the political unification of all the sectoral economic struggles which socialism necessarily aids and supports.

The organisation which first recognised these basic defects in the functioning of the revolutionary left was the International Marxist Group. It had two advantages which other groups lacked, especially in the post-1974 period. It had a healthy internal régime which enabled it to debate, on occasion in a fierce and exaggerated fashion, the strategy and tactics needed at this particular period. Secondly, the IMG was partially relieved from the oppressive and relentless pressures of British insularity through its institutionalised links with revolutionary groups in over fifty different countries within the framework of a common organisation, the Fourth International. The combination of these two features enabled it in 1977 to launch two important initiatives. The first was a non-sectarian, popular *political* weekly, *Socialist Challenge,* which attempted, not without some success, to develop an all-sided political intervention. The second was to propose the establishment of a united electoral pole, Socialist Unity, for intervening in local and national elections. This was the first serious attempt by a section of the revolutionary left to intervene *systematically* in national and local elections. It would be both foolish and false to exaggerate the importance of these initiatives. Their importance lies not so much in what they have achieved, but more in the direction in which they attempt to take the revolutionary movement. Within these initiatives there is the glimmer of a socialist alternative to Labourism — not in the sense of displacing Labour, but of regrouping the tens of thousands of militants prepared today to combat Labour policies.

In real life, parties are not built out of thin air. The birth of new mass parties reflects an important shift in working-class consciousness. "The proletariat," wrote Trotsky, in one of his last texts before he was assassinated, "may 'tolerate' for a long time a leadership that has already suffered a complete inner degeneration but has not as yet had the opportunity to express this degeneration amid great events. A great historic shock is necessary to reveal sharply the contradiction between the leadership and the class. The mightiest historic shocks are wars and revolutions." Trotsky was theorising the break carried out by the Communist Parties with social-democracy. This process was begun by the First World War and the Russian Revolution, and was completed after the Second World War. The French and Italian Communist Parties became hegemonic working-class parties only after the defeat of fascism. The crucial point here is that a revolutionary party will only come into existence when there is a breach in the traditional mass organisations of the British working class. This does not mean that socialists should subordinate their activity to the rhythms of these organisations, but it does mean that they must understand that there can be no blind leap over the shoulders of Labourism. It will, sooner or later, have to be encountered in political combat before it can be defeated or, at least, broken. Of course it is possible that a complete shift in the political boundaries and the introduction of proportional representation in British electoral practice will split the Labour Party as careerist and right-wing elements defect to safer political pastures. That will not relieve the revolutionary left of its responsibility; it will merely necessitate a rethinking of its political tactics.

It would be utterly philistine if we were to reduce the post-1968 radicalisation to the numerical growth of the Marxist left organisations. 1968 had another important political impact,

177

which can best be described as an explosion of Marxist theory. The pace at which Marxist ideas have penetrated sections of the newly radical intelligentsia has been remarkable. This development is explained by two inter-related factors: first, the fact that Marxism provided an explanation of the economic crisis and of the political upheavals that were taking place, and secondly, the complete paucity of traditional ruling-class ideology. The latter suffered a crisis of credibility, from which it has yet to recover. This was hardly surprising. A system in decline — and this decline was spectacularly manifested in Britain — will naturally find few theorists who can provide an explanation for that decline. The growing temptation is to defend the existing system by embarking on an offensive against and ideologically emasculating those who challenge the basic foundations of the system itself. This fragility of ruling-class ideology is seen in the immense care which is taken to ensure that the mass media is in the hands of those capable of exercising a degree of self-censorship. The tremendous emphasis on the "neutrality" of the institutions of the state such as the judiciary, civil service, army and police, conceals their political importance and their vulnerability. It is because they are so important for maintaining the bourgeois political order that they must be insulated from the varying temperatures of national politics. The top echelons are, mostly, ardent partisans of the Tory Party. Their politics are conducted in the network of clubs, which bring together ruling-class elements from different spheres of the State and civil society. The ranks are protected by being prevented from any participation in politics. An example of the desperate condition in which the bourgeois intelligentsia found itself was reflected in the suggestion, in 1977, by Julius Gould, a Nottingham university professor, that there should be a purge of Marxists in the institutions of higher education. The liberal opposition (typified by *The Guardian*, in particular) merely pointed out that Gould was paranoic as the number of Marxist teachers was not very large. A nastier version of a similar witch-hunt came from the fascist National Front, which demanded that all "red teachers" be sacked from schools because they defended the concept of a multi-racial society.

This crisis of ideology has hit the traditional labour movement as well. British Labourism is today without a Laski, a

Tawney, a Strachey and even a Crosland. There are pale imitations of all these figures, but their impact remains limited, even inside the Labour Party. The post-1968 developments exploded in this vacuum. The writings of Karl Marx, long dismissed as irrelevant by British Labour, were produced by the largest and most distinguished paperback publishers in the United Kingdom. Profits came before ideology. In addition, a number of Marxist publishing houses have mushroomed or expanded over the last decade. The list is fairly formidable: Lawrence and Wishart, Merlin Press, New Left Books, Pluto, Readers and Writers Cooperative, Spokesman Books, Harvester, Allison and Busby, etc. Exactly ten years after 1968, the most successful of the left publishers, New Left Books, launched Verso, a mass paperback imprint.

At the same time there was a growth of theoretical journals. While the *New Left Review* continued to dominate in the realm of theoretical debate and the development of Marxist politics, other journals in specific disciplines emerged and gathered strength. *Capital and Class* and the *Cambridge Economic Journal* concentrated on Marxist economics; *Critique* and *Labour Focus on Eastern Europe* discussed Soviet studies; *History Workshop* was edited by a collective of Marxist historians and sociologists; *Race and Class* became the focus of discussions on third world politics and ethnic minorities in the West; *Wedge* reflected the growing interest in Marxist aesthetics.

In the field of sexual politics there was the emergence on a national level of a women's liberation movement. This was a direct reflection of the recognition that women were oppressed and that this oppression was rooted in the socio-economic functioning of capitalist societies. Unlike the suffragettes at the beginning of the century, the new women militants were not satisfied with demanding equal political rights. They demanded the right to control their own bodies as well as their minds. They challenged the dominant male sexism which prevailed throughout society, including the left. They produced their own magazines — *Spare Rib, Red Rag, Women's Voice, Socialist Women* — and their own theoreticians. They resurrected old debates on the "Woman question" from the annals of Bolshevism and gave them new interpretations. There are many strands of feminism which exist today. Together they

179

constitute an autonomous current which will not (nor should it) subordinate its independence and its struggle to any political organisation.

The appearance of *Gay News* as a mass-circulation, multi-class weekly paper for homosexuals also marked a major change in attitudes to sexuality. The paper was a response to the growth of gay liberation groups throughout the country. Both the women's movement and the gay groups have an articulate Marxist minority active within them, but Marxism has never discussed these questions in any detail, nor can it have ready-made answers. The fact that it is being forced, almost against its will, to confront these issues can only be of immense benefit both for its own development and that of the particular movements.

Another development took place in the realm of art and culture. While Marxist playwrights and directors produced the best and most powerful plays for television (Jim Allen, Ken Loach, Tony Garnett, Trevor Griffiths, David Edgar, to name but a few), there was, at the same time a parallel development of the "fringe theatre". Small groups formed and decided to challenge the monopoly of the London theatres. John McGrath's *7:84* played before audiences who would never have approached a traditional theatre. *Red Ladder, Kartoon Klowns, Cast, Belt and Braces,* as well as many others, managed to reach "ordinary people". In London they were considerably aided by the existence of *Time Out,* a weekly guide to the arts in London, but at the same time espousing libertarian and anti-authoritarian politics. Its large circulation allowed it to act as a real coordinator for an alternative culture. Its anti-repressive vigilance has made it a factor of some importance in the capital city of Britain. It was the only mass journal to publicise protests against the Prevention of Terrorism Act and detail instances of how it was utilised to browbeat and harass large numbers of people, whose only crime was that they happened to be of Irish origin.

This renaissance of Marxism is by no means over. It should, however, be divided into two distinct phases. In the period immediately after 1968, the Marxist intellectuals tended to join political organisations. They felt the wind and sought to confront it from within the framework of a Marxist organisation. The Communist Party, the International Socialists and, to a lesser extent, the International Marxist Group, were the main attractions. It is worth digressing for a moment to point out that the problems confronting Marxist intellectuals are much greater today than in the twenties or even the thirties. Then the automatic choice for a Marxist was the Communist Party, where they found a home as well as direct links with the workers' movement. Intellectuals are, by definition, people of ideas. They, not unnaturally, want these ideas to be tested out, to be of some use for the struggle. In the post-1968 phase the revolutionary left groups in Britain and Western Europe had enormous potential, but none of them could offer an immediate link with the working masses. These links are now stronger than in 1968, but they still remain weak. The subsequent evolution of the larger groups resulted in the withdrawal of a large section of intellectuals: the IS/SWP was the hardest hit. The continued growth of Marxism in the seventies sees the development of intellectuals who are retreating into their own disciplines. They shun the existing far left groups and consciously confine themselves to their respective practices. They mocked the principle of "unity of theory and practice" on two counts: either the groups in question could not provide a practice or/ and their particular theory in question did not require practical verification.

Thus ten years after 1968 there are few meeting points between a whole group of Marxist intellectuals and the revolutionary militants. The latter tend to see all questions as automatically resolved simply because they are in a revolutionary organisation. The intellectuals are in turn totally contemptuous. They regard the political activity of the groups as trivial because none of them are hegemonic. This one-sidedness feeds upon itself.

The dominant theoretical tradition on the British far left is Trotskyism. In its essentials this tradition is the only one which gives a world view which can effectively combat that of both the ruling class in the West and the Stalinist bureaucracies of the USSR, China and Eastern Europe. Trotskyism was a struggle to defend the traditions of Lenin against Stalinist monolithism. Thus it is hardly surprising that Trotskyism is marked by a comprehensive and universal battle against *Stalinised* Marxism. In this lies its importance, but also its one-sidedness. This one-sidedness has succeeded in paralysing a

181

number of groups claiming the legacy of Trotsky and preventing them from developing new ideas or assessing new developments since the death of Trotsky. In the theoretical realm many new ideas are being discussed by Marxists in economics and politics. They cannot be answered or discussed by the simple repetition of timeless truths, churned out like some religious litany. That is not a tradition which either Lenin or Trotsky, not to mention Marx, would have acknowledged as their own. What characterised the generation of classical Marxists was their ability to discuss, debate and, if necessary, *change* their ideas. It was the dead weight of Stalinism which introduced theoretical and political monolithism into the workers' movement. Some of this was reflected even amongst those who were to combat it in the most vigorous fashion.

For their part the new Marxist intellectuals are often characterised by a theoretical absolutism. They search for the "ultimate truth" in their particular field, imagine they have established it and paint all those who disagree with it as "anti-Marxist". In some cases journals are established on the basis of some new discovery and around them new cliques are formed. Since they tend to exist only in the realm of ideas they can go in any direction. There is no restraint, no limit and no discipline to which they can respond, and this is their fundamental weakness. And *it* is related to their refusal to understand the primacy of politics within which the relative autonomy of theory has to be inserted. This apolitical character of some of the new Marxist intellectuals is only increased by the dogmatism and sectarianism of many of the revolutionary groups.

The fusion of these two seemingly disparate layers could be of some importance for the British left. Both have a great deal to learn from each other. An understanding of this could go some way towards reversing the critical condition of socialist politics and lay the basis for the creation of a new revolutionary socialist party in Britain. The weaknesses of the British left cannot be explained away by the recalcitrance of objective political conditions. The physicians of Marxism must cure themselves before their remedies are generally respected.

7. Reflections on Socialism and Democracy

"In one sense the House of Commons is the most unrepresentative of representative assemblies. It is an elaborate conspiracy to prevent the real clash of opinion which exists outside from finding an appropriate echo within its walls. It is a social shock absorber placed between privilege and the pressure of popular consent."

Aneurin Bevan: *In Place Of Fear*

"In a developed capitalist society, during a 'democratic' régime, the bourgeoisie leans for support primarily upon the working classes, which are held in check by the reformists. In its most finished form, this system finds its highest expression in Britain during the administration of the Labour Government as well as during that of the Conservatives. In the course of many decades, the workers have built up within the bourgeois democracy, by utilising it, by fighting against it, their own strongholds and bases of *proletarian democracy*: the trade unions, the political parties, the educational and sport clubs, the cooperatives, etc. The proletariat cannot attain power within the formal limits of bourgeois democracy, but can do so only by taking the road of revolution: this has been proved by theory and experience. And these bulwarks of workers' democracy within the bourgeois state are absolutely essential for taking the revolutionary road."

Trotsky: *The Struggle Against Fascism in Germany*

The development of representative bourgeois democracy has been uneven. Its existence has been essentially confined to Western Europe and North America. In Japan it was institutionalised through the use of nuclear weapons and an army of occupation. On the three continents of Africa, Asia and Latin America, India is an exception in terms of enjoying a period of continuous bourgeois democracy. Within Western

Europe democracy has had a chequered career. Its functioning was somewhat defective in the period following the First World War. The democratic rights guaranteed by a bourgeois democratic régime were withdrawn in a number of countries either through indigenous fascist upheavals (Italy, Portugal, Germany) or through military occupation (France, Belgium, Austria, Holland, Czechoslovakia and Norway) and on one occasion by a combination of the two (Spain). Bourgeois democracy succeeded in establishing a political continuity only after the Second World War. In the "third world" a new brand of neo-colonial, military fascism gained ground in the post-war period. Today it envelops much of Latin America and large sections of Asia and Africa — a peremptory warning of the lengths to which the ruling classes are prepared to go in order to preserve their privileges.

And yet it is worth remembering that centuries elapsed between the beginning of bourgeois revolutions and the establishment of democracy. The first of these anti-feudal upheavals was the eighty-year war between the Low Countries and the Spanish Empire in the sixteenth century. A republic based on militant Protestant principles was furtively established: Holland was the most advanced nation of the seventeenth century. Its naval and commercial strength were universally acknowledged. Its citizens enjoyed greater freedoms than the rest of Europe.

The English Revolution was the next in line. It was the first major bourgeois revolution in terms of boosting the economic ascent of a new social class. Provided that the landed gentry accepted the new role of this class and placed no fetters or restrictions on its economic development, a compromise could be agreed. The compact between the victorious leaders of the English Revolution and their erstwhile foes emasculated much of the democratic *political* content of the Revolution. At its zenith the Revolution had authorised the execution of the monarch and the leading ideological symbol of divine absolutism, Archbishop Laud. After the compact it turned upon the radical wing of the New Model Army, led by the Levellers, which was arguing for more democracy and crushed it without encountering any mass resistance. The political concordat established by Cromwell and Ireton led to a re-establishment of the monarchy, but attempts to revert to royal absolutism were rejected in 1688. The political structures of the British State were to remain thoroughly undemocratic. Universal adult franchise did not exist in Britain until 300 years after the execution of Charles I. The franchise was initially extended by a Tory leader, Disraeli, in 1867 to prevent a resurgence of chartism. The democratic programme of the chartists has still to be fully realised. Their demand for annual parliaments was never taken seriously. But it remains, nonetheless, an important democratic objective. If achieved it could considerably aid in breaking the mass apathy which exists between elections. It would also bring home to millions of working people the advantages of being able to influence political change at short and regular intervals. It would challenge the growing encroachment on democratic rights which today characterises a number of states in the West.

The first real political gains of revolutionary bourgeois democracy were established after the French Revolution of 1789. Here, too, the representative character of mass democratic institutions did not last long, though even in its short life it traumatised reactionary Europe, with the British gendarme at its head. Many of the gains of the Revolution were preserved despite the advent of Bonapartism. The last progressive phase of bourgeois-democratic upheavals in Europe was in 1848-71. The 1848 revolts were the first signs of a continental upheaval. They were halted because the liberals at their head lost their nerve and retreated. Repression soon followed, accompanied by reforms from above, though these did not guarantee the national independence of Hungary, Poland or Italy. But the 1848 revolutions left their mark on all classes in society. Marx and Engels had composed the *Communist Manifesto* a few weeks before the outbreak of the 1848 revolution in France. The document announced that the working class had emerged on the stage of history as a class by itself, that its interests were universal and that from henceforth it would be a decisive factor in all struggles. In its own fashion, the liberal bourgeoisie, too, took note of this announcement. Even though it was somewhat premature, the experience of the Paris Commune of 1871 appeared to shelve all possible doubts on the question. The Commune was savagely repressed. The new forms of democracy to which it had given birth were stillborn.

The country where democracy was extended the farthest in 1848-71 was the United States of America. The successful prosecution of the Civil War by the Union resulted in dramatic changes in the social structure of the Confederacy. Slavery was destroyed as an economic force, and political rights were granted to the black people of America. Former slaves were elected to the Congress and the state legislatures. The whole period of the Reconstruction has been vividly analysed by Peter Camejo, the American Marxist, in his book, *Racism, Revolution and Reaction, 1861-77: The Rise and Fall of Radical Reconstruction* (New York, 1976). While slavery was destroyed as an institution a political compromise was effected with the Southern ruling class: its first casualty was the democratic rights of the blacks.

American bourgeois democracy always had a strong populist content. This was partially due to its lateness, partially to the fact that it had to confront a collectivist, tribal civilisation rather than an embattled feudal aristocracy. This populism provided more vigorous democratic institutions for the white majority (a comparison between the judiciary, press and parliament of the United States and Britain would be extremely instructive) and forestalled the development of a labour movement in the European sense. American workers and trades unions have still to construct their own political party! This absence continues to provide Marxists with an irritating paradox: the country which is *objectively* the best suited for a rapid transition to socialism also possesses a working class, which has the distinction of being the most politically backward in the advanced capitalist world.

The development of bourgeois democracy received a set of severe blows with the First World War, the Russian Revolution and the post-war economic crisis. The combination of the last two created situations in a number of countries which favoured the overthrow of capitalism. But the Entente powers, while unable to crush the October revolution in Russia, were successful in isolating it (in both a political and military sense) from the rest of Europe. The Spartacist rebellion was crushed in Germany; the Bavarian Soviet was a short-lived affair; the Hungarian Commune was defeated by a Rumanian expeditionary force; the factory occupations in Italy were dismantled and by 1921 capitalism had succeeded in restoring a certain

186

degree of stability. In Italy the initiative was seized by the fascist squads. The demoralisation and despair which gripped Italy ended in the victory of Mussolini, blessed by capital and sanctified by the Vatican. In Germany the Weimar Republic was an unstable and rickety political exercise. The polarisation in German society proceeded at an alarming pace. The political tactics necessary to defeat German fascism eluded the German Communist Party and the social-democrats. From his exile, Trotsky argued cogently for a policy of united fronts against fascism. His appeals went unheard. The fascists exploited the divisions between the communists and the social-democrats quite ruthlessly. They developed a populist rhetoric; they even organised strikes. In 1933 they conquered Germany without a battle. The big battalions of the Communist and Social-Democratic parties succumbed without a struggle. At a stroke Hitler destroyed the most powerful working class in Western Europe. The defeat of Republican Spain ensured the stability of German fascism. It now embarked on a policy of conquest through war. The Iberian peninsula, Italy and Germany were all to be governed by fascist régimes. Fascism, albeit in a state of advanced senility, was removed from Spain and Portugal in the seventies.

The Second World War was thus much more complicated than the First had been. It was not simply a war between major imperialist powers for the division of the world. For a start the Soviet Union was invaded by the German war machine. Stalin's pathetic attempts to reach an accommodation with Hitler (symbolised by the Ribbentrop-Molotov pact) now blew up in his face. In addition the development of the Resistance in France, Italy and Belgium made futile a comparison between the First and Second World Wars. At the same time, however, the colonial countries ruled by Britain and France saw the development of a massive national resistance against the occupying powers. There were many wars fought within the Second World War.

The Japanese invasion of China allowed the partisans of Mao Tse-Tung to use global inter-imperialist contradictions to the advantage of the Chinese Communist Party. There can be little doubt that it was the vigorous prosecution of the anti-Japanese war which enabled the Chinese revolutionary armies to defeat Chiang Kai Shek. But in Europe there was no similar dénouement, with the exceptions of Yugoslavia and Albania. The Yalta Pact, signed by Churchill, Roosevelt and Stalin, divided Europe into spheres of influence. France and Italy were assigned to the West. The Communist Parties in both countries handed in their weapons; politically they were disarmed by Moscow. Thus, in reality, the existence of bourgeois democracy as we know it is a comparatively recent phenomenon. Its history could well have been different had it not been for the historic compromise effected in both France and Italy: the concordat between Stalinism and Capitalism. The United States did the rest. Massive amounts of capital were injected through the Marshall Plan to revive a war-damaged capitalist economy in Western Europe and Japan. The net result of these interrelated political and economic factors was a long economic boom, which spanned the two most vital post-war decades of the capitalist world. Bourgeois democracy flourished as never before under the umbrella of full employment and economic growth, though it could not conquer the congenital political instability of the French Fourth Republic. The advent of de Gaulle in 1958 signalled the beginning of new problems. The Fifth Republic was based on a drastic restriction of democratic rights.

As the economies recovered the bourgeoisie inaugurated ideological offensive. The cold war of the fifties was designed to permanently inoculate the masses against Communism. But this immunisation was effective only as long as living standards continued to rise. Once the spell was broken, as it was in 1968-69, the potential of a radical working class could put everything at risk. The late sixties and seventies have seen an acceleration of the economic crisis. Living standards have fallen throughout the advanced capitalist world. At the beginning of the seventies the total level of unemployment in the seven major capitalist countries stood at 10 million. Thus the radicals of 1968 became intertwined with a broader discontent which began to develop in the factories. The economic crisis intersected with a growing crisis of legitimacy for bourgeois governments.

By the middle of the present decade — not so much the red seventies as the cautious seventies — the governments of a number of major states had been toppled or shaken by a severe political crisis: Heath, Nixon, Tanaka, Brandt and Fanfani

188

became victims of diverse political convulsions. The dictatorships in Portugal and Spain were overthrown or dismantled; Swedish social-democracy surrendered governmental power after a reign which had lasted four decades and a general strike shook the neighbouring Scandinavian state of Denmark. Ten years after the tremors of 1968, the political and economic situation in France, Portugal, Spain, Italy and Britain can, by no stretch of the imagination be described as stable. France and Italy both have a severe political crisis at governmental level. The task of revolutionaries is, in these circumstances, to concentrate on agitating for a workers' government committed to a wide-ranging series of socialist measures.

The early bourgeois revolutions triumphed against feudalism only after extensive class struggles and civil wars. Their political aims were not to be realised for hundreds of years. The socialist revolutions, which have marked the twentieth century and opened an epoch of "wars and revolutions", took place in Tsarist Russia, Japanese-occupied China, colonised Vietnam, German-occupied Yugoslavia and a Cuba totally dependent on the United States. They were all a result of varied political, social and economic factors. Yet they shared a common characteristic: none of them confronted the central enemy of the workers' movement in Western Europe. For the social formations whose foundations were shattered by the revolution were societies where the political structures were determined by pre-capitalist social relations. The working class was a minority of the population. Even though it acquired a strategic importance in Russia and China in the first twenty years of this century, a whole series of factors helped to overthrow Tsarism and the Kuomintang dictatorship. In Russia, China, Yugoslavia and Vietnam a social revolution was carried out in the midst of war. The Bolsheviks used the *unpopular* character of the war to win over the masses. The Communist Parties in the other three countries transformed a popular war against occupying armies, into a civil war, laying the basis for a successful social upheaval. In all cases the parties of revolution had to leap over the bourgeois stage of the process in order to create a new state. Bourgeois revolution in the twentieth century could not rid the Russian or Chinese peasantry from the yoke of its traditional oppressors; it could not bring about the unification of Vietnam; it could not release itself from the fetters of imperialism in Cuba. Thus it had to be transcended with the implicit or explicit consent of the majority of the population. In Western Europe the very existence of bourgeois democracy allowed reformism and trade unionism to gain a strong base in the working class. It was the task of winning over the masses still under the hegemony of reformist politics which compelled the Communist International 1921 to develop its theses on the "United Front". The united front thus constituted an attempt both to win the mass of workers to the revolution and to unify political and economic demands against the resistance of the reformist leaders of the trades unions and the social-democratic parties. It attempted to develop a set of tactics which sought to achieve united *actions* by reformist and revolutionary workers on the problems confronting the working class. At the same time the united front permitted a total political and ideological freedom to criticise each other even while conducting common struggles. The United Front was forgotten in the late twenties and the early thirties as Stalinism captured the international communist movement. Trotsky's urgent messages from Prinkipo in 1930-33 raised the issue once again, but to no avail. German Communism ignored his advice and misled the workers into the greatest defeat to be suffered by the Western working class. After the victory of fascism, Stalin's supporters attempted to resurrect the "United Front", but in the cynical caricatures of the Popular Fronts of 1936 in both France and Spain. The Italian Communist Party's strategic thrust towards the Christian Democrats embodied in the formula of the "historic compromise" marks a further abandonment of the classical Marxist application of the United Front.

The electoral legitimacy acquired by bourgeois-democracy needed the articulation of transitional demands and institutions in the passage to socialism. "Transitional" implies that there can not be one straight leap from reform to revolution in advanced capitalist countries. Transitional demands were designed to be comprehensible and acceptable to workers not prepared for a "socialist revolution". At the same time they could not be integrated into the normal functioning of the capitalist economy. The pressure of the mass of workers would create a political imbalance and allow the possibility of a revolutionary break. Transitional demands were designed to counter the division between politics and trade unionism so loved by reformist leaders. Behind the strategy of developing transitional politics was the understanding that the masses in the West could only be won to socialism through their own experiences. It was envisaged that the fight for transitional demands would lead to the creation of transitional institutions: organs of a dual power. These would coexist with the capitalist state, but outside the capitalist economy. Finally there would be a test of strength. The approach underlined by the united front and transitional demands remains fundamentally correct. It cannot be argued that it has failed because it has still to be applied by a mass party in the West.

The bourgeois *democratic* régime was overthrown in the West. It was replaced by a bourgeois *fascist* state. It is worth recalling that those who dismembered democratic liberties and ruled through coercion and genocide were not socialists, but fascists. Democracy was dismantled by capitalism (the most recent example is the overthrow of Allende in Chile). While the fascist demagogues used a populist and anti-Establishment demagogy to establish a mass base, they stayed in power with the backing of the large capitalist corporations. Those liberal writers who argue that fascism cannot be equated with capitalism mean well, but are, of course, completely wrong. Fascism can certainly not be equated with bourgeois-democracy, but it is an extreme variant of capitalist rule — the final solution of a system unable to maintain itself in any other way. It is the punishment that capital inflicts on the working class for daring to threaten its stability and legitimacy. A look at the statistics provides further proof. The profits from all industrial and commercial businesses rose from 6.6 billion marks in 1933 to 15 billion marks in 1938! Siemens doubled its sales and its profits. Krupp tripled his takings and those of the munition barons increased tenfold. It would be a very strange capitalist who would not support a régime which made all this possible. German fascism was the only way in which the collective interests of German capitalism could be defended. The options which confronted all German workers in 1930-33 were not "bourgeois democracy" or "fascism", but socialist revolution or fascist barbarism. These questions are not just empty abstractions. They are becoming important once again as the ugly head of fascism rears itself in country after country in Western Europe.

The rise of old fascist ideas in "new" guises is now universally acknowledged. While anti-semitism remains an ingredient, the central focus of the fascists has shifted to the victimisation of black migrant workers. They have felt the lash of fascist actions: their shops have been stoned; their houses burnt and there have been killings as well. The two ideological weapons consistently used by the fascists are chauvinism and racism They represent the most vulnerable points in the armour of the British workers' movement and reformist ideology. In France and Italy the main thrust is anti-communism, though neither brand currently on display is in counterposition to the other.

In Britain the main demand of the fascists is expressed in the slogan: "If they're black, send them back." It is a sentiment which is not restricted to the fascists. It has been raised a number of times by Enoch Powell and it has support amongst the right wing of the Conservative and Unionist Party. The threat to the democratic rights of a small ethnic minority is posed by fascists and racists. The curtailment of civil liberties in both Germany and Britain ("Beruversbot" and the Prevention of Terrorism Act) have been authorised by social-democratic governments. The institutionalised discrimination practised for decades against the Catholics in Northern Ireland has been backed by the armed might of the British state. Democratic rights are certainly being threatened, but not by socialists or Marxists.

The function of a bourgeois democracy is to secure the consent of the masses to their own exploitiation and oppression. The price paid for obtaining this consent is to permit important democratic liberties such as the existence of trade unions and political parties, the right to publish and distribute every brand of political propaganda, participate in elections, etc. Political competition is permitted as long as the bourgeoisie's monopoly of legitimate violence is not challenged. Such a system is obviously the best possible way of integrating the masses into the existing social, economic and political order. The qualitative growth of the mass media, the enormous power of television, leading to a real decline in the reading habits of the masses, are all developments which enable this situation to be prolonged. It is this combined weight of bourgeois institutions — parliament, media, church, family — which represents

192

the biggest obstacle to the victory of socialism in the West. Despite the phenomenal growth in the rise of the working class; despite the rapid growth of membership of trades unions; despite the existence of mass communist parties in two major Western European countries, the strength and power of bourgeois ideology and bourgeois institutions have yet to be contested and displaced. The French general strike of May 1968, the pre-revolutionary upsurge in Portugal in 1975, the workers' upsurge in Britain in 1972-74 were not defeated by bloody counter-revolutions, but by bourgeois-democratic institutions. The distinction is an important one. Unless it is fully understood the formulation of a coherent revolutionary strategy will be impossible. The process of de-Francoisation in Spain, too, was not the outcome of a general strike, as the far left had predicted for many years, but was brought about by a series of reforms from above. They were sufficient, temporarily, to contain the potential of the mass upsurge which still exists in Spain.

The strength of bourgeois democratic institutions does not derive from the fact that they are bourgeois, but that they permit a certain degree of indirect democracy. This is important because the only alternative model that actually exists is the Stalinist model of the USSR and Eastern Europe. The negative impact of Stalinism has, till recently, been gravely underestimated by the left. What compels the mass of workers to seek shelter within the confines of bourgeois-democratic institutions is the bureaucratic monstrosity which exists in the Eastern part of Europe. The problem can be posed in a more positive fashion: if socialist democracy existed in the Soviet Union and the Eastern European states, the struggle for socialism would be infinitely easier in the West.

The reason that no democracy exists in the East has little to do with socialism, Marxism or Leninism. It is partially a result of the objective conditions which prevailed in post-revolutionary Russia in the first decade that followed 1917. Two revolutions, a long civil war, economic blockade and the defeat of the revolution in Germany and Hungary set the stage for the collective exhaustion of the Soviet working class and the tyranny of Stalinism. In the early period of the Revolution, and most noticeably in its first year, democracy did exist in revolutionary Russia. Other soviet parties were permitted, there was freedom of the press and fierce debates took place within the Bolshevik Party. *Red Pepper,* a revolutionary satirical journal, did not spare any of the leaders of the Revolution in its cartoons or barbs.

The semi-religious conformity and monolithism was to come later. In fact there was more democracy in the Soviet Union of 1917-18 than there was in Britain during the duration of the First or Second World Wars. For political activity in Britain virtually ceased during these periods. The press functioned under a severe form of self-censorship. In contrast the war was a subject of open discussion in the Bolshevik and left press in Russia. A public discussion took place as to whether or not the Treaty of Brest-Litovsk with the Germans should be signed. Lenin was in a small minority on the Central Committee. In Moscow, the Bolshevik leader, Bukharin produced a public opposition journal demanding that the Red Army continue the war. In a set of quixotic arguments this otherwise talented Bolshevik argued: better to die for the world revolution than be stifled to death by Russian backwardness. Restrictions on freedom were imposed only after the opposition had taken up arms and had refused to accept soviet legality. Even these measures were designed to be a temporary response to the civil war. Lenin specified that the term "dictatorship of the proletariat" meant precisely that and not dictatorship over the proletariat. It was the working-class equivalent of the "dictatorship of the bourgeoisie" which existed in the most advanced countries of the West, such as Britain and the United States. And lest the term be mistaken, Lenin drafted his "Theses on Bourgeois Democracy and the dictatorship of the Proletariat" in which he categorically affirmed that:

> ". . . proletarian dictatorship is the forcible suppression of the resistance of the exploiters, i.e., an insignificant minority of the population, the landowners and capitalists. It follows that proletarian dictatorship must inevitably entail not only a change in democratic forms and institutions, generally speaking, but precisely such a change as provides an unparalleled extension of the actual enjoyment of democracy by those oppressed by capitalism — the toiling classes . . . all this implies and presents to the toiling classes, i.e., the vast majority of the population, greater practical opportunities for enjoying democratic rights and liberties than ever existed before,

even approximately, in the best and most democratic bourgeois republics."

In his celebrated reply to the German leader, Karl Kautsky, Lenin even defended the rights of bourgeois parties in the soviets. He stated that the Kadets had excluded themselves by taking up arms against the new State. In other words the acceptance of soviet legality was the only condition for a party to be allowed to function, even in times of civil war. This was a far cry from Stalin's Gulag, which could only be imposed because of the specific conditions of Russia, isolated and starved in the twenties and thirties. Stalin and the grouping around him transformed the emergency measures curtailing democracy into a "socialist" virtue, institutionalised them and imposed a ruthless dictatorship, which preserved the economic base created by the revolution but destroyed its political aims and aspirations and emasculated its humanity and vision. It went further and transformed this, the most universal of all revolutions, into a nationalist nightmare.

The growing equation of the party and state apparatus led to the crystallisation of a bureaucratic caste. It had its own special privileges embodied in a total monopoly of politics. All aspects of the party and non-party life were brought under the control of the bureaucracy. The masses were not allowed to intervene. Not a single trace of soviet or inner-party democracy could be discovered in Stalin's Russia. It is well-known that Stalin carried out the execution of more revolutionaries and communists than the Tsar.

These facts are now widely accepted by the workers' movement in the West. For a protracted period, long before Solzhenitsyn discovered what Stalinism represented, the Left Opposition (associated with Trotsky) inside and outside Russia fought against the Stalinist tide. It was defeated and decimated. Three-quarters of Lenin's Central Committee at the time of the Revolution was liquidated. Its central theoretician, Trotsky, fortunately in exile, survived. His pen continued writing till an assassin in the pay of the Kremlin put an ice-pick in his skull. But Trotsky had already produced two classics. His *History of the Russian Revolution* displayed an amazing breadth of vision and culture. It remains the only detailed authentic inside account of that event. His other work *The*

Revolution Betrayed was not written in the same style, but was politically crucial. It analysed Stalin's Russia, dissected its organisms and pronounced that it was already in a state of advanced degeneration. Throughout his life Trotsky, despite the losses he suffered, continued to analyse the Soviet state as a "workers' state", a *post*-capitalist phenomenon. This definition may turn out, despite the controversy that continues to surround it, to have been the most scientific definition of the post-capitalist state. It remains a fact that the bureaucracy rests essentially on a section of the working class of its respective country. It has no independent social base. The Stalinist parties in the USSR and Eastern Europe are composed primarily of workers. Clearly the bureaucracy cultivates the more privileged workers, who are over-represented in the party. The official ideology of the State is "Marxism and Leninism". True it is deformed beyond recognition into a state religion, twisted to justify atrocities of every sort. But it remains the only possible ideology. It provides the régime with an ideological legitimacy. The Czech events of 1968 have already demonstrated that the working-class base of the party can acquire a powerful and liberating influence if a mass politics is permitted. The lessons of Hungary and Poland confirm this thesis. On another level the official seal of approval granted to the writings of Marx, Engels and Lenin can also, on occasion, produce theoreticians who understand that what exists in their countries is a miserable mutation. The emergence of Rudolf Bahro as a leading Marxist dissident in East Germany is important. His book *The Alternative* (New Left Books, London, 1978) uses the method of Marx to subject the East German "model of socialism" to a savage critique. Bahro's work will ultimately prove to be of greater value than Solzhenitsyn's politics. For Bahro, unlike Solzhenitsyn, charts a course for moving forward. He does not call for the restoration of Junker militarism.

It was Stalin, the leader of a triumphant bureaucracy on the ascendant, who provided the theorisation for a one-party state. He told an American journalist that there was one party in the USSR because there was only one class: "Where there are not several classes, there cannot be several parties, for a party is part of a class." Thus monolothism inside the party was to become the rule. Any opposition was immediately characterised as the intrusion of an alien and hostile class. All the epithets utilised, though in a more colourful and evocative fashion, by the Chinese leaders for dealing with their political opponents have their origins in this pronouncement of Stalin. The Chinese Communist Party learned this particular Stalinist lesson so well that it stretched it to its ultimate logic. Every leader who disagreed with Mao was referred to as a "capitalist-roader". Veterans of the Chinese civil war were slandered as having served the interests of Japanese imperialism. Liu Shao Chi, Lin Piao, the "Gang of Four" were all characterised in a totally unscientific and vulgar fashion. The result of this is that the services of history became superfluous. And if the revolutions in China and Russia were carried out by police spies, provocateurs, agents of foreign powers, etc., then history, indeed, has no use. It is reduced to individuals. The Russian Revolution was made by Lenin and Lenin alone. The Chinese upheaval was the work of Mao. Political parties and leaderships are devalued.

This conception of only one party for every social class is today rejected by most of the Western European Communist Parties as far as the West is concerned. For the USSR, China and Eastern Europe they continue, with some exceptions, to steer a more prudent course.

It was Trotsky who dispassionately spelt out the perverted character of stalinised Marxism. In August 1936 he completed *The Revolution Betrayed*. In it he took up, in addition to numerous other characteristic features of the Stalinist régime, its justification of monolithism and the one-party state:

"The Marxist teaching of the class nature of the party is thus turned into a caricature. The dynamic of political consciousness is excluded from the historical process in the interests of administrative order. In reality classes are heterogeneous; they are torn by inner antagonisms, and arrive at the solution of common problems not otherwise than through an inner struggle of tendencies, groups and parties. It is possible, with certain qualifications, to concede that 'a party is part of a class'. But since a class has many 'parts' — some look forward and some back — one and the same class may create several parties. For the same reason one party may rest upon parts of different classes. An example of only one party corresponding to one class is not to be found in the whole course of political history — provided, of course, you do not take the police appearance for the reality."

197

It is necessary to repeatedly stress this point. Monolithism continues to characterise every single post-capitalist régime in the world. It is true that a number of these states are more flexible in their interpretation of the old Stalinist principle, but they continue to operate it, while bearing in mind differences in national traditions, local specifities, etc.

Thus even the newest post-capitalist state, Vietnam, is governed in a bureaucratic fashion. It is an awkward paradox. After a popular social and anti-imperialist revolution, which inspired millions of people throughout the world it has a post-revolutionary government which exercises a total monopoly of information. It is undoubtedly a superior social and economic order. The living conditions of most of its people will be incomparably better than before. But it is also a fact, and therein lies the contradiction, that the citizens of Saigon and Hue had access to more information under the heavily censored press of the pro-imperialist puppet régimes than they do today.

The National Liberation Front of Vietnam fought the war not just for national independence, but also for "democracy". Its programme maintained that it was fighting in order to: "hold free general elections to elect the National Assembly in a really democratic way, in accordance with the principle of universal, equal, direct suffrage and secret ballot. . . . To proclaim and enforce broad democratic freedoms: freedom of the press and publication, trade union freedom, freedom to form political parties, freedom of creed, freedom of demonstration." This was unambiguously stated in the Political Programme of the NLF in 1967, and it was often repeated. It has still to be put into practice. It is in this context that the Stalinist origins and ideological training of the Vietnamese communists win in the end. After the seizure of state power we see a disjuncture between the propaganda and agitation used to mobilise the masses during the revolutionary struggle and what actually takes its place after victory. All the talk about "democracy" turns out to be a subterfuge, a manoeuvre to obtain mass support. Nothing more. But the future of these revolutions is bound up with democracy — a higher form of socialist democracy. Its absence distorts the internal development of the revolution even with the most benevolent and enlightened leadership (as the Cuban and Vietnamese leaders undoubtedly are when compared to North Korea, Cambodia, Albania, etc.).

This lack of socialist democracy flows from a distortion of Marxism which took place in Stalinist Russia. The response to this has taken a number of different forms over the decades. In the first instance, the experiences of Stalinism helped to revitalise and strengthen the social-democratic current in the workers' movement. The horror of the prison camps and the purges was temporarily obscured by the heroic moment of Stalingrad and the final rout of the Nazi armies. It could not be permanently ignored. Both the ruling class and its social-democratic allies utilised the tyranny of Stalinism to its maximum possible extent. The equation of Stalinism and Marxism reached its apogée during the Cold War in the fifties and early sixties. The spell was broken by the success of the Cuban Revolution and later the American war in South-East Asia. Imperialism's crimes became too blatant to disguise. They created a severe crisis of bourgeois ideology throughout North America and Western Europe.

The Communist Parties of the West were for many years the main transmitters of Stalinist ideology in the workers' movement. Their strength in some countries and their influence amongst the most politically advanced intelligentsia left behind an ideological debris which has still to be swept away. It is true that the invasion of Czechoslovakia marked an important turning point for the Western European Communist Parties. In 1956 when Khruschev had sent Soviet tanks into Budapest, the majority of Communist Party leaders had remained loyal to Moscow. As a result they were racked by internal differences — dissidents were expelled, thousands of others left voluntarily. By 1968 the political atmosphere had changed in Western Europe. The Cold War myths had been punctured by the radicalisation of important sectors of youth. In August 1968 it was the radical youth which marched to the Soviet Embassy in every Western capital with red flags and portraits of Lenin, Trotsky and Rosa Luxemburg to protest against the invasion. The Communist Parties, almost unanimously, opposed the invasion. Moscow was not supported by its usually faithful apparatuses in the West.

The decomposition of international Stalinism gave rise in the seventies to the phenomena of "Eurocommunism". The French, Spanish and Italian parties proclaimed that they were for pluralism. They now opposed a number of the bureaucratic deformations in the Soviet Union and Eastern Europe. Their press occasionally reported persecution of dissidents in Eastern Europe, and their tone became markedly hostile to Moscow. A journalist representing the Italian Communist Party was expelled from Prague by the collaborationist régime.

There were two reasons for this change. First, it reflected the total revulsion for the dictatorial methods and authoritarian character of the Stalinist régime in Moscow which was widespread in the working class. Secondly, and related to the first, the "Eurocommunist" parties were engaged in a strategic accommodation to bourgeois democracy. They were embracing formulae which represented an abandonment of Marxism even on a formal level. They were concentrating on electoral solutions to the crisis and refusing to investigate the explosive force of the crisis of the bourgeois order. Thus the electoral road needed a cleaning of the Stalinist slate. Of all the worthies of Western Communism, it was the Spanish leader, Santiago Carillo who went the furthest in breaking with Moscow. In his controversial book, *Eurocommunism And The State,* he developed an analysis of Soviet society which was derived quite openly from the tradition of Trotsky. The fact that Carillo actually acknowledged this influence was an indication of the remarkable changes that had taken place in the international Stalinist movement. On the other side there was a marked shift to the right in strategic terms. Both the Italian and Spanish communist parties claimed that it was utopian to talk of the overthrow of capitalism. They both supported austerity programmes in their respective countries. The French Communist Party waged a similar battle with different tactical nuances and, on occasion, utilised a leftist demagogy, but one its senior theoreticians, Jean Ellenstem, stated quite categorically in a debate with the Marxist theoretician, Ernest Mandel, in Brussels in November 1977 that: "The passage to socialism in France will be legal, peaceful, evolutionary and democratic or it will not take place at all."

As traditional Stalinist politics disintegrate, two tendencies struggle for dominance within it. In Western Europe the dominant tendency capitulates to bourgeois democracy. At the same time the individual party member is permitted more freedom and certain repressive features of Soviet society are criticised. On the other hand there is a truculent group that remains loyal to the original Stalinist project and still dreams of a "Czecho-slovak" path to "socialism". A crucial common denominator for these two tendencies is a rejection of the need for soviet-type bodies and a denial of proletarian democracy in the party and the broader workers' movement. The bureaucratic régime may allow individual expressions of dissent, but it excludes the organised expression of political differences within the party — tendencies and factions are not permitted. Thus an inevitable organisational split ensues (Greece, Spain, Finland, Sweden, Britain). All these different sections remain united on one level. They reject the crucial source of strength for what Gramsci re-ferred to as the "international class": namely the interna-tionalist coordination of the struggles of the working class against capitalism, imperialism and the bureaucratic usurpation in the East.

A striking feature of the development inside the communist parties has been that those intellectuals who have rejected the adaptations to bourgeois democracy and defended Leninist politics have been crippled by the partiality of their knowledge of the debates within Marxist politics. If one studies the recent writings of two distinctive French intellectuals, Louis Althusser and Etienne Balibar, one is struck by their ignorance. Both are extremely talented Marxist intellectuals. Both have sought to defend aspects of Leninism against the vulgarisations attempted by the French Communist Party leaders. Both make a number of extremely perceptive criticisms. Balibar in his book *On The Dictatorship of the Proletariat* defends many classical Marxist conceptions in an extremely effective fashion. There is, how-ever, something missing in both his work and that of his mentor, Althusser. They genuinely appear to be ignorant of the writings of Leon Trotsky on questions such as proletarian democracy. In that sense Carillo is far more advanced than Althusser, for he has, at least, not allowed his Stalinist ideological training to blind him to the works of an important and, for a period, the only major anti-Stalinist Marxist thinker. In his text, published in the British Marxist magazine, *New Left Review* 104 (July/August 1977), Althusser explicitly rejected the need for organ-ised tendencies and mounted a sophisticated apologia for the anti-democratic positions of the French Communist Party leadership:

201

"Now, *differences,* etc., are one thing; legally recognised, stable, autonomous and hence *organised tendencies* are something else. Organised tendencies did, it is true, exist in Lenin's Bolshevik Party. But in order to be serious here, it is necessary to discuss the *French Party of today.* Recognition of organised tendencies seems to me to be out of the question in the French Party. I am not speaking in opportunist terms here. One must know where one has come from and where one wants to go. I believe that the Party today expects *something else* and that is right. Communists know or feel that in the existence of organised tendencies there is a threat to the unity and hence to the existence and effectiveness of the Party. . . ."

This is not as the Editors of the *New Left Review* state, a simple "ambiguity". It is much more profound and reflects the failure of Althusser to settle accounts with Stalinist politics in a decisive fashion. Similarly Balibar's book does not discuss or defend the conception of pluralism and socialist democracy. The only serious and coherent theorisation of socialist democracy has come from the Marxist opponents of "Eurocommunism". The Fourth International, an international organisation with sixty affiliated revolutionary Marxist organisations throughout the world developed its theses on "Socialist Democracy and the Dictatorship of the Proletariat". These provide an answer to both bourgeois democracy and the confusions of Eurocommunism. They represent a novel theorisation of proletarian pluralism. The Sixth Thesis is a reply to Althusser and those like him who have, so far, been incapable of developing a strategic alternative to the reformist thrust of their organisations. Because of the importance of this thesis it is included as an appendix to this chapter.

The question now under discussion throughout Western Europe is one related to the strategy and tactics required for socialist advances. In recent years a growing assault has been made on Leninist models of "insurrection". Kautsky is being revived in some circles. A serious debate has started within the workers' movement. There is, of course, an objective basis for this debate — a fact sometimes obscured by some of those who intervene and take part in it. An economic crisis has gripped the major capitalist countries of the West. Inflation and recession have led to the biggest post-war decline in living standards throughout Western Europe. This has provoked a series of political crises which have reached an explosive stage in both Italy and France. In Britain they have led to two General Elections in one year (1974) and an increase in nationalist political movements. In Portugal and Spain they led to the dismantling of the fascist apparatus. In Sweden social-democracy was removed after being in power for nearly fifty years. All these developments have posed a set of important questions for socialists and Marxists. Is a revolutionary political strategy relevant to the struggle for socialism or should it wait in the wings while a struggle is mounted against the cultural and ideological domination of the ruling class. The two cannot be counterposed. New discussions challenging the old accepted truths have opened up. Old certainties have been displaced. Marxism can only benefit from such a process for it has much to learn. The sexual and cultural oppression of the masses has certainly to be contested, but only by being integrated within an overall revolutionary political perspective. It is wrong to imagine that there can be a "self-sufficient" project for defeating the ruling class in the field of culture and ideology without engaging in politics. The necessary struggle against the repressive and divisive structures and ideologies of capitalist societies can not be regarded as a *substitute* for proletarian democracy and a revolutionary socialist politics.

For all "cultural" movements — women's liberation, gay liberation, black self-emancipation, etc. — continually come up against the operation of the bourgeois political system. Thus any genuine anti-capitalist current will sooner or later have to face the question of the prevailing forms of bourgeois political power. In a bourgeois democracy this comprises a superstructure of governments and parties which rest on the consent of the masses, and a state apparatus which rests on armed bodies of men. Naturally it is the latter which is the lynchpin of bourgeois social relations, including the governmental system itself. Now the question which arises is how can this system be combated and defeated? A socialist revolution will either be made with the consent of the majority of the working masses or it will not be made at all.

The idea that a revolution in the West could be based on a small minority, however active and militant, is totally absurd. It is a view of revolution advanced only by those who fear the masses. Or by those products of 1968 who, despairing of the mass parties and their domination of working-class politics, have abandoned politics and picked up sub machine-guns and bombs. These latter-day propagandists of the deed are brave, but foolish people. They symbolise a pessimism and despair which have certainly gained ground over the last decade. They want to leap over mass consciousness and physically assault a few, minor ruling-class citadels. They are wrong. The actions of the "Red Army Faction" in Germany have proved to be self-destructive in both the literal and the political sense. Impatience is no substitute for politics. Those who carry out similar operations in France and Italy do themselves and what they claim to be fighting for a grave disservice. Attempts to kill journalists and trade union bureaucrats, cannot take the struggle for socialism even a tiny step forward. Tactics of this sort are a response to the reformism and opportunism of the working-class apparatus. The masses, however, cannot be ignored. Nor can they be excluded from the struggle for socialism.

How will the mass of working people be won over to revolutionary politics? Terrorism is certainly not the answer. But mere propaganda is insufficient. For the masses a break with their everyday consciousness can come only through gigantic upheavals and explosions: in their different ways Portugal, France, Chile and Czecholsovakia provide us with examples of these shake-ups in society. It is during periods such as these that revolutionary Marxists attempt, through political intervention and example, to create new and more democratic organs of power, which can organise the daily life of the people. Is this a utopia? The Communist Party in France in May 1968 could have inaugurated a situation of dual power by overthrowing the highly undemocratic structures of the Fifth Republic. It chose not to do so. Its opponents on its left will certainly attempt such a change when the opportunity next presents itself. For unless the spontaneous thrust of a mass upheaval is channelled through independent organs of power (soviets) within whose framework an alternative political and economic focus to capitalism can be discussed there will not be any real challenge to the strength of ruling-class institutions. Revolutionaries will certainly struggle for a maximum influence and strength within the instiutions of bourgeois democracy, but with the purpose of creating something which is more democratic. To put it provocatively, we can, in some countries, conceive of a parliamentary path to soviets, but never a parliamentarist road to socialism. The difference is an important and crucial one. For even a left-reformist government (Allende in Chile) will eventually, in a period of economic crisis, not be tolerated by the State. It can either die without a struggle or attempt to fight back with mass support. Naturally there is never a guarantee of success, but that is something different from the road which is normally followed and which always leads to failure. German social-democracy claimed that its tactics were the best ones because they had been "tried and tested" in struggles. And yet this old party of the German workers submitted without a fight in the face of the fascist offensive. The "tried and tested tactics" of Chilean reformism could not prevent the victory of Pinochet. When sophisticated versions of the same tactics are presented to us once again in the recent writings of Nicos Poulantzas and his admirers we can only remark that they reflect an impatience and a pessimism which are unacceptable. Poulantzas maintains that the way forward is to create a rupture *within* the existing institutions of the State by weakening and demobilising them beyond repair. It is a noble ambition, but here he makes an obverse mistake to those who have an instrumentalist view of the ruling class. For he imagines that a gradual and growing rupture will not meet with any resistance from important sections of the ruling class. They will stand to one side and congratulate those who wish to democratise the state-apparatus. This, at the very least, represents a serious underestimation of ruling-class strengths.

While it is true that in Western Europe the coercive apparatus of the State is unlikely to be weakened by interventions from without (through world wars or military occupation) nonetheless only an extremely audacious political strategy can win over the bulk of the conscripted soldiers to the side of the masses. De Gaulle understood the dangers of this in France in May-June 1968. One can agree that in normal periods we must struggle for the maximum possible enlargement of democratic freedoms: political and trades union rights for all members of the army, police, civil services, etc. We can go even further and demand, like the English Chartists of the nineteenth century, annual parliaments. This, incidentally, is a demand never fulfilled by any bourgeois democracy. The nearest is the bi-annual elections to the House of Representatives in the United States, though even here the emergence of a mass workers' party would probably lead to important changes in the Constitution. Why is this demand still feared? Because it threatens the *indirect* character of modern representative democracy. An annual general election would destabilise bourgeois rule and induce a much greater interest in political participation of the mass of voters. It would be the closest one could probably get to the right of electors to recall their representatives from any elective assembly, which is the basic principle of a soviet-type body. Aligned to it must be the demand for proportional representation, which is the most democratic way of assessing real voting strength.

An insurrection can only be successful if the State apparatus is divided and disintegrated. Portugal in 1975 provided the first post-war example of this process in a Western European country. A successful insurrection has to be based on an overall *political* strategy. This was lacking in Portugal as was the instrument which could have implemented it. Nonetheless there will ultimately be a test of strength with the élite corp of the bourgeois state. The point is to make its resistance as short as possible. But the coercive apparatus of the State will have to be defeated before the State can be transformed. We do not believe that this is a utopia and nor, incidentally, does the ruling class. But we are weak and the ruling class is strong. This situation can only be transformed by developing a strategy to win over the masses from reformism. Without that, socialism is a pipedream.

The weaknesses of what has been loosely defined as the "new left" can now be seen. What was "new" about the left which developed in the late sixties and seventies was its distance from the traditional organisations of the working class and their dominant ideologies. Thus social-democracy and Stalinism had few attractions for the radicals who challenged the ruling class on the campuses. This, of course, represented a tremendous strength. It led to a revival of creative Marxism throughout the Continent. Its weakness was that it had a small implantation inside the working class. And the latter remains the only agency for social change in the advanced capitalist countries. True, it needs allies in the new, middle groups: the technicians are important allies not just in a numerical sense, but in the concrete help they will be able to provide in any situation of dual power. But without the active involvement of those who function at the point of production, there can be no threat to the existing social order. Thus, the "new left" has to challenge the hold of the "old left" over the working classes if it is to transcend its weaknesses. This, as has been stressed, can not be achieved overnight. It requires a long and persistent struggle on a number of different terrains. Over the last decade many of the radicals of 1968 have gone in different directions. Some have retreated to the relative safety of numbers provided by the Communist parties. Others have opted for a pastoral existence which enables them to give priority to *their* personal problems without the "interference" of politics. Those who have remained politically active have confronted a number of thorny political and strategic questions. Not all of these have been satisfactorily resolved. Nor can they be by a simple repetition of the classical texts of Marxism. It is the method of the latter that needs to be developed.

In the twenties and thirties large sections of the working class were won over to the ideals of Marxism. In the sixties and seventies the process has been much slower. One major breach in the system of capitalist fortifications and everything could change overnight. 1968 saw the rebirth of revolutionary socialism in Europe. It helped to lay the ideological foundations of the new structure that is required. The task remains one of construction. The central argument of this book is that the political conditions in Europe — East and West — remain favourable, despite a number of important setbacks, for the development of mass revolutionary organisations which will put socialist democracy on the agenda once again.

Appendix

The Sixth Thesis from the "Theses on Socialist Democracy and the Dictatorship of the Proletariat" adopted by the Fourth International in May 1977. The complete text can be obtained from The Other Bookshop, 328 Upper Street, London N.1.

Among those who claim to stand for the dictatorship of the proletariat, it is only the Stalinists who advance a theoretically and politically consistent alternative to our programme of socialist democracy based on workers councils and a multiparty system within which the revolutionary vanguard party fights for political leadership by winning the majority of the toilers to its views. The Stalinist alternative is based on the exercise of state power under the "dictatorship of the proletariat" *by a single party in the name of the working class*. This alternative is based upon the following (not often clearly stated) assumptions:

    a. That the "leading party" or even its "leading nucleus" has a monopoly on scientfiic knowledge and is guaranteed infallibility (which implies the theological and scholastic conclusion that one cannot give the same rights to those who defend truth and those who propagate falsehoods).

    b. That the working class, and even more the toiling masses in general, are too backward politically, too much under the influence of bourgeois and petty-bourgeois ideology, too much inclined to prefer immediate material advantages as against historical social interests, for any direct exercise of state power by democratically elected workers councils; genuine workers democracy would entail the risk of an increasing series of harmful, objectively counter-revolutionary decisions which would open the road to the restoration of capitalism, or at the very least gravely damage and retard the process of building socialism.

    c. That therefore the dictatorship of the proletariat can be exercised only by the "leading party for the proletariat", i.e., that the dictatorship of the proletariat *is* the dictatorship of the party (either representing an essentially passive working class,

208

or actively basing itself on the class struggle of the masses, who are nevertheless considered unworthy of directly exercising state power themselves).

d. That since the party, and that party alone, represents the interests of the working class, which are considered homogeneous in all situations and on all issues, the "leading party" itself must be monolithic. Any opposition tendency necessarily reflects alien class pressure and alien class interests in one form or another. (The struggle between two lines is the struggle between the proletariat and the bourgeoisie inside the party, the Maoists conclude.) Monolithic control of all spheres of social life by the single party is the logical outcome of these concepts. Direct party control must be established over all sectors of "civil society".

e. A further underlying assumption is that of an intensification of the class struggle in the period of building socialism (although this assumption alone does not necessarily lead to the same conclusions if it is not combined with the previous ones). From that assumption is deduced the increasing danger of restoration of bourgeois power even long after private property in the means of production has been abolished, and irrespective of the level of development of the productive forces. The threat of bourgeois restoration is portrayed as the mechanical outcome of the victory of bourgeois ideology in this or that social, political, cultural, or even scientific field. In view of the extreme power thereby attributed to bourgeois ideas, the use of repression against those who are said to objectively represent these ideas becomes a corollary of the argument.

All these assumptions are unscientific from a general theoretical point of view and are untenable in the light of the real historical experience of the class struggle during and after the overthrow of capitalist rule in the USSR and other countries. Again and again they have shown themselves to be harmful to the defence of the proletariat's class interests and an obstacle to a successful struggle against the remnants of the bourgeoisie and of bourgeois ideology. But inasmuch as they had become nearly universally accepted dogmas by the CPs in Stalin's time and undoubtedly have an inner consistency — a reflection of the material interests of the bureaucracy as a social layer — they have never been explicitly and thoroughly criticised and rejected by any CP since then. These concepts continue to linger on, at least partially, in the ideology of many leaders and cadres of the CPs and SPs, i.e., of the bureaucracies of the labour movement. They continue to constitute a conceptual source for justifying various forms of curtailing the democratic rights

209

of the toiling masses in the bureaucratised workers states, as well as in those sectors of the labour movement in the capitalist countries which are dominated by the CPs. A clear and coherent refutation of these concepts is indispensable in defending our programme of socialist democracy.

First: the idea of a homogeneous working class exclusively represented by a single party is contradicted by all historical experience and by any Marxist, materialist analysis of the concrete growth and development of the contemporary proletariat, both under capitalism and after the overthrow of capitalism. At most, one could defend the thesis that the revolutionary vanguard party alone *programmatically* defends the *long-term historical* interests of the proletariat. But even in that case, a dialectical-materialist approach, as opposed to a mechanical-idealist one, would immediately add that only insofar as that party actually conquers political leadership over the majority of the workers can one speak of an integration of immediate and long-term class interests having been achieved in practice, with the possibilities for error much reduced.

In fact, there is a definite, objectively determined *stratification* of the working class and of the development of working-class consciousness. There is likewise at the very least a tension between the struggle for immediate interests and the historical goals of the labour movement (for example, the contradiction between immediate consumption and long-term investment). Precisely these contradictions, rooted in the legacy of uneven development of bourgeois society, are among the main theoretical justifications for the need for a revolutionary vanguard, as opposed to a simple "all inclusive" union of all wage-earners in a single party. But this again implies that one cannot deny that different parties, with different orientations and different ways of approaching the class struggle between capital and labour and the relations between immediate demands and historical goals, can arise and have arisen within the working class and do genuinely represent sectors of the working class (be it purely sectoral interests, ideological pressures of alien class forces, etc.).

Second: a revolutionary party with a democratic internal life does have a tremendous advantage in the field of correct analysis of socioeconomic and political developments and of correct elaboration of tactical and strategic answers to such developments, for it can base itself on the body of scientific socialism, Marxism, which synthesises and generalises all past experiences of the class struggle as a whole.

This programmatic framework for its current political

elaboration makes it much less likely than any other tendency of the labour movement, or any unorganised sector of the working class, to reach wrong conclusions, premature generalisations, and one-sided and impressionistic reactions to unforeseen developments, to make concessions to ideological and political pressures of alien class forces, to engage in unprincipled political compromises, etc. These undeniable facts, confirmed again and again by every turn of events in the more than three-quarters of a century since Bolshevism was founded, are the most powerful arguments in favour of a revolutionary vanguard party.

But they do not guarantee that errors by that party will automatically be avoided. There are no infallible parties. There are no infallible party leaderships, party majorities, "Leninist central committees", or individual party leaders. The Marxist programme is never a definitively achieved one. No new situation can be comprehensively analysed in reference to historical precedents. Social reality is constantly undergoing changes. New and unforeseen developments regularly occur at historical turning points: the phenomenon of imperialism after Engels's death was not analysed by Marx and Engels; the delay of the proletarian revolution in the advanced imperialist countries was not foreseen by the Bolsheviks; the bureaucratic degeneration of the first workers state was not incorporated in Lenin's theory of the dictatorship of the proletariat; the emergence after World War II of many workers states (albeit with bureaucratic deformations) following revolutionary mass struggles not led by revolutionary Marxist leaderships (Yugoslavia, China, Cuba, Vietnam) was not foreseen by Trotsky; etc. No complete, ready-made answers for new phenomena can be found in the works of the classics or in the existing programme.

Furthermore, new problems will arise in the course of the building of socialism, problems for which the revolutionary Marxist programme provides only a general framework of reference but no automatic source of correct answers. The struggle for correct answers to such new problems implies a constant interaction between theoretical-political analysis and discussions and revolutionary *class practice*, the final word being spoken by practical experience.

Under such circumstances, any restriction of free political and theoretical debate spilling over to a restriction of free political mass activity of the proletariat, i.e., any restriction of socialist democracy, will constitute an obstacle to the revolutionary party itself arriving at correct policies. It is therefore not only theoretically wrong but practically ineffective and

211

harmful from the point of view of successfully advancing on the road of building socialism.

One of the gravest consequences of a monolithic one-party system, of the absence of a plurality of political groups, tendencies, and parties, and of administrative restrictions being imposed on free political and ideological debate, is the impediments such a system erects on the road to rapidly correcting mistakes committed by the government of a workers state. Mistakes committed by such a government, like mistakes committed by the majority of the working class, its various layers, and different political groupings, are by and large unavoidable in the process of building a classless, socialist society. A rapid correction of these mistakes, however, is possible in a climate of free political debate, free access of opposition groupings to mass media, large-scale political awareness and involvement in political life by the masses, and control by the masses over government and state activity at all levels.

The absence of all these correctives under a system of monolithic one-party government makes the rectification of grave mistakes all the more difficult. The very dogma of party infallibility on which the Stalinist system rests puts a heavy premium both on the denial of mistakes in party policies (search for self-justification and for scapegoats) and on the attempt to postpone even implicit corrections as long as possible. The objective costs of such a system in terms of economic losses, of unnecessary, i.e., objectively avoidable, sacrifices imposed upon the toiling masses, of political defeats in relation to class enemies, and of political disorientation and demoralisation of the proletariat, are indeed staggering, as is shown by the history of the Soviet Union since 1928. To give just one example: the obstinate clinging to an erroneous agricultural policy by Stalin and his henchmen has wreaked havoc with the food supply of the Soviet people for more than a generation; its negative consequences have not been eliminated to this day, nearly fifty years later. Such a catastrophe would have been impossible had there been free political debate over opposing policies in the USSR.

Third: the idea that *restricting* the democratic rights of the proletariat is in any way conducive to the gradual *"education"* of an allegedly "backward" mass of toilers is blatantly absurd. One cannot learn to swim except by going into the water. There is no way masses can learn to raise the level of their political awareness other than by engaging in political activity and learning from the experience of such activity. There is no way they can learn from mistakes other than by having the right to commit them. Paternalistic prejudices about the alleged "backwardness" of the masses generally hide a conservative petty-bourgeois fear of mass activity, which has nothing in common with revolutionary Marxism. Any restriction of political mass activity under the pretext that the masses would make too many mistakes can only lead to increasing political apathy among the workers, i.e., to paradoxically reinforcing the very situation which is said to be the problem.

Fourth: under conditions of full-scale socialisation of the means of production and the social surplus product, any long-term monopoly of the exercise of political power in the hands of a minority — even if it is a revolutionary party beginning with revolutionary proletarian motivations — runs a strong risk of stimulating objective tendencies toward bureaucratisation. Under such socioeconomic conditions, whoever controls the state administration thereby controls the social surplus product and its distribution. Given the fact that economic inequalities will still exist at the outset, particularly in the economically backward workers states, this can become a source of corruption and of the growth of material privileges and social differentiation. Thus, there is an objective need for real control over decision-making to rest in the hands of the proletariat as a class, with unlimited possibilities to denounce pilferage, waste, and illegal appropriation and misuse of resources at all levels, including the highest ones. No such democratic mass control is possible without opposition tendencies, groups, and parties having full freedom of action, propaganda, and agitation, as well as full access to the mass media.

Likewise, during the transition period between capitalism and socialism, and even in the first phase of communism (socialism) it is unavoidable that forms of division of labour (especially separation between intellectual and manual labour) will survive, as well as forms of labour organisation and labour processes totally or partially inherited from capitalism that do not enable a full development of all the creative talents of the producer. These cannot be neutralised by education, indoctrination, moral exhortation or periodic "mass criticism campaigns", as the Maoists contend, and still less by mystifying expedients like cadres' working one day a week as manual labourers. These objective obstacles on the road to the *gradual emergence of truly socialist relations of production* can be prevented from becoming powerful sources of material privileges only if a strict distinction is made between the functional and the social division of labour, i.e., *if the mass of the producers* (in the first place those likely to be the most exploited, the manual

213

workers) *are placed in conditions such that they can exercise real political and social power* over any "functionally" privileged layer. The radical reduction of the work day and the fullest soviet democracy are the two key conditions for attaining this goal.

The present conditions, which make the problem of upholding and advancing proletarian democracy especially difficult, would of course be altered qualitatively if (or when) either of the two following developments occur: 1. A socialist revolution in one or more industrially advanced capitalist countries. Such a revolution would itself give enormous impulsion to the struggle for democratic rights throughout the world and would immediately open the possibility of increasing productivity on an immense scale, eliminating the scarcities that are the root cause of the entrenchment of parasitic bureaucratism, as explained above. 2. A political revolution in the bureaucratically deformed or degenerated workers states, particularly the Soviet Union or the People's Republic of China. This would likewise signify an upsurge of proletarian democracy with colossal repercussions internationally, besides putting an end to the bureaucratic caste and its concept of building "socialism in one country."

Following a political revolution, common economic planning among all the workers states would become realisable, thus assuring a leap forward in productivity that would help remove the economic basis of parasitic bureaucratism.

Finally, it is true that there is no automatic correlation or simultaneity between the abolition of capitalist state power and private property in the means of production and the disappearance of privileges in the field of personal wealth, cultural heritage, and ideological influence, not to speak of the disappearance of all elements of commodity production. Long after bourgeois state power has been overthrown and capitalist property abolished, remnants of petty commodity production and the survival of elements of a money economy will continue to create a framework in which primitive accumulation of capital can still reappear, especially if the level of development of the productive forces is still insufficient to guarantee the automatic appearance and consolidation of genuinely *socialist* relations of production. Likewise, long after the bourgeoisie has lost its positions as a ruling class politically and economically, the influence of bourgeoise and petty-bourgeois ideologies, customs, habits, cultural values, etc. will linger on in relatively large spheres of social life and broad layers of society.

But it is completely wrong to draw from this undeniable fact (which is, incidentally, one of the main reasons why *state power* of the working class is indispensable in order to prevent these "islands of bourgeois influence" from becoming bases for the restoration of capitalism) the conclusion that administrative repression of bourgeois ideology is a necessary condition for the building of a socialist society. On the contrary, historical experience confirms the *total ineffectiveness* of administrative struggles against reactionary bourgeois and petty-bourgeois ideologies; in fact, in the long run such methods even strengthen the hold of these ideologies and place the great mass of the proletariat in the position of being ideologically disarmed before them, because of lack of experience with genuine political and ideological debate and the lack of credibility of official "state doctrines".

The only effective way to eliminate the influence of these ideologies upon the mass of the toilers lies in :

a. The creation of objective conditions under which these ideologies lose the material roots of their reproduction.

b. The waging of a relentless struggle against these ideologies *in the field of ideology* itself, which can, however, attain its full success only under conditions of open debate and open confrontation, i.e., of freedom for the defenders of reactionary ideologies to defend their ideas, of ideological cultural pluralism.

Only those who have neither confidence in the superiority of Marxist and materialist ideas nor confidence in the proletariat and the toiling masses can shrink from open ideological confrontation with bourgeois and petty-bourgeois ideologies under the dictatorship of the proletariat. Once that class is disarmed and expropriated, once their members can have access to the mass media only in relation to their numbers, there is no reason to fear a constant, free, and frank confrontation between their ideas and ours. This confrontation is the only means through which the working class can educate itself ideologically and successfully free itself from the influence of bourgeois and petty-bourgeois ideas.

Any monopoly position accorded to Marxism (not to speak of particular versions or interpretations of Marxism) in the ideological-cultural fields through administrative and repressive measures by the state can lead only to debasing Marxism itself from a critical science into a form of state doctrine or state religion, with a constantly declining attractive power among the toiling masses and especially the youth. This is apparent today in the USSR, where the monopoly position

215

accorded "official Marxism" masks a real poverty of creative Marxist thought in all areas. Marxism, which is critical thought *par excellence*, can flourish only in an atmosphere of full freedom of discussion and constant confrontation with other currents of thought, i.e., in an atmosphere of full ideological and cultural pluralism.

Bibliography

Revolution and Class Struggle: A Reader in Marxist Politics (Ed: Robin Blackburn), London, 1977

Disaster in Chile (Ed: Les Evans), New York, 1974

The Murder of Allende by Rojas Sandford, New York and London, 1976

On the Dictatorship of the Proletariat by Etienne Balibar, London, 1977

Prelude To Revolution: France in May 1968 by Daniel Singer, New York, 1970

Democracy and Revolution by George Novack, New York, 1971

The Early Chartists (Ed: Dorothy Thompson), London, 1971

Marxism and Politics by Ralph Miliband, Oxford, 1977

Considerations on Western Marxism by Perry Anderson, London, 1976

The Technology of Political Control by Ackroyd, Margolis, Rosenhead and Shallice, London, 1977

Late Capitalism by Ernest Mandel, London, 1975

The Break-Up of Britain by Tom Nairn, London, 1977

Hidden from History by Sheila Rowbotham, London, 1973

Capitalism, The Family and Personal Life by Eli Zaretsky, London, 1976

The Legacy of Rosa Luxemburg by Norman Geras, London, 1977

From Stalinism to Eurocommunism by Ernest Mandel, London, 1978

From Class Society to Communism by Ernest Mandel, London, 1978

Dialogue on Spain by Santiago Carrillo, London, 1976

'Eurocommunism' and the State by Santiago Carrillo, London, 1977

Leninism Under Lenin by Marcel Liebman, London, 1975

Party, Army and Masses in China by Livio Maitan, London, 1976

The Protestants of Ulster by Geoff Bell, London, 1976

Northern Ireland: The Orange State by Michael Farrell, London, 1976

Trade Unions Under Capitalism, (Ed: Tom Clarke and Laurie Clements), London, 1977

The Road to 1945, by Paul Addison, London 1977

The Political Police in Britain by Tony Bunyan, London 1977

Aneurin Bevan: 1891-1945 by Michael Foot, London 1975

Why You Should Be A Socialist by Paul Foot, London, 1976

Strikes by Richard Hyman, London, 1972

Lenin by Tony Cliff (vols 1–3), London, 1978

ARTICLES

Anthony Barnett: Heath, the Unions and the State, *New Left Review,* 77

Perry Anderson: The Antinomies of Antonio Gramsci, *New Left Review,* 100

Ernest Mandel: Revolutionary Strategy in Europe, *New Left Review,* 100

Robin Blackburn: What is the "Democratic Road" to Socialism?, *International,* Vol. 3, No. 4, Summer 1977

Nicos Poulantzas and Henri Weber: The State and the Transition to Socialism, *International,* Vol. 4, No. 1, Autumn 1977

Norman Geras: Lenin, Trotsky and the Party, *International,* Vol. 4, No. 2, Winter 1977

Tom Nairn: The House of Windsor, *Socialist Challenge,* Nos. 1 and 2

Neil Williamson: The Break-Up of Britain, *Internationaal,* Vol. 4, No. 2, Winter 1977

John Ross: Capitalism, Politics and Personal Life, *Socialist Woman,* Vol. 6, No. 2

PERIODICALS AND JOURNALS

(Can all be ordered from The Other Bookshop, 328 Upper Street, London N.1)

Intercontinental Press / Inprecor, New York

New Left Review, London

Critique Communiste, Paris

International, London
Marxism Today, London
Socialist Challenge, London
Socialist Worker, London
Labor Focus on Eastern Europe, London
Rouge, Paris
Combate, Madrid
Woman's Voice, London
Socialist Woman, London
Spare Rib, London
Gay News, London

WITHDRAWN
Short Loan Collection